ARCO

MID-CAREER
JOB HUNTING

OFFICIAL HANDBOOK OF
THE FORTY PLUS CLUB

E. PATRICIA BIRSNER

Revised Edition

D1306193

Prentice Hall
New York • London • Toronto • Sydney • Tokyo • Singapore

This Arco edition is published by arrangement
with Facts on File Publications, New York, New York

Prentice Hall General Reference
15 Columbus Circle
New York, NY 10023

An Arco Book

Arco, Prentice Hall, and colophons are
registered trademarks of Simon & Schuster, Inc.

Manufactured in the United States of America

2   3   4   5   6   7   8   9   10

Library of Congress Cataloging-in-Publication Data

ISBN 0-13-508532-2

Original title: The 40+ Job Hunting Guide,
published by Facts on File Publications, ISBN 0-8160-2509-6

Contents

Preface

"In 1984, the United States climbed out of the most serious recession since the depression of 1929. During that time, business learned the bitter lesson of operating 'lean and mean.' It is still learning that lesson—and that it competes in a global economy with products produced at a lower cost elsewhere."

When I reread my preface to the original *Forty+ Job Hunting Guide*, I discovered that, unfortunately, I had been a pretty good prognosticator with statements like the one above. Much of the Baby Boom generation is over forty now, and even in this time of relatively full employment, too many well educated and capable over-forty executives and professionals have been chasing too few high-level positions.

Business has continued to downsize. Who would have predicted a few years ago the tremendous cut in big company employment and the serious financial problems brought about by mergers and acquisitions, junk bonds and various other kinds of "creative" financing. The entire financial industry has been affected (especially banks, savings and loans, and brokerage firms), automobile manufacturing, the petrochemical industry, the communications industry (where people used to look forward to lifetime employment), major department stores and retail chains, the computer industry, even the grocery chains. The economy is in a state of flux as U. S. industries continue their efforts to compete in the global economy. These factors and others (demographics, for one) have made unemployment a fact of life for the over-40 executive and professional.

In researching this book for the original edition, I talked to many over-forty executives, both employed and unemployed. We talked frankly and honestly about the emotional, physical and financial problems of unemployment. Some shared intimate problems and deep feelings of inadequacy that they hadn't been able to voice to anyone else. They told me what worked and what hadn't worked as they looked for employment.

The Forty Plus Club of New York and its members were especially helpful.[1] Many of the unemployed people I interviewed were on the Forty Plus roster or had left Forty Plus on a new job, but could remember how unemployment felt. I was also able to call the Forty Plus Educational Center when I had completed a new section of the book and ask to teach a class on that topic to "see if it worked." The participants in these sessions gave marvelous feedback. I used their "sometimes too honest

---

[1]For a description of the Forty Plus Club, see the appendix, page 241.

comments" to revise the sections—and they learned useful skills, or at least said they did!

In the intervening years since the appearance of the original edition, I have continued my relationship with the New York Forty Plus Club. They have sponsored a number of one and two day job hunting seminars which I have given for the general public. The club also continues to sponsor in-house workshops on the various topics in this book.

So many people were helpful that a list of their names is bound to be incomplete. When I tried to remember all of the unemployed or recently unemployed executives as well as the professional counsellors, personnel managers, executive recruiters (headhunters) and others from whom I gathered information, I discovered to my horror that I was missing many of the names. I also had no class rolls showing the people who served as willing subjects for the courses I taught. And some people were willing to be interviewed, but didn't want their names listed in print. So to the many people who gave me help, if I missed you and you would like to have been acknowledged, I'm sorry. Just know that I appreciated what you did and am glad I met you.

Thanks to David A. Eastman, cofounder of the Dallas Forty Plus Club, who arranged for me to present a number of two-day seminars for the Dallas group at the University of Dallas and at Southern Methodist University. At the first of these, over 140 unemployed executives and professionals showed up on the hottest day in August (it was 109 degrees!) to attend a seminar in a room which would hold 100 people at best.

From these people, and from the attendees at the many other job hunting seminars I have given, I learned what needed to be added to and changed in this book. I prepared a number of handouts to correct these, and have incorporated them into this revision. And, I have learned much from them about the current state of job hunting.

Among the literally hundreds of people to whom I owe an additional debt of gratitude, I'd like to thank: Anna Jones, President of the New York Forty Plus Board; Charles B. England, Cheryl O. Fox, Jean James, Hardy Mock, Joyce Waite, Tom Lynch, Bill Powers, Jim Bell, Greg Sloat, Stan Smith, John Lauderdale, Barrie Howard, Jack Gorman, Fred Martin, Lee Rosewitz, Don Bates, John Carney, Jack Curran, Russ Altman, Robert Anspach, Edith Arm, Bill Bender, Arthur Braun, Leroy Brown, Theodora Brown, Scott Budge, Walter Burke, Lloyd Cathey, Arthur Conescu, John Flowers, John Forbes, Warner Fuchs, Tony Gallo, Kenneth Greenwald, Bob Jenssen, Carolyn Kneip, Dave Meeker, Harold Mers, Mike Miller, Jerry Mullaney, Fred Ockert, Dan Pawling, Peter

Sloan, Rena Rappaport, Robert Reed, Elsie Richmond, Paul Stearne, S. Eric Wachtel, Peggy Woltz, Charles Whitehead, and the many current and past members of the Forty Plus Clubs of New York and Dallas who gave me wonderful support, and whose job search I'd like to think I helped. I'd also like to thank the members of the other Forty Plus Clubs who contacted me by telephone and letter with thanks, with requests for help with their personal job searches, and with suggestions for changes to the book. And I especially owe a debt of gratitude to Dorothy Wolchansky, who opened her home to me so that I could stay at no cost to the Club when conducting the Dallas seminars. The librarians at the Morris County Free Library in Morristown, New Jersey, also deserve thanks for their help in locating reference sources—and for keeping and making available an exceptionally good reference and periodical collection.

And a special thank you to New York literary agent Michael Cohn. He read an article about the Forty Plus Club in the *New York Times* and said, "Aha, there's a book in there somewhere." He contacted the club to see if any current or past member was a writer. The club officers suggested me—and that's how this book came about.

—E. Patricia Birsner

Introduction:
Middle-Aged and Out of
Work

You are middle-aged—or older—and out of work. This possibility was something "they" didn't tell you about when you were going to school. Yet, in the business climate of the 1990s, job change has come to be accepted, albeit reluctantly, as a part of business life. And it's happened to you.

A number of business trends will affect your ability to obtain a job in the 1990s.[1] What are these trends?

1. You can expect a business world in which the computer has shifted the advantage to the small company. Small companies will be able to spot emerging market trends quickly and move into new niches before their unwieldy rivals even notice the possibilities.

2. By the year 2000, 85 percent of Americans will work in a company of 200 or fewer employees. Large companies will continue to cut out layers of middle management; outside contractors will provide services once taken care of in-house.

3. Information will be a commodity. Twenty-one million new jobs generated by the year 2000 will be in the service sector, shaping information for a market of discerning consumers.

4. Opportunities will be in different industries from those which have historically provided most employment. Hot industries will be:

❐ Health care services—hospitals, nursing, social work, testing, biotechnology, ambulatory care
❐ Hospitality
❐ Personal services—buy groceries, clean house, walk dogs, shopping
❐ Entertainment
❐ Environment—pollution control, renewable energy, desert greening, earthquake testing, recycling, hazardous waste disposal

---

[1] John Naisbitt and Patricia Aburdene, "Seize the Future," *Success*, March 1990. In this article, they summarize the main trends discussed in their block-buster book, *Megatrends 2000*.

❏ Other niches—robotics, fish farming, generic drugs, ergonomics, child and elder care, outer space

5. Labor shortage of skilled employees. The skill requirements of jobs are growing faster than the skill levels of both labor and management. Employers will soon have to prospect for employees in the same way that they now prospect for customers; provide training programs for their own employees or risk ruin; look to women and minorities (they will comprise 68 percent of the total new workers between 1988 and 2000); and build multicultural, pluralistic sales forces.

6. Partnerships and alliances will develop between large corporations and small companies, between domestic and foreign companies, between profit and nonprofit, private and public sectors.

7. Companies will use global sourcing. American-based companies may carry out research in the United States, design the product in Italy, engineer it in West Germany and assemble it in South Korea. Small companies have a tremendous opportunity to flourish because they can reach pockets of demand around the globe.

8. Capital sources for growth will be international in scope, much of it coming from overseas as venture capital becomes stingier in the United States.

9. Small teams of people will get together to solve problems, instead of whole departments.

10. Many people will work from their homes. Estimates predict there will be as many as 40 million home-run enterprises by the year 2000.

11. Innovation will continue to speed up, with product lives sometimes as short as a year. Entrepreneurs will develop prototypes in hours instead of weeks, using CAD/CAM (computer- aided design/computer-aided manufacturing), CIM (computer- integrated manufacturing), and automated order processing.

12. Marketing will be of paramount importance. Consumers will be more demanding, and markets more segmented. Database technology will be essential in this market effort.

13. Entrepreneurs are "about to inherit the universe, if we can just continue to be smarter, nimbler, and more adaptable than ever before."

Some of the preceding trends are driven by demographics. World wide populations are still exploding. The 1990 U.S. Census showed that the U.S. population increased by 23 million people, or slightly more than 10 percent over 1980. The median age of the population increased from 30 to 33. The number of people aged 50 to 59 has declined though, as the relatively small generation born during the 1930s entered this age group. There are also fewer people aged 10 to 24 because of the low birth rates of the 1960s and early 1970s. During the past ten years, the number of people aged 40 to 44 grew by nearly 50 percent, while those who will soon be forty grew even more. During the 1990s, approximately 37 million (out of 250 million) people will be somewhere in their forties, an increase of over 11 million from the 1980s. The Baby Boom generation (your age group) is now in the childraising years, and the number of children under age 10 is growing.[2]

The baby boomers are the most educated generation ever. One in four has completed at least four years of college, as compared with younger people, aged 25 to 34, who are much less likely to have the same amount of education. Overall, nearly 19 percent of Americans have at least a bachelor's degree. The educational gap between men and women has also narrowed. Among people 45 to 54, 10 percent more men than women have college degrees. But among those aged 25 to 34, the difference is less than 1 percentage point.

Geographic factors also affect job hunting. At the beginning of the 1990s, parts of the Northeast and the West Coast are growing, and their economy on the whole is healthy. Costs of living are high in both. The South is growing in population by leaps and bounds, and most of the southern states are doing just fine. Living costs are still low in the South, but salaries often reflect these lower costs. The Midwest has grown little, and in fact, many of the states have lost population. However, there are bright pockets even here, and some economic progress is being made as states seek to lose their "rust bucket" reputation. The Mountain States are growing in population, but they have not really climbed out of the mid-eighties "depression." Even Texas, which was a very depressed area during the late eighties has climbed out of the doldrums, and seems headed back towards economic, as well as population, growth.

---

[2] *American Demographics*, January 1990, pp. 23-30.

What skills and abilities do you need as you look for a job now? Looking at these trends, you see immediately that being able to work comfortably with computers is absolutely essential. You have to be able to work with a wide variety of databases to extract needed information. You should know how to develop and use spreadsheets—to analyze "what if" scenarios, to keep track of budgets, to work with compensation and bonuses, to track sales trends, as the basis for decision making. Knowing how to use a graphics package such as Freelance or Harvard Graphics will enable you to turn out first-rate presentation graphics at low cost, with minimum time expenditure. You will save time by preparing your correspondence yourself on a personal computer instead of writing it out by hand or dictating it into a recorder and sending it to the word processing group or an overworked secretary.

You will have to be flexible, to be able to change the way you do things as the marketplace demands those changes. You may be permanently enrolled in training courses just to run in place, let alone keep up with the latest technologies, and the latest national and international trends.

The kinds of jobs you might obtain now are different from the kinds of jobs you took when you started working. Few over-40 executives and professionals are currently finding jobs in major corporations. They are already noticing the effects of prevailing trends. They may become entrepreneurs, starting businesses for themselves; contact owners of small businesses and find employment there; accept positions with small to mid-size corporations; enter the not-for-profit sector, which desperately needs administrators with top-notch business skills; secure civil service positions with governmental agencies of one sort or another; or become consultants or "Executives for Rent."

Some have been able to continue their salary increases, and come out of their period of unemployment with better, more interesting, and more financially rewarding positions. In some areas of the country, though, and in some industries, the over-40 executives and professionals are taking a hit on their salaries.

Marketplace turmoil and the need for companies to remain competitive has worked to the detriment of long-term employment. Job-seekers should not expect previous levels of job security. If you want to remain or to become gainfully employed, you must learn to become competitive on the job. In the decade of the nineties, it appears as though we must be prepared to accept job insecurity and change. Managers will have to learn to be flexible and adaptable to the changing job markets, to job and project assignments, career change and professional opportunities.

In spite of all of the changes going on in the job marketplace, many perceptions of the older executive in the business world remain unchanged, even though the threshold of old age has moved upward. Conventional (but faulty) hiring wisdom still says:

❒ Older executives are more expensive to hire.

❒ Older executives have reduced capabilities. They are slower, take longer to complete tasks and make more errors. They don't have the energy needed to do the job. Therefore, they are not cost effective, given their salary scales.

❒ Older executives haven't kept up with the changes in the work world. Their skills are obsolete. (Think about this: Did you perhaps lose your job because your superiors felt you had failed to stay current? Even now in the early 1990s, only one-third of middle- and upper-level managers currently joining the various Forty Plus Clubs are computer literate, and this is an age where the ability to use *Lotus* spreadsheets, financial modeling and other management tools may be critical if management is to make proper strategic decisions.[3])

❒ Older executives will be a drain on the pension plan since they will only work 10 or 15 years before they retire.

❒ Older executives cost more for medical, dental, life insurance and other benefits.

❒ Something must be wrong with out-of-work older executives because they were let go by their former employers. (This reasoning is not age-exclusive; young unemployed executives face the same prejudice.)

❒ Conversely, an older executive is overqualified for the position and won't remain on a lower level job.

❒ Older executives don't have recent "hands-on" experience since they've spent most of their recent work experience managing or supervising rather than doing.

❒ Older executives don't have the adaptability or the necessary background for the job. A company will take a chance that a younger applicant can remedy any deficits in experience while assuming that the older applicant can't learn quickly and will take too long to train and bring "up to speed."

---

[3] Most of the clubs have extensive opportunities through formal and informal classes and coaching for members to learn to use computers and computer applications. See the Appendix for information about the other work done by the Forty Plus Clubs and the cities where they are located.

❐ Older executives will not be as loyal to the company as a younger person who can be brought along to fit into the company culture.

❐ Older executives offer less opportunity to fill compliance guidelines.

❐ Companies can hire a younger minority executive who will work for less money and at the same time help the company comply with EEO requirements.

The same age prejudices are faced by both male and female executives. But women managers still do have to contend with some residue to prejudice against hiring females for executive positions. Fortunately, within the past ten years, this last prejudice against women has changed radically. In big companies, the percentage of women in middle-management positions is almost exactly the same as the total percentage of women in the company. The upper ranks of women in management are still thin, but within this decade, the increasing numbers of women who have achieved middle-level management positions will ensure that many will make it to the top. Sheer demographics and equality of opportunity, then, will also place more women managers over 40 among the unemployed.

But you want to work, you know you can work, and you can do the job for someone. As an older unemployed executive, what will you face during this period of unemployment? What can you do to improve your chances of getting exactly the right position? And how can you counter the subtle and not-so-subtle prejudices against the older employee? Read on.

Can this book get you a job? No. You'll have to get the job yourself. But it can help you get started and it will provide a framework for your efforts. Some of the hints will perhaps be things you already know—many are just common sense. Others will be things you have forgotten. And some of the advice and suggestions may differ from what you were told when you entered the job market, or may differ even from the conventional wisdom of a few years ago. The techniques outlined here do work. They've worked for many others, and if you give them a chance, you can make them work for you.

Emotional Traumas

The emotional traumas of the unemployed executive or professional job-seeker are the biggest single difference between the employed and the unemployed searcher. These traumas must be dealt with if your story is to have a happy ending.

Your feelings may run the entire emotional gamut. Some of you are angry. Your company (or bosses) are bloodsuckers. They (or he or she) were unfair, dictatorial, unfeeling. Or you may be directing your anger inward. "You dummy! How could you be so stupid! It's all your fault." You may direct your anger at society in general. "The damn government!" (Or the President, Congress, Democrats, Republicans, Governor, whatever.) You may even find that you are turning your anger on your family members—your spouse or children. You may feel vindictive, have a strong desire to "get even." (God forbid that you should act on this!) Others of you are defeated. You feel destroyed, degraded, a total failure. You are demoralized. You are embarrassed because of your "inadequacies." You've lost confidence in yourself, in your ability to do a good job, to support your family, even to look successfully for another job. You show these feelings through your very appearance, posture, dress.

Your feelings may be of disbelief. You are incredulous that this is happening to you. You went to the right schools, belonged to the right clubs, went to the right church or synagogue, and played the game of politics well (you thought). You've led a charmed life, so this can't be happening to you. (But there you are, still out on the street!)

In addition, you may be anxious and confused. "What am I going to do? How will I find a job! What's going to happen to me, to my family? Am I obsolete? An anachronism? Should I change careers?" The litany could go on and on. You may be in such a state of panic that you feel immobilized, unable to take action on your own behalf.

How about hurt and indignation? Frustration? Depression? Rejection and pain? Yes, these are also common reactions. In fact, the middle-aged, recently unemployed may feel so much pain that they suffer heart attacks, strokes or develop a panoply of psychosomatic illnesses which they must overcome in addition to the basic necessity of finding work. And frustration and depression unfortunately are ongoing problems throughout the job search.

If your entire working career (twenty years or more) was spent with one company, your reactions may be similar to those suffered by the "wronged" party in a particularly messy divorce or to those caused by the death of a loved one. Did you dedicate yourself to pleasing "the company?" Did it serve as wife, husband, mistress, lover? If so, you may feel bitter, spurned. Or the pain on separation may have left a huge emptiness, a void. You want (and probably need) time to grieve.

What about your reactions? Did you experience any of the above emotions? They represent normal human responses to traumatic events. And through all of this runs the nagging doubt that just maybe your problems are related to your age. If only you were younger, you wouldn't have been singled out. You would still be working.

You make mistakes, which can compound your problems. During a recent discussion with Forty Plus Club members, the consensus was that the most serious mistake was casting yourself as victim, instead of getting on with your search. This takes one or all of the following forms.

1. *You call your friends and present yourself as the victim.* (Poor me.) Instead, wait until you can come to grips with the situation, then contact them so that the contact experience is positive and can work for you. (See the chapter entitled "Putting Your Plan into Action" for help with "networking," which is really about helping your friends to help you.)

2. *You stay home and brood.* You feel guilty. You don't leave the house—or you spend your time fixing things around the house, hoping you'll feel better soon. You are lonely —you become self-focused instead of focusing on the outside world.

3. *You procrastinate.* You feel that you've been mistreated, and will be mistreated by other employers. What's the use, you think. You have a great deal of difficulty in preparing even a rudimentary resume.

When you think as a victim, you act as a victim. You exude a "victim aroma" which comes through loudly and clearly to all. It is deadly and can cancel out everything you've done and been.

Problems Can Increase as Your Job Search Lengthens
Your initial emotional responses may be replaced by other, more damaging ones, as the time allocated to your job search lengthens. For currently unemployed middle-aged executives, the length of time without work is usually somewhere between four months and a year, with the average being close to eight months. (This time frame is longer than that of younger unemployed executives.) However, it varies from just a few weeks to the almost chronic state of 18 months or more. And the longer the time frame, the more difficult and intransigent the emotional upset.

As an unemployed person, you tend to be at loose ends. You may not know what to do with yourself. Don't foolishly settle for the television set, the daily soap opera, the living room couch. As a current catch phrase would put it, don't become a "couch potato." To quote one unemployed person, "my brain turned into silly putty on a steady diet of the boob tube." This can happen if you do not reset your goals (for too many of us, often determined solely by our work) and don't develop a plan of action to keep going and growing.

You may feel friendless, isolated and lost. Listen to one unemployed female executive (age 48): "My existing friends didn't want to hear about my problems because they were too close to their own fears." Another woman (45): "I've always had a lot of social friends. A few of these came through beautifully, others didn't at all." A severe reaction from a long-term unemployed male (55): "I never developed any relationships or friendships. I had nothing to fall back on, to add to my feelings of self-worth." One former long-term friend of an out-of-work executive said: "I got so tired listening to that guy tell me about his troubles. All he did was bitch and gripe about what a raw deal he got...I couldn't see that he was doing one constructive thing to get his life back together. So, I just quit returning his phone calls and avoided places where I thought I might bump into him." And finally, you may simply not want to burden your friends with your troubles. So *you* do the abandoning, losing a real source of support and even long-term friendships in the bargain.

Have you gotten your anger under control so you can use that energy in your job search? Or do you still have it, lashing out at others when you least expect it? Your family and friends end up bearing the brunt of it. And it could show up unexpectedly in the middle of that critical job-hunting event, the interview. You may lose confidence to the point where you aren't sure you can do anything that anyone or any company would pay for. You may have trouble answering ads or making calls on potential employers.

Your anxiety level may rise further. And fear can enter the picture, too. Older executives have high life styles— high in fixed expenses, loan payments, running costs. You may have been keeping up with both the Jones and the Smiths. Suddenly, your income is a tiny unemployment payment (plus minuscule, or maybe slightly larger, severance pay) and your minimum requirements are in excess of $3,000 per month—and that's before you even eat! Perhaps you didn't make initial expenditure cuts, thinking your severance pay would be enough to tide you over without affecting your family during the short time you would be unemployed.

Even mundane expenditures can become major considerations and many people are unable to cope. As one sixtyish executive explained: "Older executives like me were brought up during the Depression. Bankruptcy or failure to meet one's obligations was presented to us as an absolute disgrace. Being out of work for a long time can negate all our background and destroy the actual core of our belief in ourselves. It may ruin our ethical and moral fiber. I feel like I have a runaway reactor inside me involved in a self-destructive chain reaction."

As the period of unemployment lengthens, divorce may become a real likelihood. Wives or husbands may become so disillusioned with their spouses that they file for divorce or actually go through with the divorce. This is especially true for the older man who has a wife who is not in the business work force. (It is also true for some younger men and women). The firing or job loss, coupled with the spouse's inability to get a better job immediately, has removed the "white knight" from his horse, or the goddess from her throne. They see their husbands (or wives) as losers and they want to cut their losses. Men with executive wives may hear suggestions that they do a role reversal: i.e., stay home and be "househusbands." And the female executive may be given the "why don't you just stay home now and be a housewife" comment once too often. Or be harassed because he or she isn't pulling his or her part of the weight now.

Other family members can be devastatingly cruel. Children can sneer at their unemployed parent, in-laws expect you to jump at the first low-paying non-professional job they hear about. Other family members can gossip maliciously, increasing your stress level and further damaging your self-esteem.

Both men and women may lose their interest in sex. Men see this as additional confirmation that they are too old and "out-of-it." Their wives may try to be supportive, but when they are turned away or not sought out in bed, they believe their husbands are indifferent or are freezing them out. The related experience of the unemployed older female executive is equally debilitating. They feel unlovable, unfeminine and unattractive. Since this may be occurring at about the same time as menopause, they may see the loss as an inescapable part of that natural event. Or, husbands may receive entirely too many "I don't feel like it tonight" or "I've got a headache" responses. Even now, in spite of the so-called sexual revolution, sex is still not a comfortable subject for discussion with many people in this age group. So the very real problems are not aired and may simply fester and add to the overall problem.

Loss of sexual response, though, is a very common part of depression. It occurs often enough to be one of depression's major identifying symptoms. And depression is concomitant with unemployment too often to be safely ignored. If you don't lose your sex drive, something equally dangerous to the health of your marriage may occur. Either the unemployed male or female, in a frantic attempt to shore up self-esteem, may indulge in an affair or series of affairs, completing the tearing of the marriage fabric. And if it was the first time in a long and good marriage, should the actual affair not destroy you, the guilt may.

Take action, before you lose it all.

Don't Add to Your Problems

You can damage yourself in other, more deliberate ways. You can involve yourself in any of the following self- destructive and self-fulfilling prophecies.

☐ Are you a social drinker? It's very easy to stop at the nearest bar earlier in the day for a pick-me-up. After all, you need it. Or you may start patronizing places you would never normally visit and begin your serious drinking at noon. You end up with two problems instead of one. It's far too easy to crawl into the bottle as an escape from the grim realities "out there." And if you were already a heavy drinker, these behaviors may be just enough to push you over the line into alcoholism.

☐ Cursed with anxiety? How about a few tranquilizers, uppers or downers, from your obliging doctor or—worse yet—your local purveyor of chemical pleasures? Another vicious cycle. You take the drug to reduce anxiety and tension before an interview, for example. If one is good, maybe two will be better. Then you are too loose and not quite together during the interview, and you blow it. You hate yourself and become anxious all over again. You take another drug to feel better. Round and round it goes. The first thing you know, you have a dependency. And both alcohol and drugs further depress the already clinically depressed individual.

☐ Tired of the rat race? Just drop out. Quit caring for your appearance. Don't shave or wash your hair. Quit wearing makeup and going to the beautician. Wear sloppy, casual wear or unpressed suits. Then you can be sure that absolutely no one will hire you for the kind of executive or professional jobs you formerly held. You don't look the part. You'll have to settle for a more menial position because that's the way you are presenting yourself.

☐ Doing some wishful thinking? If you just wish long enough and hard enough, a job will come out of the woodwork and you won't have to do anything about it. (Not likely!) Be defensive—take offense at everything—"you're always criticizing me," "they're just picky," "that wasn't what I meant." This also is defeating and guaranteed to make the job search longer, more difficult and less likely to be successful. And the most serious emotional problem of all—the self-destructive urge to end it all, to commit suicide.

How Do Reactions Differ?

Your sex and your marital status are related to some other major differences affecting your interior emotional climate when you are unemployed. The situations can be different for men and women, and for single, divorced or married executives. These differences need to be considered.

Male executives are often married, although when they become unemployed they find themselves without support from their wives and families. Their wives may also feel demoralized and defeated and unable to provide support. In many ways, married executives whose wives don't work have the toughest time. They have to be strong because of the very people depending upon them. They can't give way—they are expected to perform. They aren't allowed to be sad, to cry or to grieve, on the mistaken assumption that it isn't manly. The job loss may coincide with mid-life crisis. The men may feel that they didn't get where they wanted to go, they already have feelings of malaise, a vague dissatisfaction with themselves. Unemployment may occur just at the time of greatest expenditure, with one or more children in college. They aren't able to provide, so being unemployed functions as proof that they haven't "cut the mustard."

Married men whose wives work have a little more financial breathing room. They probably are going to get more realistic support from their wives. But they have less freedom to relocate than the sole-support male.

Divorced males may already feel they have failed because of their divorce. The job loss is simply additional confirmation that they are failures, that they don't measure up. They may also have lost a portion of their support group when they divorced, the married-couples network of which they and their spouses were a part.

The single male is less predictable. He may be single by choice with a full complement of male and female friends. Or, he may be a loner, married to his job. Or any of a number of other possibilities. What's most important is the strength of his support groups.

Most male executives belong to the "old boy network." At least, they usually have a network of friends and business acquaintances in place who can be called upon for help and support. They also generally have well-defined careers developed over a longer period of time than many female executives, although this isn't as true as it was even five years ago. The men may have worked for bigger, better firms. They may have started at a higher employment level than the older female executive who may have had to enter the job market in a lesser position.

Women did not have the "old boy network" tradition. However, in recent years, many have consciously developed an "old girl network" with other women executives. Even so, women's support systems are still more likely to be social, not business networks.

The divorced woman who was divorced while she still had children at home may have no network at all because she essentially worked three full-time jobs as mother, householder and wage earner. Her sole support group may have been her children. Now, even though they may be out on their own, the mother may still find she has not developed a replacement. She contacts her children for help. They react adversely—are frightened because their mother is frightened. Or, they may not be around to help. The divorced mother may also have fewer financial resources to drawn on.

The married female executive, on the other hand, may find herself in a position where her out-of-work status is not taken seriously. In fact, she may not have the severe financial problems of the single and divorced woman executive. But she still has the same ego need to work as any other male or female executive and may find herself frustrated by a lack of empathy. Her networks are also generally social, not business.

Single females are often part of a well-developed network, either business or social, or may belong to both types of networks. Their financial needs may not be as great as those of the divorced women, but their job is usually their only source of financial support.

Most out-of-work women executives feel they do have one emotional advantage over their male cohorts. They can cry, because society allows it. They can grieve and get it out of their systems. Thus, their emotional rebirth may take much less time than that of the male.

What's in This Book for You?

In the four parts of this book that follow, you will be asked to become an active participant in taking charge of your future—at least the part in which you are still among the working. In part I, you'll develop a personal action plan. This includes setting up a job search regime, organizing your time and working efficiently at the job search, taking care of your appearance and health, and putting your finances in order. You also will spend time evaluating yourself—who and what you are — and planning the contacts you should make to begin your job search. You'll also find some suggestions for coping with your number-one problem—the emotional traumas associated with unemployment—so that in the words of a recent off-Broadway show, "You can get your act together and take it on the road."

This book will present the act of getting a job as a marketing campaign aimed at selling a costly product—yourself—to a customer, your future employer. A marketing campaign consists of four basic parts: surveying the market; segmenting the market; selecting market segments that match; and positioning the product in the market. In conducting your job search, however, it is difficult to cut off the various activities and say "this is market research, this is selecting a market segment and this is positioning your product in the market place." They will overlap and you will find yourself doing several levels of activity at the same time. But in the chapters that follow, I have tried to break down the job search strategy into these steps.

Part 2 in the book is short but important. In it, you will *survey the job market in general*, and begin putting your plan into effect. You will ask yourself: what kind of job should you search for? What you have been doing—or should you make a career change, perhaps even go into business for yourself? What kind of business should you approach to work in —small business or industry or Fortune 500? Will you insist on a job on the level you just left (or higher)—or are you willing to "settle," to accept a lesser job just to work? Were you really unfairly treated? If you were, should you take legal action?

In part 3, you will work both on *segmenting the marketing place*, and *selecting a market segment* that matches what you have to offer. You will evaluate your personal communication style, and how to make it work for you in the job market. You will also consider the kinds of jobs for which you would be best suited (yes, even consider a career change), and the business and industries which your basic styles, abilities and interests most closely match.

Part 4, *positioning yourself in the market*, contains a quick course in the various "nuts and bolts" activities you will have to engage in before you are employed. You'll review the various types of resumes and how to write each one. You will also be reminded of the various ways to research jobs, to seek out agencies and employment services and job prospects. You will have a chance to update your letter-writing style so you don't present yourself as "old." You'll get help on interviewing. And finally, you'll take a look at the evaluation and decision process. When do you accept a job offer? Should you refuse it (or them) and hold out for more? What about a job contract (more and more becoming a part of accepting employment)? And finally, after you accept an employment offer, what do you do to make sure you stay on this new job?

Part I

Developing a Personal Action Plan

Coping with Your Emotions

The basis of the unhappiness and fears of the unemployed older executive is partly related to age. But much is also related to the "death" of a way of life, and to the loss of job-related relationships. It is not unusual for the newly unemployed to remark that losing their jobs "felt like they had just died," "felt like a death in the family," or "was as bad or worse than a divorce."

To become an effective job-seeker, you need to understand *why* unemployment has such an adverse effect upon you—and to learn that if affects others in the same ways as well. Then you can begin to cope with the job loss and start making the adaptations necessary for relatively normal functioning during your "abnormal" state of unemployment. By discussing the emotional problems of unemployment with others in the same boat and taking some action, you can again feel in charge of yourself and your destiny. You can arrive on the other side of unemployment increased in stature—not destroyed in person.

Emotional Stages of Unemployment

Older executives vary widely in their reaction to unemployment. But regardless of differences in personality and in ability to cope, they can be expected to go through three emotional stages during the period they are unemployed. According to Scott Budge, a group counseling specialist, those stages are: job loss, balance/dismay, and adaptation.[1]

---

[1] Much of the information in this chapter is based on interviews with Scott Budge, a group counseling specialist formerly at Pace University in New York City. During the early 1980s, Budge worked regularly with a group of unemployed executives, managers and professionals from the New York Forty Plus Club in a one-and-a-half-hour per week

STAGE 1: Job Loss.   During this stage, older executives are dis-oriented—they have suddenly lost their daily routine. They have to face telling family and friends of the loss, and anticipate their shock and anger. Family reactions are relatively predictable, and execu-tives dread these responses. In fact, many male managers go for weeks without telling their families they're unemployed. Friends, on the other hand, are almost always initially supportive; but too many of them seem to "fade away" as the period of unemployment lengthens.

Older executives' immediate reactions are generally of confusion, not depression. Some have a feeling of suspension of time—they even feel elation. They may take a vacation or time off as a means of avoiding facing what will be a severe loss. Emotionally they flip-flop between concern over economic factors (how will they get along without their income, benefits, etc.? how will they meet their expenses?) and anger over their job loss.

They begin their job search with exaggerated confidence. They're sure they'll have no trouble finding a new job. This confidence remains if they're successful, but soon evaporates if they have to spend eight months or more looking for a replacement position.

STAGE 2: *Balance/Dismay*. Most unemployed older executives make some kind of arrangements about their financial spending within two months—they reduce outgo, refinance, file for unemployment, etc. This reduces their immediate worries about money, although the worry remains just below the surface. And they achieve emotional distance from the job loss.

But the initial feeling of loss is replaced by a growing dismay that finding a job is not within their control and that the most frequent response to their job-search efforts is silence. They become puzzled and may be immobilized. Pessimism takes over. They may reinterpret their

"Rap Session." In these sessions, attendees expressed their feelings and attempted to come to grips with their emotional problems. The members of the group participated in a longitudinal study Budge conducted to establish the basis of their feelings of anger, fear and general inability to cope. Many of the insights Budge developed over this period of time are included. In addition to the interviews, Budge graciously shared a draft of an article on the same topic he coauthored with Ronald W. Janoff, director of the Manage-ment Institute of New York University. Incidentally, the Rap Sessions proved so valuable to the participants that Pace has continued providing the service to Forty Plus Club members.

preceding weeks' efforts as vain or unrealistic—or a waste of time. As one executive put it:

> I've absolutely wasted seven weeks of my life. My resume isn't any good, every contact I've made has been unproductive. I didn't have seven weeks to waste. I feel like I'm just splattering. And I've always been focused.

Self-esteem erodes from within. The unemployed become convinced that "something is wrong with me." They really feel that people can look at them and tell they are unemployed. They ask questions like: "Can anyone tell I'm out of work?" They don't sleep at night. They feel abnormal. They often become depressed.

This is the stage at which older executives seek help from professional counselors, buy self-help books (like this one), go to search firms, even seek psychoanalysis. Budge says they often address questions to counselors which are really requests to know how they are supposed to feel. "I don't sleep at night. Am I depressed?" or "Is it normal to feel this way?"

During this period, they struggle against their loss of self-confidence. A new routine which masks the pain of unemployment with the trappings of daily working life is usually the result. This is illustrated by the comment:

> You've got to get away from the house because that's death. I get up every morning, put on a shirt and tie. Then I get the hell out. I make myself do it. I have a routine and I stick to it. But what I really want to do is get back to work so the routine counts for something.

STAGE 3: *Adaptation.* The newly developed routine becomes the basis for the third stage: adaptation. The routines are a protective ritual against self-doubts and frustration. Unemployed older executives must struggle continually to assure themselves that things are OK, that everything will work out all right, even though they realize their sense of personal worth is tied up with their worth to an organization—and that to be employed is to be employed for someone, not merely by someone.

As time goes on and they still have no employment, the jobless learn to manage their days to protect their positive sense of self and to keep the realities of their situations invisible. They may increase their participation in community affairs, proceed with businesslike activity (appointments, calls) and keep to a time schedule. Their job hunt will probably be more continuous, better organized and sophisticated, even though rejection continues. Because this activity, which should be productive, is not, their notions of reward for effort and activity are upset. They worry continuously over the causes of rejection.

During the adaptation stage, a support group of some sort becomes especially useful. A group provides urgently needed feedback from peers and gives members an opportunity to vent their "hidden" fears about skills displacement, age, obsolescence, and general worthlessness.

Issues to Resolve During the Adaptive Phase of Unemployment

Whether unemployed older executives join a support group or not, they still have five major issues which they must resolve during the adaptive phase. These are: identity maintenance, loss of office, persistence of guilt, ambivalence in relationships and fear of rejection.

1. *Identity Maintenance.* Most unemployed executives refer to themselves in terms of generic job titles —I'm a planner, an information systems manager, a sales manager, a marketing manager, a purchasing manager, a controller, a program analyst, an engineer, a financial officer. They avoid reference to their former companies and to their former specific job title. They describe their skills and accomplishments in a textbook (read that resume) style. As they talk about themselves, they seem to be rehearsing for their interviews. By generalizing their skills, they also mask a worry that their specific job-related skills will melt away—that they'll be obsolete.

Even though unemployed, they still identify strongly with work roles, career direction, and with the drive and rewards that are provided by an organization. Being deprived of a job deprives them of the context in which they can formally perform management tasks, and of the organizational goals to which their very genuine skills were attuned. So, they have a real need to retain this organizational identity even in the absence of an institution.

We've got to be marketable, in tune with the '90s. Management is looking for a quick payback or they go down the tubes. So we all try to show how cost-efficient we are, how profitable it will be for a company to hire us because of our skills and knowledge.

The income is the measure of somebody's assessment of our value to them. I don't think I can afford to—or stand to—work for less than 60 grand.

I've got to do something. I want to stay in my field. I want to do something good, to work for a company. I want to be rewarded. Maybe I'm just geared to the work ethic. I always like to be busy, even if I just paint my house or start a vegetable garden. Even if I say, "OK, you're going to do nothing." I still set a goal that that's what I'll do. I've got to know what direction I'm headed for and know what my plan is. That's the worst thing about being unemployed—I don't really know where I'm going.

I've always been very goal-oriented—most of us have. We get to a certain place and discover most of our goals have been set for us by whatever business we were in. Now we don't have those things driving us and we discover we don't have any personal goals. If we don't reset some goals, we're not going to get well. We don't even know what to be challenged by.

2. *Loss of Office.* The loss of an office critically undermines the struggle to maintain executive identity. The office confers and signals status and identity. It's the forum in which executives practice their craft. But something else happens with the loss of the office. Before, home and work were separated, with home being the privileged location where one relaxed, had leisure and privacy. Now, home is neither fish nor fowl—it is neither itself nor the office. It's no longer sanctuary. So unemployed executives find they have no place that's their own: no office and no home.

In addition, all the normal, routine accoutrements of the office are no longer available. They don't have access to an answered telephone, to a typist, to a photocopy machine, even to simple supplies. They must take a great deal of time and personal initiative to accomplish even the simplest task.

3. *Persistence of Guilt.* Unemployed older executives must struggle with potentially immobilizing feelings of guilt. Regardless of cause, the job loss almost always converts into personal terms of guilt. Former President Reagan's quip that "when the other guy is out of work, it's a recession; when you're out of work, it's a depression" too often becomes a reality. As the experience of unemployment continues, depression shifts from its economic meaning to its psychological meaning and the individual is threatened with that as well.

The sense of guilt arises from several sources. For instance, most older executives have been "brainwashed," if you will, by the Protestant work ethic—you feel you don't have value if you're not being productive. It's insidious, with even routine things such as coffee breaks losing their value because you no longer have work to take a break from! The popular press and even friends and family impart a negative moral value to unemployment. Unemployment is equated with morally unjustified idleness, with laziness.

> I feel very negative about myself. My family expected more of me. I disappointed them. I'm the guilty one. But being unemployed proves Daddy was right—I am nothing. I'm scared to death to apply for a new job. I can't face new judgments.

> Every time I get turned down, I beat myself to death. I go through a whole series of why-did-I's and I-should-have's. If I'd just handled something differently, I would have gotten the job.

Unemployed older executives develop a focus of self-blame, which is disabling. They experience unemployment as a sign that they're failures. They discount any previous accomplishments. They may have an unreasonable sense of "destiny" which says that fate caused their unemployment because they were inadequate. They may develop a circular pattern of blame. "I am no good because no one will hire me. But that's the way things are. The economy is changing so fast that the company got in trouble. It had to let people go. But why me? I may really be no good. After all, no one has hired me…" They have a nagging sense of worthlessness which dogs their steps.

Each interview, then, becomes a personal test on a deep level. They worry whether the interviewer "saw" their lack of value. And this anxiety may cause them to present themselves in an artificial and constrained manner, undermining their interviews.

But older executives must fight their feelings of personal worthlessness and daily affirm the value of work and of working by actively seeking employment. The actual act of looking for work may help harness the feelings. So, the ritualization of an imitation of working—dressing, commuting, maintaining a visible aspect of a working routine—becomes extremely important. It represents control over the situation, a sort of magical force working for the individual to counteract the feelings of being lost and worthless.

4. *Ambivalence in Relationships.* The unemployed older manager's role is strained by the conditions of unemployment. Relationships with family and friends become ambivalent. Even if the individual

joins a group whose stated purpose is to help the person get work, relationships tend to be awkward and a little constrained, simply because unemployment may be "contagious." One man said it well: "Friends ask how you're doing, but they're petrified they may also lose their jobs."

This ambivalence further aggravates self-doubt and causes people to have an almost perpetual preoccupation with the impression they are making on others. They are particularly concerned with the impressions they're making on interviewers.

> I'm feeling negative about myself, so I think I'm being abrasive. I'm sending out negative signals and getting negative feedback. I haven't had such negative feedback in years. I've even had out-and-out run-ins with people and I've been decimated. My God, if that's the way I'm coming across, how can I possibly go out and get a job?

They are also profoundly lonely. Even though many older managers may be out of a job, they are out of work *by themselves*, not out of work as members of a labor group, who are *all* out of work because of a layoff, or some other temporary work stoppage. And when older managers do get jobs, they also get them alone—by themselves.

Budge describes unemployment as a group phenomenon by using this analogy: Unemployment is like a group of commuters waiting for a bus. Each line of people (job applicants) is waiting for a bus (job) to come in, without knowledge of the bus driver's (employer's) exact position or even whether the bus (company) has broken down (layoffs, belt-tightening, hiring freezes). The bus driver is just doing a job (hiring) and doesn't know the passengers (applicants), nor in any way grasps their individual concerns. When a bus does finally arrive, if it isn't one's own, the destinations of its passengers are irrelevant.

5. *Fear of Rejection.* This fear stops far too many job-seekers cold and keeps them from trying. The scenario is something like this: "I've already failed once (or twice or a dozen times). If I try hard again, they'll simply tell me, 'No.'" This anticipated "No" finally becomes so big that many stop going out on interviews, or even trying. They just stay put—and do nothing.

Stanley Wynett, writing in the *National Business Employment Weekly*,[2] says that many job-seekers are unaware that they fear "the Big

---

[2] Stanley Wynett, "Overcoming the Big No," *National Business Employment Weekly*, May 21, 1989, pp. 9 +.

No." They may still go out and make contacts, but after one or two tiny rejections, they quit for the day—or the week. They no longer "feel in the mood."

Dr. Herbert Fensterheim says in his best seller, *Stop Running Scared* that "persistent fear of an object or idea that originally does not justify fear, usually prepares you for the three Fs: flight, fight or freeze." He calls avoiding job interviews "fear-maintaining escape behavior." You can't keep the fright from occurring in a given situation, so you avoid the upsetting event that brings it on. You use every excuse under the sun to avoid getting and going on interviews. You don't face your fear and give yourself a chance to find out that what you think is going to happen won't happen and is only in your mind. According to Fensterheim, at some point, you have to take a stand and face your fear.

Some Guidelines to Handling the Emotions of Unemployment

Since managerial identity is threatened by unemployment, the development of ritual activities, of a job search routine, buffers the psychological ill effects. The following are particularly helpful:

❒ Accept that unemployment is a contingency in your career. Deal promptly with family and income problems to avoid destabilization. Maintain professional contacts and professional visibility as an aspect of working life that you can mobilize during unemployment. Continue your leisure-time activities, a hobby, small business or community activity and investigate them to see if they are exploitable reserve resources.

❒ Locate and associate with others who are also unemployed. Such relationships are inherently unstable, but they can be incorporated into a ritual of businesslike activity which is focused on getting a new job. It also helps substitute for informal work relationships and keeps alive the feeling of a peer group apart from family and friends. Such a group helps individuals discharge their constant feelings of worthlessness. The group gives consolation to the hurts and indignities of rejection, and provides a place where you can display your unemployed status without damage.

❒ Assess and reassess your status as a means of reaffirming the values of the business system without accepting any personal guilt. Decide for yourself which of the values you accept and which no longer are important to you. You may find you are hanging on to outmoded values, or worse yet, to values which were never your own but were foisted on you in your childhood, in college, in your marriage or on earlier jobs.

☐ If you seek professional help, seek it wisely. Most of the problems of unemployment result from the condition itself. Many therapists and counselors lack a clear understanding of the determinants of these problems and may unwittingly enlarge an individual's feelings of self-blame. Many professionals have therapy models which are not based on work, and they are themselves peripheral to organizational life. Few have had training in problems related to work life. They may apply clinical models, mistaking the mechanical depression of unemployment for physiological depression. As a result, they may misdiagnose and give inappropriate treatment. (Frequently, depression clears up immediately when older executives are reemployed. If the depression were physiologically caused, this would not be true.)

Older unemployed executives often have a real need for emotional support. You need an opportunity to vent your feelings without becoming maudlin and without fearing that a judgment will be made against you. These are some ways to get this emotional support.

1. *Join an existing support group for unemployed older executives guided by a competent professional.* This has several advantages. First, the others in the group are your peers. Second, the composition of the group is fluid, varying from meeting to meeting with the entrance of new members and the departure of old members to jobs. Thus, it is easy for someone to fill a niche in the group. Third, the very fact that you are going to the group on a temporary basis may enable you to come to grips more readily with some deep feelings and real problems. Have you ever met someone you've never seen before and don't expect ever to see again with whom you developed instant rapport? During the course of your conversation, did you discuss inner secrets and feelings you'd never before bared to anyone? These groups operate somewhat on the same basis. You know you'll be understood—and you know what you say will not be held against you at a later date or under other circumstances. If such a group is available in your vicinity, join immediately. Don't wait until you are discouraged by an unproductive job search. The group will help you feel ready to begin your search; and most importantly, the group will shore up your business identity.

2. *Your family.* If you have a family, this may be a good alternative to a support group. However, whether family is a reliable source of

support for you or not is situational. Do you already have open lines of communication with your spouse and/or children? If so, you are in a position to discuss your current feelings. In fact, the occasion of unemployment can act to draw families back together and to reopen formerly closed avenues of communication. This does require extra effort on your part and you may feel that in your situation, it wouldn't work.

Brothers, sisters and cousins (who are, after all, built-in peers) may make a better support group than those with whom you reside. You have a common experience base, and they may have been unemployed at some time or other. So, if you have family members around, at least try to draw upon these lines of support.

3. *Friends.*   You may encounter problems in using friends as a basis of support. But you still should try. Use care in approaching them. Don't make them feel threatened about their own status. Also, keep in mind that some people may be embarrassed if you attempt to use them as a "crying towel." Most, however, are willing to listen and will help if you can tell them how. Perhaps those friends best able to give you support and good advice are those who have, at some time in the past, grappled with unemployment themselves. Review your friends for this kind of experience. Then perhaps invite several who fit this criterion over for an hour or two, or phone them to talk.

Should any of your friends or acquaintances happen to be currently unemployed, you have a real opportunity to develop a mutual self-help organization with a broader purpose than just that of your own personal needs.

4. *Other existing sources of support.*   If none of the preceding is available, check in your area to see what is. Call the business librarian at your local library. Contact one of the business editors or the librarian at your local newspaper. Approach your priest, rabbi or minister. Stop by the Chamber of Commerce, the YMCA, YWCA, YMHA, YWHA. Check with local college counseling services, the human resources department of your former employer (if you parted under amicable conditions). Local mental health agencies are another possible contact. And, at least discuss the question of this kind of support with a counselor at your local unemployment office.

Keep in mind, though, that the kind of emotional support you are looking for is likely to be different from that needed to further your job search.

For those few of you whose drinking or substance-abuse habits may have contributed toward your current unemployed status, don't overlook the very real help and support of groups such as Alcoholics Anonymous and other substance abuse organizations. Numerous AA members have already struggled with the twin problems of alcohol addiction and unemployment. Locate meetings whose attendees will most likely come from the executive, professional or managerial ranks.

For some of you, prayer may be a means of getting support. In the strictly secular setting of unemployment, people tend to forget that other avenues of help exist. If you have a religious background and some experience with prayer, try it. It could be healing.

5. *Set up your own mutual support group.* If none of the above will work, then locate other unemployed older executives and set up your own group. Run an ad in a local paper or put up a notice on the community bulletin board. You can probably arrange to have a preliminary meeting in donated space—a church, a school or someone's office after hours. (In many communities, banks and savings and loan organizations have meeting rooms which they'll make available free of charge to worthy community groups.)

To get such a group off the ground, you'll have to use your organizational, managerial and problem-solving skills. But you'll end up helping both yourself and others. And you'll get the sort of support and lift to your self-esteem which you need.

This last alternative requires more commitment than the others if it is to be made to work. You will need to recruit someone to serve as a facilitator—perhaps a minister with counseling training, a high school counselor with special skills for working with groups, or someone who regularly facilitates other types of group therapy. The group should be organized so that it can be ongoing after you get your own long-awaited job. Otherwise, it could be a disservice both to you and to the very people you want to recruit as members.

Above all, you need community. You *must* reach out for contact with other human beings. Remaining isolated and alone during this time is a prescription for failure.

How Do You Begin Your Job Search?

When you were employed, you disciplined your activities and structured your time. The external requirements of the job plus your own internal desires forced you to get up at 6:30 every morning, shower, shave or put on makeup, eat breakfast, then commute to work. You organized the rest of your day similarly, and culminated your day with a regular evening regime and bedtime at a reasonable hour. You probably always considered yourself disciplined and work-oriented, and may have looked down a little on others who were not.

Make this lifetime of good habits continue to work for you. Avoid the temptation to take some time off for good behavior. Don't go off on a vacation (unless it has been planned for months and you'd lose the cost of the tickets) or take the first few weeks off to take care of some of the things around the house that have needed doing for years. A friend calls this "fixing-up" desire the "bathroom syndrome." When he became unemployed a few months ago, he spent the first month getting up every day and looking at his bathroom, planning the changes he was going to make on it. Then he spent the next month making those changes in a leisurely fashion. He had been unemployed a full three months before he got back to the really important matter at hand: finding a job.

By then, this man had geared down so much, that he had great difficulty gearing *up* for a concerted job search. But you don't feel like looking for a job, you say? You want time to lick your wounds and get yourself in shape? You're down in the dumps, and you don't want to see anybody while you're feeling like that? Some other time, but not now. Pick yourself up by your shirt collar and *get started*.

Consider first these personal aspects of your job search. How are you going to keep up your spirits, present your best side to potential employers? How are you going to get your act together? The trick is to approach the job search with energy and use your time effectively, but that can be difficult to do unless you have a job search strategy that works on a daily basis.

A Job Search as a Marketing Campaign

Begin by thinking of yourself as a "product." You are one, you know, whether you like the idea or not. You have a certain set of skills—of features, benefits and attributes—that you need to make appealing to a potential "purchaser," a new employer. Your job search, then, is really a marketing effort, in which the product you are going to market is yourself. Your marketing campaign includes all elements of marketing: marketing research; advertising (your letters and resumes); packaging; prospecting for "customers"; and that very important part, personal selling (the interview), which includes closing the sale (getting the job).

In a job search, each one of the marketing phases has a corresponding function particular to looking for a job. Some of the elements in each section are:

1. Surveying the Market in General

   ❏ What is the general economic situation?
   ❏ What are conditions in this market (location)? Should I consider another market place?
   ❏ What are the market segment(s)?
   ❏ What does the job market look like? What are possible markets for my skills?
   ❏ Where are the jobs? (Geographical location, business/industry/non-profit/government)
   ❏ What are areas of greatest opportunity?

2. Segmenting the Market

   ❏ What do the market segments look like?
   ❏ How many companies are in the segment?
   ❏ What do the particular market segments need? (Skills, background, general and specific abilities)

3. Selecting a Segment with Matches

   ❏ Which segment(s) do my skills most closely match?
   ❏ What can I do best for which position in the segment?

4. Positioning Your Product in the Segment

❏ Goals and objectives (What am I looking for?)

❏ Market Research (What kinds of activities do I need to engage in to get a job? What kinds of jobs are available? Where are they?)

❏ Product research (What are my strengths and weaknesses? What do I like to do? What do I want to do? What do I need to learn? What changes do I need to make?)

❏ Budget (Time, finances, energies)

❏ Developing new skills

❏ Prospecting for possible employers (lead generation)

❏ Presentation (Resume, letter campaigns, preparing for interviews)

❏ Personal selling (the interview)

Time Management—Working Efficiently

Job hunting is time-consuming and exhausting. You must use your time as effectively as possible. You were used to managing time on your job. But when you're unemployed, everything else is out of whack, and it's easy to quit managing your time, too. This section on time management isn't meant to be insulting—it's meant as a reminder to continue managing your time wisely.

One of the most efficient time-management tools is the list. Begin by writing down as many job-hunting activities as you can think of, basing them on the suggestions shown above in the market survey section. Then prioritize the activities, using an A, B, C. system (A for the most important activities, B for those which are important but can wait a while, C for those which might be useful, but which can be done later, provided doing the A and B items doesn't get you a job.) Then, for those rating an A priority, number them in order of importance and/or immediate need.

Let's say your list looks like this:

❏ Read job-hunting books.

❏ Talk to other unemployed or recently unemployed executives or professionals to find out what worked for them.

❏ Write a preliminary resume.

❏ Make a list of your accomplishments on the job—what you did that made money or saved time or money for your employer.

❏ Write brief job descriptions for each position you held.

❏ List responsibilities for each position held.

❏ Review your strengths in technical, business and interpersonal skills and write them down.

❏ Evaluate your technical, business and interpersonal weaknesses. Decide if you have any areas where you should take corrective action. Write down both.

❏ Determine and write your job objective(s).

❏ Write a thumbnail description highlighting your business abilities.

❏ Prepare drafts of your final resume or resumes. You may need several different kinds and may go through several drafts of each before you come up with something you can use.

❏ Get personal stationery printed.

❏ Avail yourself of a personal computer/word processor. (If you don't have one, check at a nearby quick-copy shop. Many of them will allow you to use a word processor for a small fee or can arrange to have someone input your resume so that you can produce a professional-looking document.)

❏ Review your personal wardrobe for job-hunting suitability.

❏ Find a place to work outside your home—the office of a friend, the public library, a community facility—some place with permanence.

❏ Arrange to have your telephone answered—an answering service or machine, someone's office.

❏ Apply for unemployment compensation.

❏ Review your financial obligations and finances.

❏ Prepare a budget for six months or longer.

❏ Have your resume drafts reviewed by knowledgeable people in your field, or by people whose opinions you value.

❏ Prepare answers to possible interview questions.

❏ Go through at least one and preferably more mock interviews with friends, acquaintances or other job-seekers.

❏ Discuss your situation fully and honestly with your family.

❏ Seek help from a counselor.

❏ Contact all of your references, preferably in person, or by telephone.

❏ Make contact with a self-help group.

Obviously, this list is incomplete. But you could use it as a starter, supplementing it with items of your own. You can see that all of these can't be done in one day, one week, or even one month. After all, you aren't superman or superwoman! But some of them must be completed before you should even think of going on an interview.

Concentrate initially on those items that you will need immediately and tag them as having an A priority. Here is one possible A list, shown in prioritized order (your own list will be different):

Priority	Activity
A1	Apply for unemployment compensation.
A2	Write a preliminary resume.
A3	Review your financial obligations and finances.
A4	Discuss your situation fully and honestly with your family.
A5	Get personal stationery printed.
A6	Locate a computer you can use.

Then, at the start of every day, list the activities you should work on for that day, reprioritizing them according to the A, B, C system. Be sure to include personal-care activities like getting a haircut or going to the beauty shop, shining your shoes, taking clothing to the cleaners, etc.

As you complete each essential preliminary activity, check it off on your personal checklist. This will both keep you on target and give you a sense of accomplishment. Then, continue to make lists and check off activities as you enter the later phases of your job search.

Keep in mind another point about time management. The time-management experts say, "Do it now." In a job search, it's entirely too easy to procrastinate and spend hours "fiddling around" or otherwise wasting time. Instead, consider your job search to be your full-time employment—perhaps the most important job of your life, since it will determine your continued success. Let's face it. At this age, there's a terrible temptation just to give up and let everything go. Fight it!

Get up in the morning at your regular time. Eat a good breakfast. Get dressed in your business togs (and be sure you look good, even if you're just going to the library). *Get going.* Leave the house with your briefcase and your list for the day. Then, put in at least a six-hour work day toward completing your A priorities—those activities you identified as most important *today* toward your job search. By doing this, you are making an active commitment toward finding a job.

Keep accurate and complete records. These should include financial records such as mileage, interview expenses, support group costs, supplies, printing, etc.; records of resumes and letters sent and which forms you used; lists of contacts; interviewers' names and the dates you interviewed. (Many states require that you turn in a list of all job contacts and interviews before they will pay you your unemployment—and they do check on your statements.)

Your Appearance and Health

Your appearance and the way you project yourself physically are the ways you are currently packaging your product i.e., "advertising" your worth. After your years in the executive or professional ranks, reminding you that appearance is a critical hiring element may seem presumptuous. This section serves only as a reminder of the importance that appearance plays. So, take a good look at yourself as others see you. It is an absolute fact that if your appearance doesn't measure up to some interviewer's preconceptions, you've provided them with an automatic deselector. Nothing else that occurs in the interview really counts. The first five to fifteen seconds of an interview set the tone for the rest of the interview and ultimately determine whether you get the job or not. You are an actor on a stage when the interview begins. You must project vitality, confidence and attention to detail in the way you dress, your grooming, your posture.

But paying special attention to your appearance each day has another, perhaps more important and personal value. That is, "the better you look, the better you'll feel." Spending the time it takes to look good is a way of whistling in the dark, of keeping up your spirits.

S. Eric Wachtel, president of Wachtel Associates, New York City, a firm specializing in executive recruitment and organizational planning and development, laid it right on the line when he said:

> Far too many older executives reinforce the stereotypes which produce hiring prejudices. They don't pay attention to their personal appearance and general presentation. I continue to be astonished at the number who come into this office needing a haircut and wearing messy shirts with frayed collars and cuffs. Their suits are rumpled and either lack taste or are out of style. Their entire appearance—lack of general grooming, poor posture, low energy level—screams, "This person is a poor risk. Don't consider hiring him or her." They appear defeated, and reinforce this impression when they speak. Their voices are weak and shaky; they are either obsequious or overly engaging—too "up". They completely fail to sell themselves, to present a positive image.

Clothing. Begin by taking a really good look at your wardrobe. Check each garment for pulls, loose buttons, frayed cuffs, etc. Then put on the suits that pass muster and stand in front of a full-length mirror. Make sure the suits fit smoothly, without wrinkles or unusual bulges.

Consider: How long has it been since you bought a good new suit? If your answer is a year or more ago, this is one place where you shouldn't economize. Go to a first-class shop and buy a new suit, complete with new shirt or blouse, shoes, and other appropriate accessories. Buy in tasteful, muted, somewhat conservative colors (blues, grays) in natural fibers (wool, silk, cotton). Your clothing must match and blend harmoniously. If the store has a wardrobe coordinator, ask for his or her help and accept the recommendations he or she makes. Then, have the suit tailored to fit. Don't cut corners here. A few years ago, the exact same advice was appropriate for business women. Stylish and feminine clothing designed for business women is now available, and some dresses are suitable for an interview, especially in the summer. Still, women can't go wrong with a good, solidly tailored business suit.

What you wear tells the world the state of your self-esteem. If you have lost weight, get your suits retailored. Don't just throw on any old thing, even to go to the library. Dress to increase your self-esteem—as though you were going to a most important business meeting. It does matter.

Hair.   Look at your hair. Are you waiting too long between haircuts? Go to a barber or hairdresser and get a good stylish cut. Consider carefully your present hairstyle. Can it be a deselector? Anything which interviewers look on unfavorably or which hits on any of their preconceptions or prejudices should be avoided. Some possible deselectors: Males wearing their hair too long or with sideburns may be viewed as messy, unkempt or failing to keep current. Women who wear their hair long and "down" may give the impression that they are trying too hard to look youthful. (If you like wearing your hair long, then at least put it up into a businesslike chignon or in a clasp at the nape of your neck.)

Men: If you've been going to the corner barbershop for years just because it's handy—then find out who cuts the hair of the person you know with the best-looking hairstyle—then go to that stylist to get your own cut.

Women: Continue your regular visits to your hairdresser. Consider cutting your hair and wearing it in a short, softly waved, natural style. Don't wait to get a permanent or begin doing your own hair as a money-saving measure unless you are good at it. You need to look your very best. If you haven't been going to a hairdresser regularly, invest in hair care to improve your overall image.

Job counselors, employment agency personnel and executive recruiters disagree on whether to color grey hair or not. It may be a matter of personal preference. But many job-hunters feel that anything which might give them an appearance edge in locating a job should be considered. If you decide in favor of coloring, be careful. If you had black or dark brown hair, don't dye your hair back to its original dark color. It always looks artificial and gives a harsh, unflattering edge you don't need. Instead, go for a lighter, softer brown than your natural color, or have your hair "highlighted" (slightly lighter streaks of color). Since you will already be coloring, at least go for the most flattering effect. The distinction between male and female hairdressing has blurred, so the place to have your hair color treated would be at a first-rate salon with a colorist. Above all, don't attempt to color your hair yourself. The results will not be the effect you desire, and may even prove to be a deselector. If you do decide to color, pay special attention to the roots and get touch-ups every two or three weeks.

A decade ago, hair coloring would have been out of place for male managers, although acceptable for women. However, today's executives are more adaptable—and hair-coloring is a way to present a slightly more youthful appearance. Another hair question which must be dealt with is what to do if your hairline is decidedly receding (or, let's face it, if you're bald). Again, the general impression is better if you just accept the bald spot instead of doing a a fancy trick of combing eight- inch long side hair over the gleaming top, in the vain hope that the shine won't show. It *always* shows, and this hairstyle is rarely flattering. Sometimes the part is so low that almost no short hair is left above the ears. The question of wearing a toupee or wig is in the same area of taste. If you have a very good hand-tied toupee or wig of real hair which fits exceptionally well—and is the same color as the hair over your ears and at the nape of your neck, then wear it. But take a critical, honest look at the image you present in the mirror. Is it obvious that you are wearing a "rug?" It's your decision if you want to continue wearing it, or whether you want to go to the expense of getting a really good hairpiece—which costs several hundred dollars.

General grooming.   A couple of other appearance notes. Spend more time on general grooming. Take extra care during your bath or shower. Keep your nails trimmed and buffed, or have a regular manicure. Business women can now wear polish (muted colors, please, but it doesn't have to be an insipid pale pink). Keep your shoes polished and have new heel lifts put on as soon as the heels begin to wear. Have your suits cleaned and pressed more frequently. And take the necessary time to exercise and keep yourself trim. It's awfully easy just to give in to gravity and let everything sag.

Body image and body language.   Posture projects self-image. Even if you don't feel like it, put on your best posture whenever you leave your house. Gather your body together: lift your chest, relax your shoulders, tuck under your derriere and straighten your spine. See, you already look better! Finish the good impression by keeping your head up, ready to look the world in the eye. Stride when you walk—project energy, but the energy of a strong body, not nerves.

So what if that isn't the way you feel? Fake it. Act. You are doing a very important selling job—selling yourself into a job. And that has to begin by selling yourself on yourself. After you force yourself to present a lively appearance, you will find that the reality will soon come to approximate the projection, and you'll feel better for it. Practice walking, sitting and standing with energy. Then check the way you look doing this in a full-length mirror. (That full-length mirror has to function as your toughest critic.) As you walk down the street, observe yourself in store windows as you pass by. Make constant adjustments to keep up your posture and your positive appearance.

Health and physical well-being.   After you have your external appearance under control, consider your internal being. Get a physical to check on your general health. Find out if there is a physical cause for your general malaise or lack of energy. Check on your nutritional status—when you are "down," it's too easy to skimp on your meals and fail to get adequate amounts of vitamins, minerals and other nutrients. It's one of those vicious-cycle things—you don't feel well, so you don't eat well. You don't eat well, so you don't feel well. And, of course, check on the condition of your heart and vascular system.

If you have been troubled by impotence or a total lack of interest in sex, don't accept for one minute that this is entirely due to your age, or is completely tied in to your unemployed state (although that can definitely bear on the problem). Bring up the topic and discuss it fully and frankly with your doctor.

If you are not having any physical problems, you should still get a physical exam. Just knowing that your general health is all right, or that you are doing something about it, will be of value and will help increase your self-esteem.

Voice.   Record your voice and listen to it. Your voice must be pleasant and full of energy, not loud, but dynamic. Articulate more carefully so that you'll be easy to understand. (Mumbling unfortunately goes along with the general blahs that afflict the unemployed.) And take the extra effort to organize your thoughts carefully.

Put Your Finances in Order

Your income for the immediately foreseeable future has been drastically reduced. Even if your last employer gave you a healthy severance package, you're not prescient. You don't know how long you will be unemployed. The length of unemployment for managers now averages somewhere between eight months and one year. In some industries (the financial industry, for instance) the length of unemployment has been much longer than that. Of course, some executives and professionals find immediate reemployment. But for each person in that happy circumstance, someone else has already been searching one year to eighteen months, depending to some extent upon the health of the business or industry in which he or she is searching for work.

So taking prudent financial steps immediately is essential, even if you'd rather just continue the way you are. Don't be an ostrich—instead, be realistic, as you review your situation.

l. *Apply for unemployment compensation immediately.* Far too many older professionals fail to apply soon enough for this income source out of a misplaced sense of pride. They feel degraded by the process. This is especially true when they've heard horror stories of applicants being treated as nonpersons, beneath the notice of the personnel in the state unemployment office. Worse yet, they resent the time that is wasted on routine processes not applicable to managerial-level people. When these people finally do apply, they discover they cannot recover the funds that would have been available to them between the end of their employment and the time they did apply. If you didn't go because you had accrued vacation time, the unemployment divisions of the various states automatically take this into account in calculating when they will begin paying benefits. There is always a period of delay between filing and the first check. So run, not walk, to file your application. You shouldn't lose any of the funds to which you are legally entitled. These funds were paid by law by your employer and, in some cases, by you. Also, some states do have effective and beneficial programs for executive-level personnel.

2. *Go over your current budget.* If you don't have one, check your actual expenditures for the last six months to determine your current spending levels.

❏ List essential expenditures—food, utilities, mortgage, health insurance, tuition payments. (If any of your children are still in school, you will want to avoid taking them out of college if you can, since this will probably be upsetting to you and them. However, you might insist they get a job to help with expenses.)

❏ List other expenditures for which you are obligated —car payments, loans, etc.

❏ List expenditures you think you'll have to make during your job campaign. Don't cheat yourself and the success of your campaign by trying to cut corners on these. You must have resumes prepared; you should have personalized stationery and you'll need routine operating expenses—car, bus or train fare, lunch money. Also include personal-care items such as needed new apparel and more frequent haircuts and/or beauty shop appointments.

❏ List items which are discretionary and can be cut. Cable TV, liquor, entertainment and country-club dues fall into this category.

3. *Identify* and list available income and other funds you will have for at least the next six months. Include unemployment compensation and your spouse's income.

4. *Reinvest your pension funds.* Take whatever action is necessary to reinvest your pension funds if you aren't vested in your former employer's pension system. You have only 60 days to rollover these funds into an IRA account. Don't miss the deadline. If you do, you won't be able to shelter the funds and you'll have to handle the money as regular income on your tax return. One other point: They're always there as a backup if your financial situation becomes desperate. Cashing in IRAs should be your absolutely last resort, however, since there are sizable penalties for early withdrawal of funds from these accounts.

5. *List other possible sources of funding.* Include the borrowing value of your life insurance, what you might get from refinancing your home or taking out a home equity loan, your stocks and bonds, IRAs, etc. You hope you won't have to tap these sources, but be realistic. What liquid resources do you have? (A house or other property is really not a liquid asset!)

6. *Work out a revised six-month budget.* If funds are going to be tight, contact your creditors and try to defer or rearrange payments on some of your major bills. Most creditors would prefer to know this in

advance so they don't continue to push too hard. Notifying them also shows your "good faith intentions." You can avoid potential credit problems by taking this step early and working out a minimum payment schedule until you are employed again. Utility companies will often work with you, as they do with others, to equalize payments during this time.

7. *Set up an accounting procedure to keep track of your job-search expenditures.*   Many of these will be tax deductible.

8. *Discuss your projected budget fully with other family members.*

☐ *Men*: If your wife hasn't been working, perhaps she will be willing to help tide the family over during this time by finding short-term work. If she is already employed, she may be able to help in many ways, taking over the health insurance obligations for the family through her employer's health benefit package, for example.

☐ *Women*: Discuss your revised budget and curtailed spending needs with your husband. Work out future spending together, since he will also have to work on a limited spending plan.

☐ *Families with children*: Consider what contribution children remaining at home can make to the budget. At your age, they should be old enough to understand what is going on. Be sure to let them know what the problems will be, without scaring them unduly. They will be more helpful and less demanding if they know reality rather than having to conjecture about the situation themselves. They also need to know that you aren't "crying wolf." They may be able to take care of some of their own needs through part-time jobs or entrepreneurial pursuits such as yard work, window washing, baby sitting and so on. Older children who are working but still living at home should be required to contribute at least enough for their own support.

☐ *Single people*: If you have no family responsibilities, then sit down and have a talk with a friend or relative—or with yourself—about your financial situation.

Whatever you do, come out of your deliberations with a workable financial plan that takes your situation fully into account, and has been "bought into" by your family. By doing so, you'll have your credit rating and the major portion of your resources intact at the end of this period of unemployment. And you'll accomplish something else as well. Financial problems exacerbate the bad feelings you already have because you're unemployed. Developing a financial plan and taking action is positive and productive, and will give you a needed boost.

Recreation and Leisure-Time Activities

The stress of daily living is much harder on the unemployed than on someone who works 40 hours a week. Susan Barstis, a clinical psychologist with the Kaiser Permanente medical program in Los Angeles suggests that the out-of-work need vacations more than people who are employed. But because most unemployed shouldn't spend the money for a typical vacation, she suggests less costly alternatives such as gardening, painting or carpentering—for a couple of hours each day. She says this will help relieve the trauma of job loss and perhaps can even ward off depression.

Older executives often are active in community affairs. There's a terrible temptation to withdraw from these activities when you're unemployed to avoid embarrassment. Don't yield to this temptation. Continue to participate exactly as you did before. You'll get reinforcement of your continued worth—the organizations need you just as much now as they did before. And you'll have natural opportunities to meet other executives, and may even get valuable leads on possible employment. Besides, when your unemployed period is over, you'll want to continue these desirable activities. If you drop them now, you'll find them difficult to resume later. That said, a word of caution: Don't let organizations and volunteer activities take over your life. You can't afford to spend all of your time on these to the detriment of your personal job search.

Continue with your hobbies and with normal social activities. But keep these in perspective, too. You won't want to indulge in expensive entertaining or take up costly new hobbies. But accept social outings, even if you really don't want to, and spend some time on those hobbies (the inexpensive ones) which give you the most pleasure.

Do take up some new hobby or activity—a free or inexpensive one. Go to the local museums on free admission days. Go to the dollar movie house instead of the seven-dollar-a-ticket first-run theater. Participate in free activities going on in the community. Don't overlook the activities in the religious community of your choice. You need to do these things as stress-relievers. Enjoy them without guilt.

Part 2

Surveying the Job Market

Putting Your
Plan into Action

When you're working on your self-marketing campaign, you're really not working with a linear process. You'll move back and forth through different kinds of activities as your job search progresses and your situation changes. But the first thing you must do, in any event, is to put together some kind of a preliminary resume, then begin work on some of the activities suggested in Chapter 2, "How Do You Begin Your Job Search." Carry on those activities and the ones outlined in this chapter at the same time. That way, you'll move your campaign along faster and make the most efficient use of your time. Both make contributions to more than one phase of the job search—and some of them will stand you in good stead later when you're again among the working.

Early in your search, you're likely to have a tremendous desire to stay at home and lick your wounds. Don't. You need to get yourself ready as quickly as you can to make the necessary contacts to get things moving. Still, you may make a grave error if you begin contacting people and companies before you really know exactly where you should be heading. You need to organize yourself and develop your marketing strategies first.

Find Out Who and What You Are
At this time in your life, your goals and your life in general have undergone major changes from what they were when you were younger. Before you rush into a new job based on your old goals and life style, evaluate carefully where you are right now—and where you want to go. Chances are that you should change your life goals. You probably no longer really want the job that was your ultimate goal 10 to 20 years ago. Or, you may have already reached your initial goal and it's time for you

to reset your goals instead of drifting aimlessly through this period. Take the time and effort to study yourself now. You may be surprised to find out how different your current needs and wants are from those you had in your twenties, thirties and even early forties.

Don't rush into a new job that is unsatisfactory for you just because you want to be employed. Far too many people who do this find themselves unemployed again after a short time. They may quit or be terminated—or remain in an unhappy and possibly dead-end situation.

You don't want to repeat their errors. You want to deal with the reasons other than general business conditions which explain why you were terminated from your previous position. You need to take enough time to determine the work environment in which you will be most successful. You should adequately survey the job market, and determine what you could do best in that market. You also need to take the time to determine what market segments exist, then select the market segment which best matches your overall life goals.

There are at least two ways you can determine what to do with the rest of your life. You may contact an industrial psychologist or counseling firm—or you can study this on your own. Most job-search specialists suggest that the most useful study is the one you undertake by yourself. But many people can't successfully complete this alone, either because they procrastinate or because they don't know where to start.

If you've already tried on your own and have decided to go for help, your first step is to locate a good, competent psychologist or counselor who isn't going to charge you an arm and a leg. Most universities have psychologists on their staffs who do this kind of counseling on a full- or part-time basis. You can also check with the American Personnel and Guidance Association for qualified practitioners in your area. In their *Directory of Approved Counseling Agencies*, they list those agencies in the various states which maintain high professional standards. Take the time to check, because the whole realm of counseling is an area which has attracted a large number of quacks. Especially in these times of relatively high executive job instability, someone is always around to take advantage of those who are experiencing adversity.

What should you expect from counseling? First, the counselor should suggest that you undergo a battery of psychological and skill evaluation tests. Then you will undergo a series of relatively structured interviews where you will review the results of your tests—your strengths, weaknesses, areas of interest and so on. Only then will you be ready to discuss and evaluate your job goals and objectives. This process should help you find out:

❐ If you are suited to the work you've been doing.
❐ What shortfalls or deficits you have that you can do something about.
❐ What your strengths are.
❐ What your interests are.
❐ What you should be doing.

If you decide to do this study on your own, begin with several sheets of paper. Head one sheet *Skills*, another *Strengths*, a third *Weaknesses*, a fourth *What I Want Out of a Job*, a fifth *Life Style*, a sixth *Accomplishments* (subdivide this one into past, current and what I hope to do in the future), a seventh *Goals and Objectives* (subdivide this one into past, current and projected), and an eighth *Problems I Had on Earlier Jobs*. Keep a couple of other sheets handy for additional headings and for notes. Then answer the following questions for yourself on the paper with the appropriate heading:

1. Is my existing career obsolete? Must I change careers because jobs are no longer available in my existing one?

2. What skills do I have? What do I do well? What do I enjoy?

3. What are my weaknesses? Have these caused me difficulty on the job? Which ones can be corrected—or should be corrected? Will this be costly in terms of time, effort or money? What training or self-improvement efforts have I undertaken to increase my value to a prospective employer?

4. What problems did I encounter in earlier jobs? If I was fired or terminated, what are the reasons? (Be honest here. If it wasn't due to weakness on your part, say so.) What can I do to avoid these problems in the future?

5. What time spans are built into present decisions? (For example: How long would additional training take? How much longer are your kids going to be in college? What risks are built into those decisions?)

6. What goals, values, priorities do I already have?

7. What do I want to accomplish before I die? What do I perceive my life's mission to be? What have I already accomplished? (Include both business and personal accomplishments.)

8. What do I want out of a job? (Do you like line or staff work, large or small companies? What about nonprofit organizations or government? Do you prefer to be a specialist or would you rather have broad responsibilities? What kind of people do you like to work for and with? Can you be satisfied with a restricted job or do you require continual challenge? Do you prefer to "do" or to manage those who do? What about going into business for yourself?) What about travel? Overtime or long hours on the job? What about long-term prospects for advancement?

9. Where do I want to work? (In a major city, a suburban or rural area? What region of the country—the Northeast, Southeast, Midwest, Mountain States, Northwest, West Coast? International? If so, where?) Will I be willing to relocate or do I want to stay where I am?

10. What about my life style? (Are you willing to make changes in it, or are you happy with your current life style and unwilling to change if you don't have to?)

After you have answered these questions (and others that you think of yourself), analyze your answers carefully. The last step in completing your analysis is to write your new goals and objectives. You may also want to write a narrative or summary statement which capsulizes who and what you are and where you want to go. You will find a partner useful in this endeavor. Ideally, this should be someone who knows you well, say your husband, wife, brother or sister or a long-term friend. But you and another unemployed executive might find it helpful to undertake a mutual self-help study, using each other as partners and critics.

This activity is *not* "make work." You're dealing with the rest of your life, and a little soul-searching is in order. As an older executive, it's especially important that you rethink your life goals and objectives. You're not the same person you were 10, 15 or even 30 years ago. You may be shocked to discover that you've been conducting your life on out-of-date, even archaic assumptions about yourself. Time spent in getting reacquainted with yourself can be invaluable.

Make Valuable Contacts
Since it may have been years since you've looked for a job, let's review the importance of using your contacts. This is an important part of surveying the market and determining the market segments that currently

exist. It is also one area where you as an older executive have a leg up on younger job-seekers. You already *know* many people in your industry and your community, and have most likely developed a larger range of acquaintances and business associates than the younger person.

As you're aware, two job markets exist, the *visible job market*, represented by jobs listed in newspaper advertisements, with state employment agencies, through executive recruiters, employment agencies, trade associations and college placement services; and the *invisible* or *hidden job market*, containing jobs which will soon be available due to retirements, expansion, under staffing, budget increases, or which might become available if the right person applied. These latter jobs are usually known to only a few people within an organization. Even the human resource departments are often unaware of their existence. At any given time, about 75 percent of the job potential is in this invisible market. Entry to this market is largely through personal contact. (Not what you know but who you know is often what counts here!)

In the early stages of your job search, you may not yet be aware of possible employment opportunities. You may have been so buried in your own job or situation that you haven't kept abreast of employment options in your industry or area of specialization, let alone in the general world of employment. Your first inclination is to buy the Sunday paper and begin searching there. That's a valuable activity, but not nearly as likely to be immediately productive as is looking for information through the people you know. In keeping with the idea that you are marketing yourself, you should survey the job market—and part of that is to survey the market through the eyes of your friends and acquaintances.

Your purpose: to get whatever information they might have about the job situation. You aren't begging them for a job, but just their assessment of what is happening in their business or industry. Ask them to give you the names of friends or acquaintances of theirs who might be willing to provide information and possible leads to companies that are hiring. Then use the first group of friends' and acquaintances' names as an entree to the next group of people.

Don't restrict the number of people you talk to. You need to get the big picture of the job market. Almost all your managerial skills are transferable to other businesses and industries, so don't just investigate the business or industry you've recently left. You also need to be aware of possibilities which you could qualify for with minimum additional training. Investigate small businesses of all types; city, local, state and federal government possibilities; the nonprofit sector; and start-up industries as well as big business.

Most of the new jobs these days are in small- and medium-size business and industries where you will have a better opportunity to access decision-makers directly. And where—as an older employment prospect—you will have a better opportunity for employment.

Networking requires basically a five-step approach, as follows:

1. *Prepare a contact list.*   Include not just important decision-makers, but everyone who may be able to help you. You never know who is going to give you that golden lead. Also consider the kinds of contacts/referrals that would be most likely to help you accomplish your new goals (if you have gotten that far with your self-evaluation). Without doubt, you have at least 50 friends or acquaintances who might be helpful. How many of these present contacts might be able to help you? Consider the following list for starters:

❐ Family members—father, mother, brothers, sisters, in-laws, aunts, uncles, cousins.
❐ Friends from the past—coworkers from earlier jobs, neighbors, customers, military friends, fraternity or sorority members, former schoolmates. No matter how old, don't overlook them. Whether or not they can help you immediately, they will be delighted to hear from you, and may come up with useful leads later on.
❐ People from your most recent job—employers or employees, fellow workers, competitors, salespeople, customers or clients. If necessary, mend your fences. You may want to use some of these people for references as well as for information and possible leads.
❐ People from your social contacts or organizations—church, synagogue, lodge or club members, sports groups—bowling, tennis, golf, sailing, hunting, etc.—hobby groups, contacts made through your children (little league, band parents, etc.).
❐ People whom you've contacted through charitable or public service groups.
❐ Professionals who have provided services for you —bankers, lawyers, doctors, dentists, accountants, etc.

2. *Send a resume and cover letter to each of your primary contacts.*
Even if a contact happens to be your brother, you're making a mistake if you assume that he knows all there is to know about you and your career. If you do not have time enough to send your resume before you meet with the primary contact, take along your resume and leave it. You may even want to ask them for suggestions for improving your resume.

3. *Use your contacts effectively.* Be aware that your network contacts will usually think more in terms of jobs that are open or not, than in terms of your individual skills and background. Help keep each contact focused on you—on what you have done before and can do in the future.

❐ Consider each contact as a resource whose time is valuable. When you ask for a meeting, be very specific about the length of time you'd like to talk to them (no longer than fifteen to twenty minutes). Then, be on time for the meeting, and after your specified time is over, thank them for meeting with you, and leave. Only stay longer at the insistence of the contact—and even then, be careful not to overstay your welcome.

❐ When you ask him or her for referrals, specify exactly what kind of organizations, departments, specialties or persons you'd like to be directed to, and specify which of your skills would be appropriate.

❐ Be especially careful when friends have gone out on a limb to help you by arranging interviews with others. Go to the interviews prepared to meet new friends and to present yourself in the best possible light as a worthy representative of your friends. One note of caution: since your friends may never have had to look for jobs, they may arrange some interviews which appear to be nonproductive from your standpoint. You still owe it to your friends to put your best foot forward so that you don't blow friendships by making them look bad.

❐ Go to your meeting with each contact armed with a prepared list of questions you'd like answered.

4. *Always ask permission to use the name of your contact.* Then do just that, both in phone conversations and in correspondence. Nothing drives the networking process more quickly and more effectively than a personal reference.

❐ Try to develop other possible leads from each new contact. Ask if they know someone who might have information about a particular field, or who has exceptional knowledge about an area in which you are interested. However, don't press in such a way that he or she becomes uncomfortable.

5. *Follow up.* Allow your contact to set the schedule. Just be certain that you adhere to it and recontact each person within the agreed-upon

time. Report back to your contact when a lead pans out. Always send a short and gracious thank-you letter.[1]

You may not find out all the information you need on these initial visits. But you'll meet some nice people—and find that these meetings force you to think and to focus more closely on the market segments that might match your "product attributes," as well as on your overall employment goals and objectives. Also, devote some part of the meetings to mining the possibilities for secondary contacts. Try to get the names of at least one (or more) people who might more directly be able to help you. Contact these new people, again using the name of the referral as an entree. In this way, you can use your current network to build a new network that might enable you to locate a job that's "just right."

Business or Professional Organizations

You can make very useful contacts through the business or professional organizations to which you belong or for which you are eligible. If you're a marketing executive, for example, you may have been paying dues for the Sales and Marketing Management Association, but not attending meetings. Or you may have felt that belonging to such organizations and going to meetings was a waste of time. In either event, change your tactics. As part of your survey of the current job market, find out where and when the meetings are held, then go. You'll stay current in your profession or area of specialization, find out the latest in the field—and you may get important leads. Joining and paying your dues can be considered essential expenditures, and are tax deductible. However, don't expect these organizations to help you get a job. The personal contacts you make at the meetings and the networking that goes on before and after the sessions is where you'll get the most help.

Job Search Organizations

Another excellent way to make contacts, and get help writing your resume, advice on setting up your job campaign and support in working your way through the emotional traumas of unemployment is to join a self-help organization for the unemployed executive or professional. There are a number of these around in various parts of the country, and they provide a very valuable service. However, be aware that most of

---

[1]The five guidelines for networking were suggested by Kenneth and Sheryl Dawson, writing in "The Total Job Search System, Part 2," *Chemical Engineering*, May 1989, pp. 165-170.

these job-search organizations are general in nature; they do not focus on the special problems of the older out-of-work executive.

A few organizations do provide services exclusively for the older executive. For instance, the seventeen Forty Plus Clubs in the United States help only unemployed executives who are over forty. If one of these clubs is in your area, you may find that it will provide the kind of support you need to get your job search campaign off the ground.[2]

Other Groups That Might Help

In some areas, state unemployment commissions provide some useful services, such as help with job search techniques, for the older executive and professional. Their job counselors may provide leads or information on places you can get help in your area. Since you have to go there anyway to collect your unemployment compensation, at least check out what assistance they might have and any job opportunities they may know about. Ask if other unemployment offices provide different services from those that your center provides. (In major metropolitan areas, executive and professional services are provided from one or at most, two or three centers. If you don't happen to go to that particular center, you may never find out what assistance is available.)

In some cities, the chamber of commerce conducts job forums, either alone or in conjunction with service organizations, sales executive clubs, advertising clubs or other such groups. These forums are usually free or charge a nominal fee. Consult your local chamber about availability.

Colleges and junior colleges frequently provide ongoing assistance to the unemployed through short courses (example: writing your resume, interviewing) and counseling. Many also have special Saturday or evening meetings especially designed for "networking." For example: a number of business and professional organizations for women meet under the auspices of the local junior college, and attending these meetings has proved to be useful in getting job leads. These organizations also provide good speakers who discuss worthwhile business topics, and may provide useful insights vis a vis the status of business in your area or general business trends.

Checking back with your own college or university placement bureau may also be helpful. While these placement bureaus are generally geared

---

[2] A description of the way the Forty Plus Clubs operate, their addresses and those of other job search organizations are included in the appendix. The author can attest to the effectiveness of the Forty Plus Clubs. She became a member in 1981, and has maintained an associate membership in the club since that time, just in case she should ever require the services of the club again.

toward recent graduates, they are particularly useful in some disciplines, such as education.

Many local high schools have gone into the "adult evening school" business. They frequently offer helpful one- or two-evening seminar sessions on topics of special interest to job-seekers.

For women, CATALYST for Women, Inc. (250 Park Avenue South, New York, NY 10003), has current, up-to-date information on job counselors and organizations providing assistance in all parts of the United States. They can be contacted in person, by mail or by calling (212) 777-8900.

Most large public libraries have developed extensive collections of job-search materials and have access to computer data bases; and their employees are delighted to help you locate information that will help in your search. The computer data bases are especially helpful when you are into the last phase of your marketing effort, and need information about specific companies with whom you will be interviewing.

The business editorial staff members of city newspapers have proven to be surprisingly helpful to many job-seekers. They know what's going on in your community, and can point you to job seminars, self-help groups and other available assistance.

Recently a number of organized religious groups have become concerned about the effect unemployment is having upon their adherents. In some areas, they sponsor inter-faith self-help and/or counseling groups. These function primarily in a support role, giving members an opportunity to air their fears and come to grips with feelings so they can learn better ways to cope with the pressures of unemployment. Call your local minister, priest or rabbi to see what is available in your area. The YMCA, YWCA, YMHA and YWHA also provide similar services in some parts of the country.

You can also "let your fingers do the walking" by checking in the *Yellow Pages* for the listings under executive recruiters, management consultants, employment agencies, executive marketing and outplacement companies. These resources will be discussed in more detail later in this book.

Finding Out Where the Jobs Are

How long has it been since you looked for a job? Twenty or 30 years? When you first got out of college? If you changed jobs before, the chances are that the job came looking for you; it was a great opportunity and you were actively recruited to take the job. As an older executive, you have probably met and interviewed many job-seekers over the years. You may think that you know the ropes. But—and it's a big but—the shoe's on the other foot now. You're the one who's seeking work.

Looking for a job is a marketing problem. And you market yourself partly through your resumes, letters, telephone calls and interviews. But first, you need to discover what the job market really is, then segment it to determine exactly which part of the market (which jobs) match your qualifications and interests. You must be a detective as well as a marketer. It's true that many job opportunities are never listed in the want-ads, with personnel agencies or even with headhunters. You know the reasons. The positions aren't open long enough for a public listing. They're filled by internal promotion, by people recommended by company personnel. And they're filled by applicants who keep their "ears to the keyhole," taking advantage of networking to make contacts and send in their applications and resumes before positions are even posted.

Jobs are located in two places: the visible market (positions already open and showing in advertisements and human resource department postings) and the invisible or hidden market (jobs not open but that will be opening soon because someone's retiring or leaving, the organization is expanding or new positions are being created). Or the position may not even have been considered yet. You may have an opportunity to plant the idea for the position in some executive's mind.

What percentage of jobs are filled from each market? According to some experts, the invisible market handles about 75 percent of all available jobs, with 25 percent of the jobs coming from the visible market. Others say the ratio is closer to 80:20 in favor of the hidden market. Depending upon the year, surveys conducted by various personnel magazines and journals report responses indicating that human resource departments recruit from 25 percent to almost half of their new employees through the visible market. (Note, however, that particularly in small companies, human resource departments do not recruit and hire all employees, although in mid- to large-size companies, they do recruit and screen candidates for all but the very top two or three positions.) Take your pick of the percentages. They still mean that you're going to have to try both markets.

Finding Opportunities in the Invisible Market
You approach the invisible market differently from the visible market. The suggestions on networking and using your contacts provided in Chapter 3 are valid ones for approaching the hidden market. The best way to locate a hidden job *is* through networking—the referral of a friend or business acquaintance. In fact, some companies are convinced that the best employees they hire are those that are recommended by their own employees. Their experience has been so good that they offer employees bonuses of $1500 and more for recommending candidates who are hired and retained on the job after the usual trial period (say, six months or so). As an older executive, you probably have more opportunities for this kind of referral than would a younger job-seeker. Networking is generally the most fruitful when you are looking for the same type of work you've been doing and not contemplating a radical career change.

But you can approach the hidden market in other ways. None of them is easy, and all require that you expend effort and energy.

Researching Jobs
You may not yet know if you are in the right field, industry or part of the country. You may be thinking about changing careers, and want to know more about various career options. You want to find out as much as you can about what is available in your geographical area; you may want to investigate opportunities in other areas. What are the sources you can utilize during your research to locate the names, addresses, telephone numbers and other information on possible employers? The following sources have provided excellent "market research" information for many other job-seekers. They will be useful now, when you are researching the entire market; they will prove useful when you begin to narrow down your search, to determine the "niche" or segment to which you will

market yourself; and they will be useful as sources of background information when you are positioning your "product" in the market segment, and are preparing for interviews with specific employers.

Organizational Sources of Information

❐ *College and City Libraries.* Ask for the collections on employment opportunities. Included will be books on job-hunting, directories of all kinds, information sources (including clipping files) on local and national businesses. A key resource, which shouldn't be overlooked, are the knowledgeable librarians who know how to locate the information you need and who are usually willing to help.

❐ *Chambers of Commerce.* These were mentioned earlier as a possible source of help through their job-search seminars and presentations. The various chambers also have full information on local businesses, including their general size, their addresses, the names of local corporate offices and owners. And often, chamber officials know about specific local hiring needs and opportunities.

❐ *Better Business Bureaus.* This may not seem like a good source. But if you locate a company in which you are interested, or are being considered for a position with a company about which you know little, contact the Better Business Bureau of the area where the organization is located. It will provide you with the results of any investigations it has made. The reports are cautiously written to avoid possible lawsuits, but they provide food for thought, and may prevent you from making a disastrous mistake. Truthfully though, this source will be more useful to you in latter stages of your job search than in the beginning.

❐ *Fortune, Forbes* and *Business Week 500.* Once a year, *Fortune, Forbes* and *Business Week* complete independent nationwide surveys of all major corporations doing business in the United States. They also are now conducting the same kinds of surveys on international businesses. Each firm is ranked by size, primarily on the basis of the past year's business performance. Included are the firms' asset bases, profits, increase or decrease in business compared with the preceding year, the major officers and their incomes plus other information that might be of interest to investors. This information is more up to date than the information contained in most of the standard reference directories, but is not as detailed. (See directories later in this chapter.)

❐ *Value Line Investment Survey.* Value Line provides current up-to-the-minute information on the securities of specific companies. Primarily produced as a source of detailed "insider type" investment information, it still provides good background information on companies looking for turnaround specialists, growth specialists or other types of management help. Your stockbroker will have copies that you might be able to look at, and libraries with large business collections frequently subscribe to the service.

❏ *Trade and Industry Associations.* Begin with the associations you already belong to and those for your industry. Get copies of their publications (or read them in the public library). Open positions are often announced in the help- wanted ads in the back of the journal. Or you can sometimes get leads on openings by looking in the promotions columns to see if a job might be open because someone was promoted out of it.

❏ *State, Local and Federal Job Information Centers.* State capitals and major cities have state and federal job information centers where openings for government jobs are posted. Since many high-level positions require that you take a civil service examination, you can obtain information at the centers about taking the tests. Positions in local government are also posted, although some of the higher level positions are political in nature, and dependent upon an individual's political skills, activities and networking. Federal Job Information Centers (FJIC), operated by the Office of Personnel Management (OPM), are located in many major U.S. cities. They provide regional job vacancy information and will answer questions about application procedures.

❏ *Annual Reports.* Some libraries keep these on file as do stockbrokers and financial planning groups. You can also write to companies in which you are interested and ask for copies.

Using Books as Information Sources

Some really excellent books are currently available for use by the job-searcher. The following are recommended.

Kathryn and Ross Pelras, *Jobs '90*, Prentice Hall. This is an excellent paperback source of companies in all parts of the country that are most likely to hire in the near future. Full addresses for locations are provided, along with contacts, telephone numbers and a variety of other information about possible employment. Addresses of employment agencies, executive search firms and other job-help groups are included. This book is only $14.95, and is readily portable. If you are going to buy only one other book (besides this one!) this is the one to get.

Heinz Ulrich and J. Robert Connor, *The National Job-Hunting Guide: A Directory to Where Jobs Are...Anywhere in the U.S.*, Dolphin Books.

This book gives addresses and telephone numbers for employment agencies and executive search firms, by state and city, lists special opportunities for the various areas and corporate information on the major employers in the area. An excellent source, but may be slightly out-of-date.

Diane Wheeter Strauss, *Handbook of Business Information*, Libraries Unlimited. This book is available in almost every library. It lists every conceivable type of business information source and describes what can be found in each. Discussed are directories, basic reference sources, periodicals and newspapers, on line data bases, vertical file collections and electronic business information. Look here first for guidance in locating sources of business information.

Anne Boe and Bettie B. Youngs, *Is Your "Net" Working?: A Complete Guide to Building Contacts and Career Visibility*, Wiley. Most of this book deals with networking on the job (you can use that after you get back to work), but one chapter in particular, "Using Network Referrals to Build Career Visibility" is filled with practical advice on career moves and job searches. This chapter also has a section on referrals and how to determine ahead of time whether people will give favorable references.

Kenneth and Sheryl Dawson, *Job Search—the Total System*, Wiley. This book is another look at how to search for a job. It deals with executives and professionals, but not specifically with executives and professionals who are already out of work. It has a particularly good section on networking.

John Lucht, *Rights of Passage at $100,000*, Viceroy Press. Recommended as helpful if you are looking for high visibility and high dollar positions.

Lester Korn, *The Success Profile: A Leading Headhunter Tells You How to Get to the Top*, Simon and Schuster. Among other topics, discusses the essential qualities headhunters look for when recruiting an executive, the personal attributes that go with successful careers, suggestions for selecting an industry, company and career best suited to your talents, career planning for the executive woman and professional tips on job hunting.

Gene R. Hawes, *The Encyclopedia of Second Careers*, and *The Career Changer's Sourcebook*, Facts On File. These two books provide a survey of a variety of career fields to be considered, discuss the type of work, the various levels of positions in that field, and the approximate salaries. Hawes suggests ways of preparing for that new career and how one might go about seeking that job. Since the books are inclusive, some of the careers are at lower levels than those you might be looking for, and the salary information is slightly out of date. However, if you are considering a career change, these books are a good place to browse before beginning more in-depth investigation.

U.S. Employment Opportunities, Washington Research Associates. This resource is a looseleaf binder divided into eighteen different industry segments. Covers current career news, recent economic/technological developments in the industry. Lists places where opportunities are best, gives list of resources for that industry—association names, periodicals and current books which will aid in research on a specific industry. Good for browsing, especially if you're interested in a career change.

Joseph and Amy Lombardo, *The Job Belt: The Fifty Best Places in America for High-Quality Employment Today and in the Future*, Penguin Books. Includes a discussion of the area, its economy, population, climate, location, housing, cultural and recreational opportunities; employment projections and salaries; private employment services; state job services; and major employers.

Robert Levering, Milton Moskowitz and Michael Katz, *The 100 Best Companies to Work for in America*, a Plume Book, New American Library. Analyzes what the writers have determined to be the 100 best companies to work for from an employee's viewpoint.

The National Job Bank, Bob Adams, Inc. These books are published yearly, and are designed for use by managers and professionals, the major company listings are by state. Lists company names, person or title to contact, telephone number and brief information on products and business sectors. Includes number of employees and location of corporate headquarters. In the back of the book is an industry cross-index, arranged by generic type of business, and listing the companies by state and location that fit that particular industry classification. Job Bank books are also available as individual state titles.

Job Bank Guide to Employment Services, Bob Adams, Inc. Summarizes employment services and opportunities available nationwide. Includes employment agencies, temporary services, executive search firms and state/local/federal employment offices.

Everybody's Business, the Irreverent Guide to Corporate America, Harper and Row. This book provides readable and entertaining histories and profiles on 317 major companies. These are especially useful in preparing for job interviews. The histories and profiles include both the good and the bad. The book has not been updated recently, but the historical information is still valuable.

CPC Annual, College Placement Council. Produced every year, the book includes general articles on the job search process, directory listings of major employers of engineering, science, computer, administrative, managerial, and general business personnel. Company listings include a brief description, employment opportunities and employee benefits.

The 1988 National Survey of Executive Compensation, Arthur Young. Includes hiring and compensation trends in industry, as well as a very good picture of the going compensation in a number of industries. Will help you get an idea of what you might be able to negotiate for in terms of perks and added benefits.

Jack Anderson, *The Plum Book: The Official United States Guide to Leading Positions in Government, Presidential and Executive Appointments, Salaries, Requirements, and Other Vital Statistics for Job Seekers*. The book is as advertised. "Useful for federal job lookers."

Ronald L. and Caryl Rae Krannich, *The Complete Guide to Public Employment*, Impact Publications. Useful for browsing. Several sections are similar in intent to the *Forty Plus Job Hunting Guide* in that they discuss major aspects of the job search, but with the public sector specifically in mind. Lists multiple sources to contact.

Federal Jobs Digest, Washington Research Associates. Lists over 3,000 vacancies countrywide each issue (published every other week). Includes addresses to contact for application.

Federal Times Newspaper, available from Federal Times in Washington, is a weekly publication intended for present federal employees, although useful for those seeking federal jobs. The emphasis is heavily on department of defense and senior executive services positions.

U.S. Government Manual, U.S. Government Printing Office. Provides information on federal job classifications, required qualifications and associated duties.

How to Get a Federal Job, Facts On File. Written by a government personnel manager, Krandall Kraus, this is a definitive job-hunting bible for anyone seeking entry into federal civil service.

Using Directories to Get Information

Numerous business directories provide much information about specific businesses, industries, organizations and governmental agencies. Good places to begin looking are Klein's *Guide to American Directories*, which tells you where you might locate information in different published directories; the *Encyclopedia of Associations*, which lists the major incorporated national-level (and some state-level) business, trade and nonprofit associations, along with the addresses and the names of officers; Marlow and Thomas's *The Directory of Directories*, which lists 9,600 plus business and industrial directories, business rosters, data bases, and other lists and guides under 16 broad subject categories; Constance Winchell's *Guide to Reference Books*, American Library Association, which lists every conceivable reference source and often provides leads to information in unlikely places; and The *Encyclopedia of Business Information Sources*, which includes a wide variety of useful information, and divides information by industry and type of business.

Standard and Poor's Register of Corporations, Directors and Executives is a three-volume annual, kept up to date during the year with three supplements. Employers are listed alphabetically, numerically (by Standard Industrial Classification [SIC] code), and geographically. The listing for each includes brief information about the corporation, its chief business, telephone number, number of employees, names of board members and major executives. The listings in *Standard and Poor's Register* are very large incorporated businesses. For that reason, very large private businesses are not listed, nor are smaller corporations who don't meet the size requirements of the register. The headquarters address may be the only one given, and the locations of the individual executives are generally not noted. However, for major corporations, it's a fine source of relatively current information. Standard and Poor's also publishes other information (for example, *Standard and Poor's Stock Reports*), but these are less widely available.

Moody's Industrial Manual lists large industrial (manufacturing) companies whose securities are traded. Employers are listed alphabetically, along with a description of their location, line of business, size and officers. If you're interested in a position in the industrial sector, this book would be a better source for you than *Standard and Poor's Register*.

Standard Directory of Advertisers: Classified Edition. Describes companies that allocate at least $75,000 annually for national or regional advertising. Discusses media uses, names of key advertising, marketing and sales executives. Companies are arranged by broad industry categories. Includes "Tradename Index," a list of brand names and companies that own them.

Moody's Public Utility Manual, Moody's Transportation Manual, Moody's Bank and Finance Manual, and *Moody's Municipal and Government Manual* contain information for other sectors similar to that in *Moody's Industrial Manual*.

The *Thomas Register of American Manufacturers* provides about the same information that's in *Moody's Industrial Manual*, except that in its 12 volumes, it covers nearly every product and product line and nearly all U.S. companies engaged in manufacturing, not just those traded on the stock exchange. Either directory will be of value to you, and you might want to consult both.

Dun and Bradstreet's Million Dollar Directory and *Middle Market Directory* provide information on smaller companies. Companies are listed alphabetically, numerically (by SIC code), geographically and by product classification. Indicated are the company's location, telephone number, line of business, sales, total employment and the names of executives.

Dun also produces a number of other useful business information sources. *Dun's Business Identification Services* is a microfiche collection of the names and addresses of all the companies for which Dun and Bradstreet has credit reports, and lists names, addresses and officers for more than one third of all U.S. business enterprises. *Dun's Business Rankings* presents the top 7,500 public and private U.S. companies, ranked by number of employees and sales volume. *The Career Guide*, an annual, provides an overview of numerous major businesses, discusses employment opportunities, gives a list of disciplines hired, the address(es) and name or title of person to contact. Excellent resource.

Fortune's Plant and Product Directory will give you national information on who makes what and where if your experience and interest is with a specific product or product line. Fortune also publishes an annual *Fortune Directory of U.S. Corporations*, which contains the information from Fortune's annual Fortune 500, plus additional information.

A number of states publish directories on the businesses they've licensed for operation. For instance, the *New Jersey Industrial Directory* lists by county the businesses and industries doing more than a million dollars worth of business in the state. Information includes business location, name of the officer in charge, headquarters office address and top executive, number of employees at the site, preceding year's sales, and general type of service or products.

Other useful directories and sources of job information:

State and Local

Chambers of Commerce Business Directories
Human Resources Directories (put out by some cities)
Industrial Development Guides
Job Bank books. These are published for numerous cities and areas, (and also in a national edition discussed earlier). Examples:
    The Boston Job Bank
    The Greater Chicago Job Bank
    The Southwest Job Bank

Membership rosters for various trade and manufacturing organizations
State Education Directories (published yearly or every other year). These
list school districts and schools, members of the board of education, the
superintendent of schools and various supervisory personnel. Useful for
people considering education as a second career, as well as for professional educators. Many of these membership rosters can also be accessed
through the various data bases, and are listed in the *Directory of Directories* discussed earlier.

Phonefiche. A microfiche collection of the white and yellow pages
of the telephone directories for many U.S. cities and towns. Libraries
may have this resource if they do not have paper telephone directories.

National

America's Corporate Families: The Billion Dollar Directory	Dun's Marketing Services
Gale Directory of Publications	Gale Research Co.
Directory of Corporate Affiliations	National Register Publishing Co.
Directory of National Voluntary Organizations	The Allstate Insurance Companies
Directory of National Women's Organizations	The Allstate Insurance Companies
The Foundation Directory	The Foundation Center
Occupational Outlook Handbook	Bureau of Labor Statistics
Polk's Bank Directory	R.L. Polk & Co.
Research Centers Directory	Gale Research Co.
The National Job-Finding Guide	Dolphin Books
Training and Development Organizations Directory	Gale Research Co.
Women's Organizations and Leaders Directory	

International

America's Corporate Families and International Affiliates	Dun's Marketing Services
Bottin International: Inter- national Business Register	
Directory of American Firms Operating in Foreign Countries	Simon & Schuster

Directory of Foreign Firms Operating in the United States	Simon & Schuster
Directory of Foreign Manufacturers in the United States	Business Publications Division, Georgia State University
International Directory of Corporate Affiliations	National Register Publishing Co.
Kelly's Business Directory	Kelly's Directories Ltd.
Polk's Worldbank Directory	R.L. Polk & Co.
Principal International Businesses	Dun & Bradstreet
Who Owns Whom	O.W. Roskill, London

Using On-Line Computer Data Bases as a Source of Information

Many libraries today are equipped to do computer searches on a variety of public and business data bases such as GEnie, CompuServ, DIALOG, BRS, ORBIT, NEXIS, Dow Jones News/Retrieval, NewsNet, and others (libraries appear to be somewhat partial to DIALOG and NEXIS, although many subscribe to other services as well or instead). If you have a home computer with a modem, you can subscribe to one of the services (CompuServ is the least expensive of the major services at the time this book is being written, although that can change quickly), and use it to obtain the information you desire. The biggest advantage of on-line data base services is their availability. They provide information that even the biggest libraries may not have in their collection, they provide more information than is available in the print version of their data bases and, more importantly, the search process usually takes just a few minutes.

Some particularly useful data bases/electronic information sources are:

Electronic Yellow Pages (EYP), produced by Dun's Marketing Services. The EYP includes a Construction Directory, Financial Services Directory, Manufacturer's Directory, Professional's Directory, Retailer's Directory and Wholesaler's Directory.

The Electronic Yellow Pages Index on DIALOG references the EYP. *The TRINET Company Database* references trade journals, census bureaus, state and industry directories and other sources to present information on companies with 20 or more employees (includes SIC codes, number of employees, locations, principal products, etc.). *The TRINET Establishment Database* provides similar information for branch locations. Both TRINET data bases can be accessed through DIALOG.

Many or most of the directories listed in the Business Directory section can also be accessed by one or several of the major data-base services. Some full text data bases for major magazines and journals can also be searched on the major data-base services. DIALOG, for example, has full text for many articles from Harvard Business Review, McGraw-Hill Business Backgrounder (the full text from a number of McGraw-Hill business periodicals); Trade and Industry ASAP (the full text of 125 or more trade journals and regional business periodicals); and Business Dateline. Some newspapers are indexed or available in full text versions electronically. Among those newspapers of most use during a job search are Barron's, Commerce Business Daily, Financial Times, Investor's Daily, New York Times, Wall Street Journal, Washington Post, and wire services such as UPI News and Business Wire (the full text of business news releases issued by corporations, research institutions and other organizations).

A number of indexes to periodicals are also available on line. The most useful business indexes are *ABI/Inform, Management Contents, Business Periodicals Index*, and for special industries, *PTS T&S Indexes, PTS PROMT*, and *Trade and Industry Index*.

Using the Telephone

The telephone is an excellent marketing tool for contacting the invisible market. Telephone the people referred to you during your networking activities and ask for an opportunity to speak with them in person. Use the telephone as a part of a two-pronged search activity. Write a letter to the people and companies you identified during your initial research, then follow-up with a telephone call asking for an interview. The telephone is useful in contacting people in the visible job market, too. Call company human resources offices to ask if they have job openings in your specialty. Ask to be interviewed for positions advertised in the newspaper (if a telephone number is given, call first before sending them a resume). Call employment agencies and recruiters.

Many job-hunters don't "bother" with the telephone during their job search. Why? Because they're afraid of a turndown. This is the same kind of fear which keeps salespeople from making "cold calls." But judicious use of the telephone can save you hours of driving and walking. And you can make more contacts in a shorter time than you can by any other method.

Cut down on your anxiety by writing a script or outline to use in making your calls. Scripting is what enables telemarketers to make hundreds of cold calls each day. (It also enables them to talk to the people they want to talk to—and to sell them what they want to sell them!) Scripting also keeps you out of trouble when you get cold feet in the middle of a call and can't think what to say, or what the next point is that you'd like to make.

You can write a complete script in which you write down every word you'd like to say. That's a good thing to do if you are just beginning. If some of the wording doesn't work, then you can correct it as you make other phone calls. Even if you are comfortable with the telephone, you should at least outline the points you want to make, and the order in which you want to make them. Both types of scripting will help you keep your calls on target—and short.

Begin writing your script by planning the main points you want to make. Generally, you want to make no more than two to four points. Any more than that, and the call gets too long and loses its effectiveness. Your main points might include 1) your background; 2) why you are looking; 3) how your accomplishments might be of value to their organization or some other organization that they know about.

Then, write the beginning—the introduction, in which you tell why you're calling—and finish by writing the conclusion of the call. That can be a request for an interview or for information of some kind.

Here's how you might write a script to follow up a letter campaign:

Purpose	Your Script
Why you're calling	Hello, (name of person you have called), this is Betty Graves. You may recall that I sent you a letter and a resume last week in which I explained that I'm looking for a position as a computer systems analyst with management responsibilities.
Your background	For the past two years, I've been working as a computer analyst with the direct marketing services group of AT&T. I've been a team leader on a group which developed a new direct marketing system integrating inbound and outbound telemarketing with billing, accounts receivable, credit, warehousing, compensation,

electronic mail and automated office systems needed by a state-of-the-art direct marketing operation. This and other projects for which I have been team leader provided me with a strong background in my field.

Why you're looking

We will be finished with this project within a short period of time, and I want to broaden my responsibilities. I'm looking for the names of firms that might be able to use my skills. You may recall some of the strengths I mentioned in my letter (mention one or two of the best ones).

Accomplishments

I'm wondering if you know of any situations in which an organization:

1. Has growing pains and needs an experienced analyst to determine its computer hardware and software needs and develop, purchase and implement cost-effective programming.

2. Plans to update existing computer systems and programs.

3. Wants to develop systems that will integrate the data bases of related departments, divisions or activities.

4. Has an existing data processing department and wants to update its functionality to that of an information management group.

Request

Are you aware of any organizations in these situations, which you would be willing to share with me?

Close	I appreciate your willingness to help. Thank you for the information, or, I'm sorry you don't know any group that needs that kind of help. I appreciate your willingness to listen, anyway.

You might write a similar but less formal script when you've been referred to someone by a friend or acquaintance. That kind of script might go like this:

Introduction	Hello, my name is Jane Compton. Bill Groggan from Taos Eyewear suggested that I call you.
Purpose	I'm currently looking for a position as a product manager in the optometric products line. Bill says that you are extremely knowledgeable about the job opportunities in this area.
Aim of conversation	I hope we can get together and talk. I'd like to talk with you about this, and to see what suggestions you might make that could help me in my job search. I can come at whatever time is convenient for you. (Set time and date.)
	or
	I'm sorry you won't be able to see me. Can you suggest someone else who is knowledgeable about the industry who might be willing to offer some advice?

A good telephone/letter campaign can get interviews, as can using your networking contacts for referrals. In the beginning, you'll be referring to your script. But as you continue, you'll find that you'll be more comfortable and won't need the script as a crutch. You'll also find that you'll get more tangible leads as you follow through on referrals, and some of them will be for interviews for the hidden jobs you've uncovered.

The best time to call? Between 9:00 and 11:00 a.m. on Tuesday through Friday. If you're calling human resources departments, Friday morning is particularly good, since people don't make too many hiring decisions on Friday. But Monday morning is bad, and Friday afternoon is even worse. That's the time the department conducts its exit interviews for departing employees (and you don't want any part of that activity).

Approaching Jobs in the Visible Market

Don't ignore the "unhidden" market. Thousands of managers and professionals get jobs in this market. They locate their jobs through the classified ads, listings with recruiting firms, placement agencies, corporate human resources departments, civil service offices—and yes, even the state employment services.

Prospecting

Prospecting in the visible market is a little easier than in the hidden market. The resources you'll use are more accessible. You'll need the newspaper, lots of stationery and postage, the telephone directory, good soles on your shoes and persistence.

Human resources offices. Human resources departments are now involved in hiring all but the very top executives in major companies, and in many small- to mid-size corporations. Telephone calls and visits to the offices of companies you'd like to work for can be productive. And conceivably, you might get the jump on a new position by your persistence. Jobs are often requisitioned several weeks or even months before they open. Then they're announced internally for two or three weeks before being advertised in the newspaper. You visit an office, complete an application and ask for an interview. Because the interviewer is aware that the job opening is going to be available, you will be interviewed for a position that's essentially still "hidden." Human resources people from different companies also talk to each other. You might obtain a lead on jobs they know are available in another company.

Answering Newspaper Advertisements. Newspaper ads are not always valid leads to jobs. Some companies put ads in the newspapers because they have someone they're unhappy with, and want to shake the trees to see what they can find. But the majority of ads are for legitimate jobs. You shouldn't ignore them as a source of leads.

Some organizations spend big bucks on display ads in the business section of the newspapers; others put little bitty one-inch ads in the classifieds for jobs that pay as well and are every bit as good as those in the display ads. Companies may also place ads in trade and association journals and magazines and in local area newspapers. Regardless of the way they look, ad copy is written in a number of different ways:

1. Ads that are completely unintelligible. You read the ad and you still don't have any idea what it's for. If it has the job title that you're looking for, it's worth a telephone call to find out what the job is that they're really advertising, but it isn't worth spending a whole lot of time on. You could be doing something more immediately productive with your time.

2. Ads that are intentionally misleading. These are often for the so-called "glamour" industries, for positions that sound as though they are high-level management, marketing or human resources positions, or they may be designed for the greatest possible response. Sometimes, the ad is misleading because the interviewer who wrote it didn't realize that the ad was ambiguous—or may have had a hidden agenda. You may never get a response to your letter and resume, but you could still take a chance and send them. This type of ad, though, really belongs in the "caveat emptor" ("buyer beware") ranks. If you should be asked to come for an interview, play it cool and cautious.

3. Ads that don't say enough. They don't list essential duties, or they use current buzz words as a substitute for substance. You have to study these ads carefully, and "read between the lines" to see what the ad is really about. The ad may have a theme. Use it in your response.

4. Ads that say exactly what they mean. They include job duties and responsibilities and list the minimum requirements for hiring. They may include enough information about the hiring organization that you would know whether or not you'd be interested. To even get an interview on this kind of ad, you'd have to meet or exceed every criteria. But these employers know what they want, and their jobs are worth pursuing.

5. Ads that don't say who the employer will be. These ads may or may not describe the job accurately. But they definitely don't describe themselves. You are asked to respond to initials, to a blind box address at the newspaper, to a box number or a street address. Why don't these employers identify themselves? They may be looking to replace an employee but don't want to signal their intention in advance; they may have marginal jobs, but want them to sound big; or they may simply want to get the resumes without having to respond to the ones that don't interest them or having people show up in person to respond to an ad.

6. Ads in which the employer says very little about the available job, other than the job title, and devotes almost all of the ad space to selling the company as a desirable employer.

7. Ads placed by executive recruiters. The ads list the position(s) for which the company is recruiting, a very brief explanation of the job, and often a salary range. Sometimes the ads list only job titles and salary range. These are almost invariably valid jobs, although sometimes firms may simply be looking to replenish their stock of resumes.

Agencies and Employment Services

Contacting agencies and employment services for assistance can be thought of as somewhere between the invisible and visible market. Employment services really run intelligence agencies. They seek information about existing jobs and try to locate people who fulfill the requirements of those positions. Then they try to get the two together, for a fee.

Executive Recruiters. Employers pay for the services of executive recruiters. They may be retained at a definite fee to work on an exclusive basis to fill a position. Or, they may work on a nonexclusive, contingency fee basis. (They only get paid if they locate someone that can fill the position.) Recruiters are most successful when they work in specific industries or markets. They understand hiring practices and policies and they generally have complete knowledge about the companies who use their services. As mentioned, executive recruiters often advertise positions that they're trying to fill. But their ads usually provide only the position title and a salary range. If the ads give more information about the position, they generally disguise their client enough so applicants (or other agencies) can't go directly to the company to apply.

Executive recruiters are good sources to contact. They retain resumes on file if the candidates are well qualified and present themselves well. Since they're working for their clients and not for you, you may not get any action from your visits to them. On the other hand, if you fit the needs of one of their clients, they'll work hard to help you get hired.

Executive recruiters are most frequently located in major cities. You can locate them in the *Yellow Pages* under "Executive Recruiting Consultant," "Technical Search Firms," "Executive Search" or "Executive Search Consultants," or some variation of these headings. Some newspapers also have a section that lists recruiters. And you can often get an idea of the agencies that recruit for your field by reading the help-wanted ads.

For additional information about executive recruiters, you can order the *Directory of Executive Recruiters*, published annually by Kennedy Publications, Fitzwilliam, NH 03447. Another source of names of executive recruiters: the membership list of the Association of Executive Search Consultants, 30 Rockefeller Plaza, New York, NY 10012.

Employment Agencies. Until the mid 1970s, most employment agencies charged applicants a fee to get a job. But since then, most of the agencies have changed to an employer-paid fee. Their ads now say "paid." The primary difference between employment agencies and executive recruiters is in the level of the staff they're recruiting. Employment agencies generally specialize in clerical, administrative, semi-skilled and entry-level positions. However, many agencies have more than one division, with one part of the agency recruiting lower-level employees while another division deals with managerial and professional workers. Some regular employment agencies now include temporary placements, managerial and professional as well as clerical. For this reason, if you need temporary work to tide you over, an employment agency might help. Temporary work has another advantage. It gives you a chance to get inside a company and look around. And you just might find a job there.

Another possible source of work is the temporary employment agency. Many "rent-a-body" firms now exist for the sole purpose of providing temporary, but high-level "consultants" for short, well-paid assignments. You become an employee of the agency, and are paid by them. Many large, medium-sized and small firms who don't need a full-time writer, or a full-time marketing department, or a staff of computer programmers will hire consultants from an agency for the time needed to complete the work. It's a good deal for everyone. The work is never dull, often challenging, and can be very satisfying. And frequently, good people who are hired only for the length of the project are asked to stay on for additional assignments, or are hired outright. The agencies generally make some kind of insurance available to their employees, and while they don't usually have pension plans, they do frequently have 401k plans.

Management Consultants. Some management consulting firms also do limited executive recruiting. However, they almost never advertise the positions they're looking for, since they're generally on a retainer or the recruiting is being done as part of a larger project. Management consultants do specialize in certain kinds of businesses and in certain areas of expertise (accounting, computers, planning, etc.). If you know of a consulting firm working in your area of specialization, you might send them a resume. But you'll only be asked to come in for an interview if they think they could use you themselves or if your resume fits a position for which they are recruiting at that moment.

State Employment Services. When you applied for your unemployment insurance, one of the requirements was that you visit the State Employment Services for an interview and "help." The services seldom have listings for middle- and upper-level managers. But occasionally, they'll be knowledgeable about business in the area and will provide a good lead. Since you have to go there anyway, you might as well try to get some good out of the experience.

Professional Associations. Some professional associations have placement bureaus as a part of their service to members. If you don't know about the associations to which you belong, write or call to see if they offer this service.

College Placement Services and Alumni Associations. Don't overlook the services your college may be able to give you. Call or write to see if it has a placement service available to older graduates. For teachers and school administrators, for instance, the college services are perhaps the best source of job leads. And jobs for people with professional degrees are also frequently listed.

Other Ways to Look

Outplacement Services. The outplacement specialist is a relative newcomer on the job market. Many of them are hired by companies to help terminated employees look for a job. Essentially, outplacement services are marketing services. They help you learn to market yourself. They'll help you write your resume (which may be like those of their other clients), write letter campaigns, prepare you for interviews, give you advice on your search, etc. But they do not get you a job. If you go to an outplacement service on your own, you will get help. But—and it's a big but—you'll pay plenty for it. The charges are often a twelfth to a tenth of your potential salary. And it's payable in advance, not after you get a job.

Ads in Professional and Trade Publications. Some people have had good luck advertising their availability in newspapers and in professional and trade publications. To be effective, the ads have to be well written, with a selling punch. Newspaper ads seldom draw any responses. Ads in professional and trade publications fare somewhat better. The primary disadvantage is that you can end up spending quite a bit for advertising with no results.

Part 3

Segmenting the Job Market— Selecting an Area That Matches Your Skills and Experience

Personal Communication Style and How You Can Make It Work for You

Your ability to communicate impacts on every aspect of your job search. You *must* communicate effectively if you want to be hired—you must be precisely understood by your audience, i.e., the person who interviews you, a potential manager or a C.E.O.

Unfortunately, three times out of four, you'll fail to do your best selling job, to convince the person with whom you're speaking, because you aren't communicating in a manner familiar to them. You'll fail to apply the communication golden rule: "Thou shalt communicate with others in the manner through which *they* best understand." To apply this rule, you must determine their communication style, then deliver your communication to match the style that they understand best.

Communication Styles

People communicate in a vast array of styles. You may not be fully cognizant of these differences because your department or industry was peopled with clones who communicated in much the same way as you. As a boss, that was your prerogative. You may have preconceptions and prejudices about people who communicate differently. You may distrust people who are glib and facile. You may have had a long-term feud with salespeople or marketing people whom you felt were careless of facts or didn't pay enough attention to details. Or conversely, you may dislike people whom you feel are too concerned with detail and have difficulty communicating the big picture.

No one is going to try to revamp your own personal communication style. That's impossible anyway, since your basic style was probably set before you started school, as was the style of everyone with whom you will come in contact.

To avoid miscommunication, however, you must first understand how *you* communicate and the way in which your communication style reflects your personality. Next, learn about other styles and how to spot them. Then you will be able to identify potential employers' communication styles so that you can estimate the best way to approach them. Discover better ways to use your communication strengths and to modify those behaviors that can lead to problems with people communicating through other styles. Learn how to sell yourself in ways that are acceptable to others and yet compatible with your feelings about yourself.

In a nutshell: Don't try to make yourself over. You can't. You have no choice but to retain your own basic communication style. But you can learn how to modify your presentation to match the preferred style of others.

Background of Communications Styles

A number of years ago, Dr. William Marston, a psychologist at Columbia University, studied "normal" behavior in people. He developed a system of identifying behaviors and related communications styles which is especially appropriate for older executives. By studying the way normal people reacted in all kinds of situations, Dr. Marston concluded that two sets of factors interact to determine behavior. The first is related to the environment: people will respond differently in what they perceive to be a favorable environment than they would in an unfavorable environment (and being unemployed is decidedly an unfavorable environment). The second factor is the "style" of reacting in a given environment. People can react in only two ways. They can be active or passive.

The environment can be represented as a continuum, from extremely unfavorable to highly favorable. People's reactions can also be represented as a continuum from highly active to extremely passive.

When these two factors are combined, four basic communications styles result. You can be: active in an unfavorable environment; active in a favorable environment; passive in a favorable environment; or passive in an unfavorable environment.

Figure 5.1 illustrates these four environments.

Basic Behaviors

The upper-left quadrant environment is *unfavorable* or antagonistic, and the people who perceive themselves to be in that environment are *active*. Individuals who behave this way work to overcome unfavorable condi-

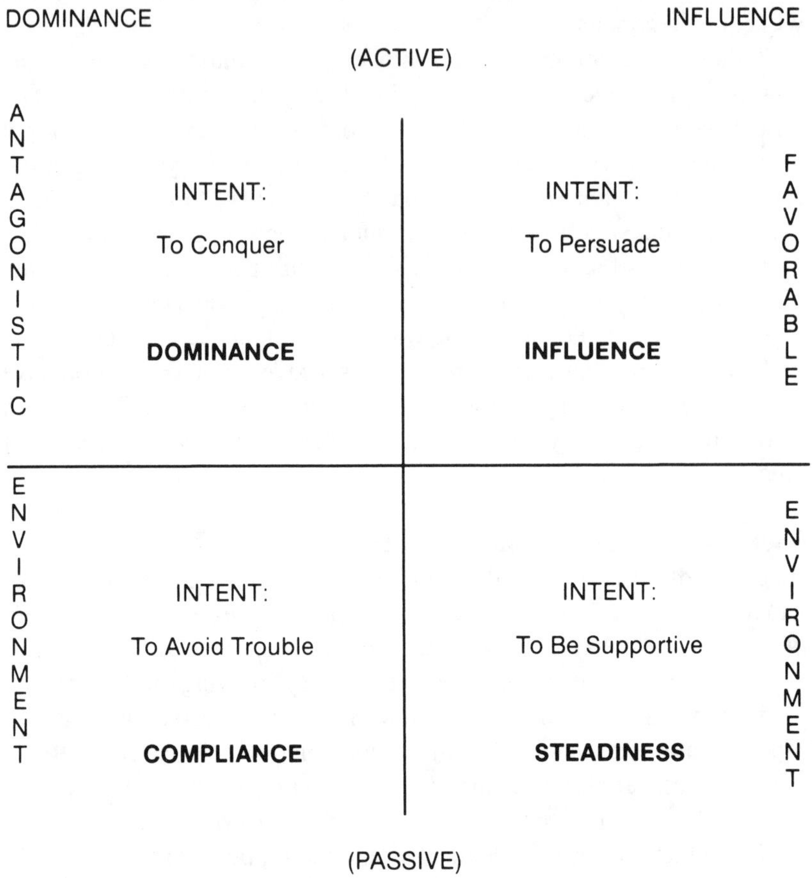

DOMINANCE INFLUENCE

(ACTIVE)

| A N T A G O N I S T I C | INTENT:

To Conquer

DOMINANCE | INTENT:

To Persuade

INFLUENCE | F A V O R A B L E |
| E N V I R O N M E N T | INTENT:

To Avoid Trouble

COMPLIANCE | INTENT:

To Be Supportive

STEADINESS | E N V I R O N M E N T |

(PASSIVE)

Figure 5.1. William M. Marston's Four Factor Behavioral Model

tions—to win. Their intent is to dominate. This behavior can be referred to as "High D" (for "dominate").

The upper-right quadrant environment is *favorable*, and some people are *active* in that environment as well. Their behavior is outgoing, persuasive, gregarious. They love to communicate. They're glib and facile with words. They convince and persuade. Their intent is to "influence," so their behaviors are characterized as "High I."

The lower-right quadrant environment is *favorable*, but the people in this quadrant tend to be *passive*. They're friendly, but in a low-key way. They prefer to sit back, work quietly but steadily, and provide support. They like to be thought of as steady and reliable—and they communicate in this way. Their intent is to be supportive, and this behavior is, accordingly, called "High S." High S behaviors are "people" oriented, but in a less aggressive way than the High I.

The lower left-hand quadrant is an *unfavorable* environment in which people choose to respond *passively*. These people follow the rules and do things right because it keeps them out of trouble. They're very careful about what they say; they're concerned about facts and details. They comply with what is expected of them. This style of behavior is referred to as "High C" behavior, and the intent is to comply.

But you may say, "I behave differently at different times. I can see myself at times in each of those quadrants." Yes, that's true. Everyone has an interesting and different mix of behaviors from all four quadrants. Your ability to use the behaviors of a particular style may be high in one quadrant and very low in another. But for a short period of time, you could behave in the manner characteristic of any quadrant if you find yourself communicating with someone exhibiting the behaviors related to that style.

In any given situation, you will react according to the way you perceive the environment. If you perceive that the environment is unfavorable or antagonistic, and you are generally active in an unfavorable environment, you'll exhibit the characteristics of High D behavior and communicate very aggressively. You may antagonize. If you tend to react passively, though, you may be so low key and unassertive that you fail to make any impression at all. And it is always important to remember that while you're reacting, other people are also reacting and communicating according to their perceptions of the environment.

As an unemployed person, you may fail to present yourself at your best because you may perceive that you are in an unfavorable environment, and communicate accordingly. But what if an interviewer perceives that the same set of cues is a favorable environment? Your communication approach will be pitched to the wrong environment and may come across either as too harsh or as over-cautious, and turn the interviewer off.

Spend enough time observing the interview situation to make a preliminary judgment about the interviewer's view of the environment and the style in which he or she is communicating. Then, you can match your presentation to that style. Most of the time, you will be right. But should you have misjudged, you can always shift your style later.

How do your communication behaviors stack up and where do you fall in the four quadrants? Figure 5.2 contains a list of 24 sets of four words. Each of these sets of four words represents a group of behaviors. For each set of four words, choose the one word which is most like you, and place an X in the M column.

Figure 5.2

Personal Concept

READ CAREFULLY: In the three columns below there are eight four-word groups. Select two words in each group--one which is MOST like you and one which is LEAST like you. Use an (X) to mark your choices.

EXAMPLE:

	M	L
AUTOCRATIC	X	
CONGENIAL		
STABLE		
EXACTING		X

	M	L
EXPRESSIVE		
COMPLIANT		
FORCEFUL		
RESTRAINED		
FORCE-OF-CHARACTER		
CAREFUL		
EMOTIONAL		
SATISFIED		
CORRECT		
PIONEERING		
EASY MARK		
INFLUENTIAL		
PRECISE		
DOMINEERING		
WILLING		
ATTRACTIVE		
EVEN TEMPERED		
STIMULATING		
FUSSY		
DETERMINED		
TIMID		
DEMANDING		
PATIENT		
CAPTIVATING		
OPEN MINDED		
COMPANIONABLE		
KIND		
SELF RELIANT		
AGREEABLE		
SELF CONTROLLED		
PLAYFUL		
PERSISTENT		

	M	L
HIGH SPIRITED		
TALKATIVE		
GOOD NATURED		
SOFTSPOKEN		
CONTENTED		
IMPATIENT		
CONVINCING		
RESIGNED		
RESPECTFUL		
GOOD MIXER		
AGGRESSIVE		
GENTLE		
POISED		
CONVENTIONAL		
NERVY		
ACCOMMODATING		
CONFIDENT		
COOPERATIVE		
ARGUMENTATIVE		
RELAXED		
RESTLESS		
WELL DISCIPLINED		
INSPIRING		
CONSIDERATE		
DIPLOMATIC		
COURAGEOUS		
SYMPATHETIC		
OPTIMISTIC		
EAGER		
POSITIVE		
LENIENT		
GOD FEARING		

	M	L
ADVENTUROUS		
ENTHUSIASTIC		
ADAPTABLE		
LOYAL		
HUMBLE		
GOOD LISTENER		
ENTERTAINING		
WILL POWER		
LIFE OF THE PARTY		
OBEDIENT		
TOLERANT		
COMPETITIVE		
CAUTIOUS		
NEIGHBORLY		
VIGOROUS		
PERSUASIVE		
RESERVED		
OUTSPOKEN		
STRICT		
ELOQUENT		
OBLIGING		
ANIMATED		
DOGGED		
DEVOUT		
ASSERTIVE		
GREGARIOUS		
NONCHALANT		
DOCILE		
OUTGOING		
BOLD		
MODERATE		
PERFECTIONIST		

Next, choose the one word from the remaining three which is least like the way you normally behave, and put an X in the L column beside the word. Continue in the same way through all 24 sets of words. When you finish, check to see that you made only one choice for the word *most* like you and one choice for the word *least* like you for each set of four words. Then, read the next section before scoring your response.

To learn to identify the different communications styles, let's start with Shakespeare's admonition to "know thyself." As you read the following descriptions, you will note that each is described in terms of a set of recognizable behaviors—behaviors that you can observe. We aren't dealing with motivations and nebulous feelings here.

HIGH D

Behaviors: High D people are self-starters who get going when things get tough. They thrive on challenge, conflict and competition. They are direct, positive and straightforward. They say what they think, and can be very blunt and to the point. They can cope with chaos, they are "change agents."

They like to be center stage—they are take-charge people. They fight hard for their beliefs and ideas, but can accept defeat and don't hold grudges. After a battle, they don't understand why others are still angry or holding a grudge.

They prefer variety, the unusual, the adventurous. They will lose interest if their jobs become routine, so must constantly be involved. They are prone to make job changes, especially early in their careers. When they find the challenge they need, they'll stay.

They are individualistic and self-sufficient. They demand a lot of themselves and of others. They may be discontented and dissatisfied with the status quo.

How they appear: They will probably be running late. They may be—or may appear to be—rude. They may interrupt you, take phone calls, read letters, call to their secretaries or otherwise interrupt you as you are talking. ("Go ahead, I'm listening.") Their offices may appear disorganized, with stacks of papers sitting around.

Impulsiveness and impatience are the keys to recognizing High D behaviors. Dress may or may not be a clue. If their secondary behaviors are active in a favorable environment (High I), they will be well dressed. But if they are low in I characteristics, they probably don't care much about their external appearance, so may be sloppy, or at least unstylish. Messy offices, careless dress and sloppy grooming are a dead giveaway to a High D.

How to communicate with people showing High D characteristics: They want you to be brief, so get to the point quickly. Stress what you can do for them or for their company. They want you to be sure of yourself, so be firm, don't pussyfoot around. Level with them. Emphasize the bottom line. They'll act on impulse, so hit them quickly and hard—but not argumentatively. In short, communicate with them in the same manner which they project.

Many top executives exhibit High D tendencies. That's what got them ahead. Your interviews with them will be short, to the point. They'll leave the details for someone else to fill in.

HIGH I

Behaviors: High I people are outgoing, persuasive and gregarious. They strive to persuade others and make their opinions and beliefs prevail. High I people are very comfortable in "one-on-one" situations. Their outgoing nature and the image they project is that of the so-called "natural salesperson."

High I people are basically interested in other people. They are poised and meet strangers easily—and people respond easily to them. They inherently trust and accept people. They are incurably optimistic. For that reason, they may misjudge people's abilities and intentions, with occasional disastrous results.

They are easy conversationalists, doing everything they can to put others at ease. They sell themselves well. In business, they are friendly competitors and they're optimistic, though not too well-organized as managers.

High I people normally dress very fashionably. They join organizations for prestige and for personal recognition. They usually have a broad range of acquaintances and tend to "name-drop".

How they appear: Their ego is apt to be all over their offices. The walls will be covered with pictures of *them* getting awards, plaques with *their* names on them, certificates, trophies and so on. You will know exactly who occupies that office. They will be friendly, outgoing and enthusiastic. And, of course, their dress is a good clue. Above all, the key to recognizing High I people is their ego. You will even hear this because they talk constantly, and use that word "I"—*"I did this, I did that."* They will tell you how wonderful they are, how wonderful their company is and so forth.

How to communicate with people with High I characteristics: They like the special, the novel—if it's new, it's exciting. Since they like to talk about themselves, let them tell you about what they've been doing. Don't attempt to dominate the conversation. (You couldn't anyway—they'd interrupt you. You don't want to try for one-upmanship, in any event.) They want to be the first to do something, and above all, they want recognition. Emphasize the ways in which you can help them get what they want, the recognition they want (and need). Compliment them (sincerely) on their office, their organization, whatever. Use a broad brush in telling them about your accomplishments and omit the details. Details are boring to a High I.

Many High I executives have made it to, or near to, the top, especially in sales and marketing, public relations, advertising and people-intensive businesses.

HIGH S

Behaviors: High S people are usually amiable, easygoing and relaxed. Most of the time, they are even-tempered, low-key and unobtrusive. They hate to be singled out in a crowd. They tend to be complacent, are frequently lenient with others, but emotionally mature.

They are warmhearted, love their homes and are excellent neighbors. They work at friendship and probably have retained the same friends they made years ago.

They tend to be undemonstrative and controlled. They conceal their feelings from others—and they hold grudges. The saying, "I don't get mad, I get even," is true for the High S.

High S individuals strive to keep things the way they are and dislike change. Once under way, they work steadily and patiently. They dislike urgency and the pressure of deadlines.

They seldom argue or openly criticize, but they can quietly resist and slow things down. They're normally passive resisters, but pushed to the wall, can be implacable enemies.

They tend to be very possessive and develop strong attachments for things, family, coworkers, their departments and companies. They will often refer to the company or their work group as "we" or "our".

How they appear: They will be very low key. Their dress is usually conservative and neat. Their offices will also be neat, but not compulsively so. They will have no more than a few papers or folders on their desks. The pictures in their offices will be of their possessions—their spouses, their families, their houses, boats, airplanes, summer cottages and so on. Their possessiveness is usually evident in nameplates on both their desks and their doors. They may also have labeled Scotch tape dispensers, staplers and other objects on the desk or in the room. Don't touch anything in the room—they may resent it. They will appear to be very easygoing, but are reserved in their judgments. They are also very security conscious.

The High S style is the most difficult to identify because these individuals are so good at masking their emotions. If you don't see anything in their behavior or in their office that identifies them as High D, High I, or High C (the next style to be discussed), they're probably High S, and you can make that as a tentative identification.

How to communicate with people with High S tendencies: Sell yourself first, in a low-key, non-dramatic way. You must win them as friends, then they'll go along with you as a friend. Don't move too fast at first; let them move at their own pace. Don't push or hurry them. They may resent it (which you won't know because they are masters at hiding their feelings) and you will have blown the interview. Talk security, service, dependability and backup. Don't talk about turnarounds or instituting changes. These are threatening. They expect you to take a sincere personal interest in them and their company. Provide all the details they want and be prepared to answer their questions fully. Don't attempt to take over the interview to try to move it ahead. They'll get where they're going in their own good time.

More High S people are middle managers than top-level executives, not because of lack of ability, but because they don't consider the pressured life style desirable. You're likely to find them in human resources departments. *You must get past these people before you can hope to get a job.* They may not make the hiring decision, but they can prevent you from being hired—or even seen by someone who does make the hiring decision.

HIGH C

Behaviors: High C individuals are characterized by orderliness. They are precise and attentive to detail. They strive for a neat, orderly existence and tend to follow traditional procedures and established systems. They are reserved, conservative, adaptable, open-minded (to a point) and diplomatic. They are careful with people because they stay out of trouble that way. They prefer to adapt to situations and to compromise, if necessary, to avoid conflict and antagonism. They work to stay out of hot water and to avoid stepping on toes. They tend to document, document, document. They go by the book.

They are naturally cautious and tentative in decision-making. When they are convinced by fact and detail, they will make up their mind and may be rigid should unexpected change be necessary. They try hard to be what others want and expect them to be. They have high personal standards and live up to them. They expect others to meet the same high standards they set for themselves.

How they appear: Their offices will be neat and orderly. Their desks will be clear. They will appear to be unhurried. If there are pictures in the office, they will probably be of things—landscapes, still lifes, abstracts or attractive photographs. They will be prepared for your visit, will be on time and will have read your letters, resume and/or job application. They'll be courteous and diplomatic, but will have detailed, precise quesitons to ask. They will be dressed conservatively and will almost always be very well groomed.

How to communicate with people with High C tendencies: Be precise and technically correct—don't generalize. Be sure you answer all questions carefully and completely. Use facts and include the how's and why's, if asked. They're interested in research and statistics. Supply all the details they want, but don't get caught trying to manipulate the facts and figures in your favor. The key to recognizing High C executives is their precise manner and that they organize everything. So prepare your answers accordingly.

Because they are cautious, avoid telling them about the massive changes you made on your last job unless you set the framework first. Talk in detail about the research and preparation that it took before you could make such a far-reaching change. Their extreme caution makes them want quality, reliability and precedent. Show that you followed the rules and helped your employers reach their stated goals. If you leave a resume, give them one which includes a full listing of prior job responsibilities.

Low D, Low I, Low S and Low C Behaviors

You will be low in a particular set of behaviors in at least two, and sometimes even three quadrants. How low you are in a particular quadrant also tells us something about your behaviors and your overall communication style.

Low D Behaviors: Those who have few D behaviors tend to be meek or unassuming, and may fail to speak up and be counted. They don't like to assume leadership roles.

Low I Behaviors: People with few I behaviors tend to be quiet and reserved, very low key. They tend to be logical and analytical, to prefer facts to people.

Low S Behaviors: People with few S behaviors tend to be in high gear, alert and fast-moving. They may be erratic, or at least sporadic, and may be very intense. They may choose to engage simultaneously in many different kinds of activities.

Low C Behaviors: People with few C behaviors tend to be nonconformist and independent. They may be fearless risk-takers, and enjoy getting into trouble.

Determining Your Style

The answers you gave on the quiz you took in Figure 5.2 can be used to plot a profile that will tell you how high or how low you are on each of the four sets of characteristics. You can place these answers on a graph and produce a picture that represents generally how you'll appear to others when you communicate. A sample profile might look something like Figure 5.3. The person with this profile has a primary High D set of behaviors, is low in I behaviors, has a secondary set of High S behaviors, and is really low in C behaviors. This person would be identified as a High D in an unfavorable environment, but might behave as a High I if the environment seems favorable enough.

Look at the list of words in the Figure 5.4 answer key to check your answers. For each group of four words, one word is representative of a D behavior, one an I, one an S and one a C. Go back to the answers you marked on Figure 5.2. Next to each M answer and then next to each L answer, write the letter (D, I, S or C) that corresponds to your answer.

Next, count the D responses you made in the M column. Go to the chart in the center of the graphs in Figure 5.5 and place that total in the M column on the D line. Repeat your count with the I answers, the S answers, and the C answers. Add the number of responses that you counted to see that you had 24. If not, go back and recount to find out what you omitted.

Repeat the counting procedure for the responses in the L column. Count the D, I, S and C responses and put the numbers in the appropriate boxes in figure 5.5 under the L heading. They should also total 24 responses.

Subtract the responses in the L column from the number of responses in the M column to find the difference between the two. Put that number in the appropriate boxes under the A heading. You'll have positive and negative numbers in the A column if you did it right. To check: add the numbers in the A column. They should total zero.

Now you'll convert these scores into three sets of profiles—a public concept, a projected concept and a private concept. Note that on either

Figure 5.3. Sample Profile

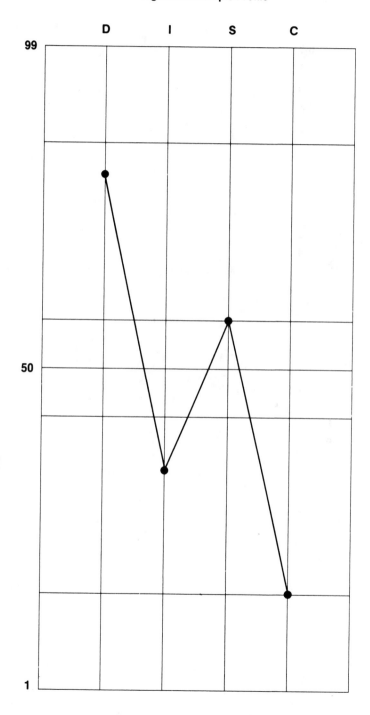

Figure 5.4. Answer Key to Communications Styles Quiz

EXPRESSIVE	I	HIGH-SPIRITED	D	ADVENTUROUS	D
COMPLIANT	C	TALKATIVE	I	ENTHUSIASTIC	I
FORCEFUL	D	GOOD-NATURED	S	ADAPTABLE	C
RESTRAINED	S	SOFTSPOKEN	C	LOYAL	S
●		●		●	
FORCE-OF-CHARACTER	D	CONTENTED	S	HUMBLE	C
CAREFUL	C	IMPATIENT	D	GOOD LISTENER	S
EMOTIONAL	I	CONVINCING	I	ENTERTAINING	I
SATISFIED	S	RESIGNED	C	WILL POWER	D
●		●		●	
CORRECT	C	RESPECTFUL	C	LIFE OF THE PARTY	I
PIONEERING	D	GOOD MIXER	I	OBEDIENT	S
EASY MARK	S	AGGRESSIVE	D	TOLERANT	C
INFLUENTIAL	I	GENTLE	S	COMPETITIVE	D
●		●		●	
PRECISE	C	POISED	I	CAUTIOUS	C
DOMINEERING	D	CONVENTIONAL	C	NEIGHBORLY	S
WILLING	S	NERVY	D	VIGOROUS	D
ATTRACTIVE	I	ACCOMMODATING	S	PERSUASIVE	I
●		●		●	
EVEN-TEMPERED	S	CONFIDENT	I	RESERVED	S
STIMULATING	I	COOPERATIVE	C	OUTSPOKEN	D
FUSSY	C	ARGUMENTATIVE	D	STRICT	C
DETERMINED	D	RELAXED	S	ELOQUENT	I
●		●		●	
TIMID	C	RESTLESS	D	OBLIGING	S
DEMANDING	D	WELL-DISCIPLINED	C	ANIMATED	I
PATIENT	S	INSPIRING	I	DOGGED	D
CAPTIVATING	I	CONSIDERATE	S	DEVOUT	C
●		●		●	
OPEN-MINDED	C	DIPLOMATIC	C	ASSERTIVE	D
COMPANIONABLE	I	COURAGEOUS	D	GREGARIOUS	I
KIND	S	SYMPATHETIC	S	NONCHALANT	S
SELF-RELIANT	D	OPTIMISTIC	I	DOCILE	C
●		●		●	
AGREEABLE	C	EAGER	I	OUTGOING	I
SELF-CONTROLLED	S	POSITIVE	D	BOLD	D
PLAYFUL	I	LENIENT	S	MODERATE	S
PERSISTENT	D	GOD-FEARING	C	PERFECTIONIST	C

Figure 5.5. Personal Concept Scoring Form—Communication Style

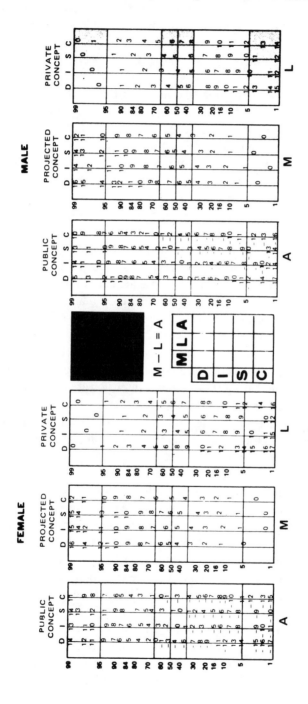

side of Figure 5.5 are three sets of graphs. The graphs on the left are headed *Female*, the graphs on the right, *Male*. The left-hand graph in each set is marked *Public concept* above and has the letter A underneath. The center graph is marked *Projected concept* and has the letter M underneath. The right-hand graph is labeled *Private concept* and has the letter L underneath.

Transfer the scores from the M column of the chart onto the center graph in the set of graphs you're using, and circle the corresponding number. If the number of the score you made isn't on the graph, extrapolate between the two nearest numbers.

Similarly, transfer the scores from the L column onto the right-hand graph marked *Private concept* and the scores from the A column onto the left-hand graph marked *Public concept*.

Finally, join the scores together—D to I to S to C—on each graph to get the profiles representing your communication behaviors.

So far, so good. But what do those three different profiles mean? Basically, your M responses and the projected concepts indicate the way you *think* you should act and communicate to be successful. This profile is heavily influenced by your general economic situation, your last job, your family, etc. It can also show the stresses you are placing on yourself to try to accomplish your objectives.

Your L responses and the private concepts profile reflect the way you respond when you know people well or are in the privacy of your home. It may also represent the way you respond when you are severely stressed and your project concepts "mask" slips.

The public concepts profile and the A set of numbers generally represent what the public sees—and reflects the interaction between the concept of yourself that you're projecting and the way you communicate and behave in private.

To repeat: most people have strengths in two of the quadrants. For example, the person represented by the profile in Figure 5.6 has a primary strength in the S or steadiness quadrant, and a secondary strength in the C or compliance quadrant. Both behaviors are passive. The person will exhibit High S behaviors in a favorable environment, and will communicate in the High C style in an unfavorable environment.

Almost an exact opposite set of communication behaviors is exhibited by the person with the profile shown in Figure 5.7. This person is active in both the unfavorable and favorable environments, exhibiting High D behaviors in the unfavorable and High I in the favorable. Interestingly enough, the two people represented in Figures 5.6 and 5.7 will have a terrible time communicating with each other unless both make adjustments in style and are aware of and respect the differences in style. (In marriage, however, opposites really do attract. High D people often marry High S spouses, and a High I will often marry a High C. That way, they cover most communications bases. What one can't do, the other can.)

Look again at your graph labeled *Public concept*. Circle the one or two scores that are above the horizontal line marked 50 (this is a percentile score at the left side of the graph). These are your natural style(s). The highest one is your preferred style, the other score (if you have one —you may have been so overwhelmingly high in one area that the other three scores are below the fiftieth percentile) is your secondary style.

Note which one of these you use in a favorable environment, and which you use in an unfavorable environment. If you had only one above the line, you probably use this style exclusively in all situations—which can get you into trouble on occasion.

Now, reread the descriptions for your primary and secondary styles. These are the ones which you can use easily. You can also use without too much stress any style in which you score in the midrange between the 50th and the 35th percentile. This does not mean that you can't use a style that scores below the 35th percentile—it just means that you have to do it deliberately, and work at it. Also check what kinds of behaviors the low scores generally reflect.

To assist you further in understanding the possible strengths and weaknesses in your own style, transfer the *Public concept* profile you developed in Figure 5.5 onto both the probable strengths and the possible weaknesses graphs in Figure 5.8. Use the horizontal lines and the percentile markings at the side to approximate the profile positions. Begin on the D column, then continue on to the I, the S and the C columns. To read your strengths, locate the center horizontal line marked 50. If the score is located above that line, read all the words from 50 up to and including the charted point; if the marking for a set of characteristics is below 50, read all of the words from 50 down to and including the charted point. The first list of words describes the way you might appear to people who like you (probable strengths); the second list of words describes the way you might appear to people who don't like you (possible weaknesses).

If you've done everything according to the directions so far, you should have a profile of your overall style with which you will pretty much agree. One further note: When the projected concepts profile is radically different from that shown in your private concept, the public concept may not give a completely true picture of your basic self. You

76

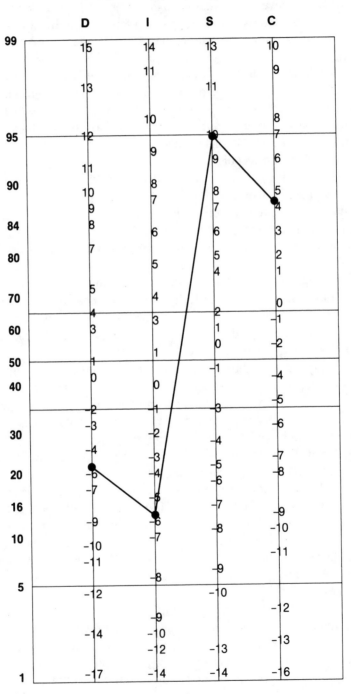

Figure 5.6 Public Concept

A

Figure 5.7 Public Concept

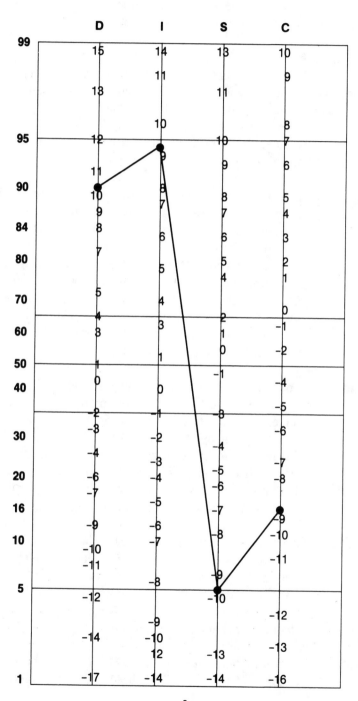

A

may want to try overlaying your *Private concept* style on the charts in Figure 5.8 as a further check on what your style might be without the added stresses of the concept you're attempting to project.

Problem Behaviors

Most people's basic styles are set during childhood, and it's very difficult to make a substantive change in style. What's far easier to handle, though, is to find out what behaviors in the different quadrants can most heavily impact on others. Read the following descriptions that apply to you. Then, modify those that you know you've had problems with on a situation-by-situation basis.

High D   You are impatient and don't give others an opportunity to think and to assimilate. You tend to be impulsive, to blow up when things go wrong, but you get over your anger fast. (This behavior is a disaster with a High S. The High S will brood about it and not get over hurt feelings.) You may fail to consult or share. You are probably a one-way communicator—you tell, not ask, and are a poor listener. You may not be sensitive to the feeling and needs of others. You may try to dominate and override others, or to intimidate them. You may be too blunt.

High I   You are too global—and you may find detail difficult. You may act without thinking, be too optimistic. You may be perceived as too talky, too superficial. You may not give other people an opportunity to respond. You like people and may trust too much. You probably give poor directions. You may not listen enough and may cut others off because they don't respond quickly. You tend to "wing it," to go off on tangents. You may be too outgoing, too effervescent.

High S   You may be seen as too indirect, as lacking conviction, or as not forceful enough. You may spend too much time on tasks and lack a sense of urgency. You may be too slow to respond, and too patient. You may spend too much time listening and not enough time asking or telling. You may be stubborn or clam up when pushed.

High C   You may talk too deliberately, concentrate too much on details and the "small" picture. You want everything in

Figure 5.8 Public Concept, Probable Strengths

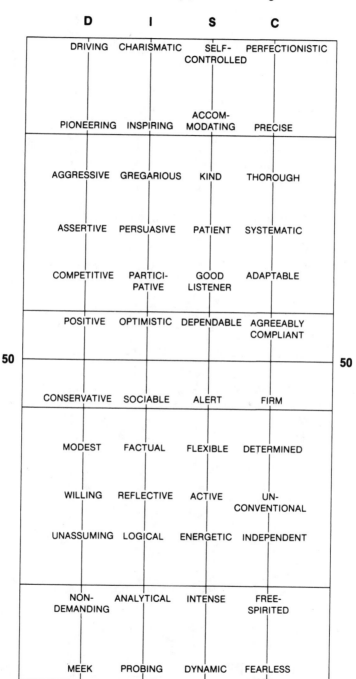

Figure 5.8 Public Concept, Probable Weaknesses

D	I	S	C
BELLIGERENT	SELF-PROMOTING	PHLEGMATIC	OVERLY DEPENDENT
DICTATORIAL	SUPERFICIAL	INDIF-FERENT	EVASIVE
ARROGANT	OVERLY OPTIMISTIC	TOO LENIENT	WORRISOME
DEMANDING	GLIB	POSSESSIVE	DEFENSIVE
NERVY	OVERLY CONFIDENT	COM-PLACENT	NIT PICKER
HASTY	POOR LISTENER	NON-DEMON-STRATIVE	TOO COMPLIANT
HESITANT	RESERVED	RESTLESS	OPINIONATED
SHY	BLUNT	IMPATIENT	STUBBORN
OVER-CAUTIOUS	SUSPICIOUS	PUSHY	IMMOVABLE
HUMBLE	ALOOF	TENSE	REBELLIOUS
FEARFUL	PESSIMISTIC	IMPETUOUS	DEFIANT
INTIMIDATED	WITHDRAWN	HYPER-ACTIVE	RADICAL

50   50

exactly the right form, which others may view as picky. You may move too slowly and cautiously. You want things written rather than told. You will ask (and ask) rather than tell. You may be too sensitive to possible slights, yet be critical of faults in others.

Business Needs All Communications Styles

A well-rounded organization needs all communications styles represented for balance and productivity: High D's for their goal orientation and attention to the bottom line; High I's for their people skills, intuitive understanding of the effect decisions will have on the people involved, and their ability to sell ideas and get commitment from others; High S's for their calmness, their unflappability, their personal commitment and their ability to work well with almost anyone (they also are usually able to concentrate well on the task at hand); and High C's to keep the organization "honest." High C's are concerned about details, about risk, about possible problems and often come up with the tough "what if" questions. They are also needed for their diplomacy and tact. Both the High S and the High C communicators are stabilizers, and help keep the group on track.

Unfortunately, many organizations are not balanced as far as communications styles are concerned. Decision-makers far too often "clone" themselves—they hire people with the same communication style that they have because they have had no trouble talking to them.

Determining Personal Stress

Unemployment is obviously a time of considerable stress for everyone. Anything you can do to lessen your internal stress will make it easier for you to concentrate on the important elements of your job search.

In making your choices for your communications style, you have already shown whether you are stressing yourself in the communications area. The differences between the respective scores on the M and L profiles/scores show whether you are under minimum, average or high levels of stress.

To illustrate how this process works, look at the M and L profiles of one unemployed executive in Figure 5.9. At the left of each profile is the column of figures representing the percentile rankings of the various scores.[1] Look at the D scores in the M and L profiles first. On the M

---

[1] No doubt by now, you have identified the scoring process as a variation of the Bell curve of distribution. The middle portion bounded by the three horizontal lines in the center of each profile represents the "averages"—those scores within one standard deviation from the mean, while the portions delimited by the top and bottom horizontal lines represent the extremes on the scores.

profile, the D percentile is 84, while on the L profile, it's about 46. The difference between these two scores is the number of stress points (38 points). On the I scale, the score on the M profile is about 55, on the L profile, about 75; the difference is 20 stress points. The difference between the two S scores is 20 points (30 and 20), and the C difference is 12 points (48 and 36). To determine the total stress points, add the four differences together.

$$D + I + S + C = \text{Stress Points}$$

$$38 + 20 + 20 + 12 = 90 \text{ points}$$

Generally speaking, anywhere between 0 and 40 stress points represents minimum stress, between 41 and 80, moderate stress, above 81, high stress. Please note that this means stress that you are placing yourself under—not stress that's imposed from outside.

To explain the kinds of stress the executive in the example is undergoing: The basic underlying style of this executive is a High I one (the private concept). But this person feels that to be successful, he must be aggressive and assertive, so he pushes this aspect of his personality—which is already in the "average" range. (Incidentally, pushing for High D characteristics is difficult, almost impossible, for those people whose underlying D scores are below 50. They could project a High D behavior for a short period of time, but could not maintain it for long without causing personal stress. What they should do is to determine when the High D behavior is absolutely essential, use it when they identify that type of situation, and immediately drop the behavior.)

But what he is doing with his basic High I characteristics is especially revealing. In this instance, the executive is basically an outgoing person who really likes people. But to be successful, he feels that he must hold back on this behavior. Almost invariably, reducing one's outreach to people has come through bitter experience. The individual trusted someone or something too much, and was sadly disappointed.

Executives often try to change the S scale. On the Private Concept profile, this executive has an extremely low S rating, which generally reflects a perception of time. He probably moves quickly to get things done and is very active. But the higher rating in the Projected Concept suggests that he is trying to be more patient, to be less demanding of the people he's managing (or was managing). He's trying to cut down on his expectations that people "get things done yesterday." Since this execu-

Figure 5.9. Stress Points, Male, Projected Concept

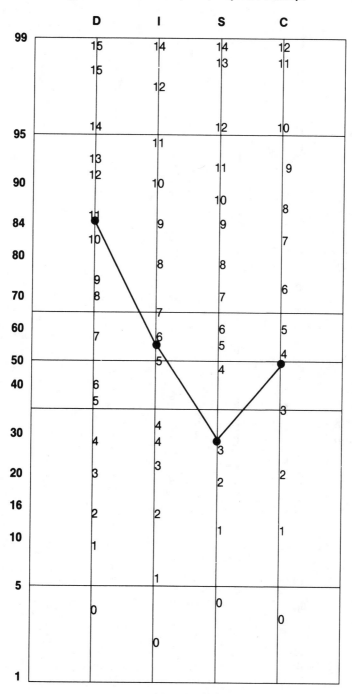

M

84

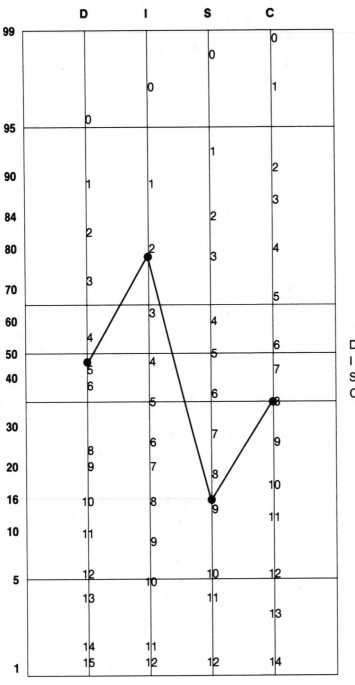

Figure 5.9. Stress Points, Male, Private Concept

Differences:
D 84 – 46 = 38
I 55 – 75 = 20
S 30 – 10 = 20
C 48 – 36 = 12

tive is unemployed, it could also mean that he's trying to be more patient in a situation in which he is not in control and can't hurry the results.

Finally, the C changes may tell either or both of two things: the executive is trying to become less independent (the higher the C score, the greater the dependence), and/or he is trying to pay more attention to details to be sure that nothing falls through the cracks.

Now, compare the D, I, S, and C percentile scores on your *projected concept* and *private concept* profiles, and calculate the differences. You are concerned with absolute differences, not plus or minus differences. Add the D differences, the I differences, the S differences and the C differences to determine your stress points. If your stress points are in the medium high to high range, take a good hard look at the *projected concept* to see whether you need to stress yourself. If the answer is yes, then ask yourself further: Do you need to stress yourself all the time, or can you be situational?

Making Adaptations in Style to Match Job Search Requirements

As you begin your job search, evaluate the communication styles of the people you meet. Make guesses about the best way to interact with people that are not connected to your job search. Then practice communicating with members of each group in the style you perceive them to prefer. Then ask yourself: Were you right? Was your interaction easier?

You'll find your judgments get better as you go. Practice may not make perfect, but it will surely improve your track record. In any event, by tuning in to their words, actions and surroundings, and paying attention to them as individuals, your communication will be more rewarding. Why? Because your attention is concentrated outward toward them, rather than inward toward yourself.

You'll also want to use different styles of resumes, different kinds of letters, and different ways of interacting in interviews, based on your judgments about styles. Those adaptations will be discussed in later chapters.[2]

---

[2] For a fuller explanation of your individual communications style than is possible in this chapter, send photocopies of Figure 5.2, Personal Concept, and Figure 6.2, Position Concept (in the next chapter), showing your responses, along with a check or money order for $10.00 to Jack Mohler Associates, Box 153, Garwood, NJ 07027-0153.

Also available: Provolator, a computer scoring version of the D.I.S.C. quizzes in this and Chapter 6, can be ordered from Prowess, Inc., 9563 Crestedge, Dallas, TX 75238.

What Kind of Job Should You Search For?

After completing the exercises in the last section, you have a good idea of your skills, strengths and weaknesses; goals and objectives; and your communication style. You still may not know what job you are best suited for or what you should search for.

Part of this is related to your basic makeup. It's more comfortable and less effort to look for the same kind of employment you had before. Radically changing job types can be a great personal risk. Can you face the challenge of a second or even third career at your age? Or should you stay in the same kind of job because you aren't ready to risk that much?

Now really is the time to consider whether or not it's time to change the direction of your work life. A well-known executive recruiter conjectured early in 1990 that executives and professionals working today can expect to have at least six job changes during their working careers, four of which will be involuntary.[1] Some other interesting statistics (and not so interesting, if you happened to lose your job at the time) also tend to lend credence to this idea. At the end of 1989, you couldn't pick up a newspaper without reading about a major company entering Chapter 11, going out of business, closing down a location or locations, laying off a number of employees, or offering older employees early retirement. Big business lost more than two million jobs, while small business and new business start-ups were responsible for the creation of over 22 million new jobs.

---

[1] William J. Morin, president, director and CEO of Drake Beam Morin, Inc., in an interview with Consuelo Mark on "Wall Street Quarterly," CBS, January 17, 1990.

Harry Levinson, a famous industrial psychologist, writes frequently on career topics and career changes.[2] In numerous articles, he has pointed out that the most critical factor for people to consider in choosing a second career is their "ego ideal." The "ego ideal" is central to people's aspirations, and is an idealized image of the way they hope to find themselves in the future.

People strive throughout their lives for their ego ideals, but never fully achieve them. When people feel they are progressing toward their ego ideals, they feel more positive about themselves. The closer they get to their ego ideals, the better they feel about themselves. The greater the gap between their ego ideals and their current self-images, the angrier they are at themselves, and the more inadequate, guilty and depressed they are apt to feel. (This loss of the ego ideal is one of the worst features about being unemployed.)

When careers help satisfy ego ideals, life and work are rewarding and enjoyable. When careers do not meet these self demands, work is a curse. The desire to attain ego ideals is the most powerful motivating force. Delivering on the promises you make to yourself, then, is an extremely important aspect of choosing a new direction.

What Is Your Ego Ideal?

Levinson suggests that reviewing your family history, school and work experiences can help you to outline the needs that are critical to your ego ideal. Answering the following eight sets of questions will help you know your ego ideals and help you recognize your own sense of purpose.

1. What were your father's or father-substitute's values? Not what did you father say or do, but what did he stand for? What things were important to him? What was the code he lived by? Similarly, analyze your mother's values.

2. What was the first thing you did that pleased your mother? (This is important because usually the first person that children try to please is their mother. Later, pleasing their father becomes important, too.) For women, the mother's value system may have more weight in forming their values (question 1), while the activities they did to please a parent (question 2) were more often performed with the father in mind. These two questions should give you insight into the way you have formed your current values system.

---

[2] Levinson wrote at length about the ego ideal in the *Harvard Business Review*, May/June 1983.

3. Who were your childhood heroes or heroines? Did you idolize athletes, movie stars, or political figures? What kind of people do you now enjoy reading about or watching on TV? What kind of achievements do you admire?

4. Who are and were your models—relatives, teachers, scoutmasters, preachers, bosses, characters in stories? What did they say or do that made you admire them?

5. When you were able to make choices, what were they? What was your major in college? What jobs have you accepted? (These may appear to be random, but they were not. Look at them carefully to find the pattern.)

6. What few experiences in your lifetime have been the most gratifying? Which gave you the greatest pleasure and sense of elation? The pleasure you took in the experience was really the pleasure you took in yourself. What were you doing?

7. Of all the things you've done, at which were you the most successful? What were you doing and how were you doing it?

8. What would you like your epitaph or obituary to say? What would you like to be remembered for? What would you like to leave as a memorial?

After you complete your answers, review your occupational activities to determine those that fit the way you like to behave—to do your job or deal with your coworkers. Ask yourself: In what environment am I comfortable?

Try discussing your answers to these questions with a friend. During your discussion, also explore these other areas of your personality.

❐ How do you handle aggressive energy? Do you channel it into the organization and administration of projects or do you bottle it up?
❐ How do you handle affection? Do you enjoy interacting with others or do you feel more comfortable keeping your distance? Can you express your emotions to others? (Thank them, praise them, give them a pat on the back?)
❐ How to do you handle dependency? Can you make decisions or do you honestly prefer that someone else make them? Do you want to be in charge, be a team member or work independently?

You are really trying to answer for yourself: Do I want to continue as a manager—or would I have a better life, with less frustration, doing something else? If your answer is yes, ask yourself what that something else should be. This last question is one of the soul-searchers of all time. You are asking yourself to start over, or at least, to enter uncharted territory.

After serious reflection, if you discover that you really don't want to leave the field in which you've been working to start a new career, you still have a number of other questions to answer.

❐ Where do you want to look (locale)? Are you willing to relocate? (Before you can answer that one honestly, you must discuss this thoroughly with your family, since their desires have to be considered in such a momentous decision. Especially now, with so many two-career families, the question of "where" becomes crucial to a successful job search.)

❐ What size company do you want to work for? Fortune 500, small business or industry, consulting firm, nonprofit organization, civil service or other governmental agency?

❐ Do you want to be an entrepreneur, to start your own business?

❐ Should you look for a management position, or are you willing to accept a lesser position if the long-term prospects look good?

❐ Are you willing to "settle," to accept almost any job, just so it is interesting and will last long enough for you to reach retirement age?

Still not ready to make a decision, or you don't yet have enough direction? Read on. By the time you complete the exercises in the following pages, you should know enough about yourself to decide whether to change careers or to look for more of the same.

Matching Communication Styles and Jobs

When people plan their careers, they are generally attracted to job areas and professions which in some way match their communication styles. As they advance in business, however, the job demands are different, and the ability to use different communication styles is needed. Managers succeed or fail on the basis of their ability to adapt, to match their communication styles to the requirements of their jobs.

In essence, this means that jobs, like people, have "personalities" and communications needs. The managerial positions you want and are qualified for demand that you make constant adjustments to your basic style. That's a "given" for success in managing people. You'll be happier—and better able to make the needed adjustments—if you understand whether you have a natural fit for the job (and must therefore make only minor adjustments in style) or whether you must constantly watch for situations where you'll have to make major adjustments in your style.

Figure 6.1 illustrates how careers fit into the four DISC quadrants. It shows some of the major career areas that are compatible with the different kinds of communications styles. Beginning with the D quadrant: the positions in the bottom portion of the quadrant are high D positions in which some measure of high C would be valuable.

Figure 6.1. Careers Matching Communication Styles

D | I

High D, High I

Executive
Manager
Production Planner
Business Developer
Controller
Corporation Lawyer

High D, High C

Credit Person
Audio-Visual Producer
Engineer
Inventor—Product Developer
Scientist
Author

High I, High D

Sales Engineer
Salesperson "Tangibles"
Labor Negotiator
Management Consultant
Salesperson "Intangibles"
Account Executive

High I, High C

Contact Person
Public Administrator
Recruiter
Fund Raiser
Community Recreation Director
Personnel Director

C | S

High C, High D

Actor
Commercial Artist
Architect
Chemist
Data Interpreter
Tool Designer

High C, High S

Detailer—Draftsperson
Automation Programmer
Statistician
Actuary
Quality Control Coordinator
Mathematician

High S, High I

Psychologist
Underwriter
Investment Counsellor
Methods Analyst
Claims Adjustor
Market Analyst

High S, High C

Arbitrator
Trust Officer
Survey Analyst
Accountant
Skilled Specialist
Editor

In the top part of the quadrant are positions requiring High D behaviors with a lesser measure of High I style. Over the line into the top of the I quadrant are the positions for which High I behavior, pushed by lesser amounts of High D, are helpful. These positions are frequently in the sales area. High I positions, which require some measure of supportive High S behavior, are shown in the bottom part of the sector. In the High S quadrant, the jobs shown at the top of the quadrant are High S jobs requiring occasional outgoing High I behaviors. The bottom of the segment shows the High S jobs that have a High C component—generally positions in which services are provided. At the top of the High C sector are positions requiring High C attention to detail along with some High S supportive behaviors. And finally, at the bottom of the C quadrant are those positions that require High C attention to detail, but also some assertiveness and overcoming of obstacles.

Determining the Communication Style of Your Desired Position

To determine the communication style of the job area you're considering, take the simple quiz in Figure 6.2. Think of the characteristics of the job. What kind of requirements does it have? Would you be making many contacts? Initiating action? Taking risks? Or would the position be such that you couldn't accept risks? Must perform without error? Serve others? Pay attention to detail?

The quiz in Figure 6.2 has 24 different job factors that have varying degrees of importance on a job. For each factor, decide its importance and rate it numerically. If the factor has a very low importance, rate it a 1. Give it a 2 if it's low, a 3 if the job has an average requirement for that factor, a 4 if the requirement is high, and score a 5 only for those factors for which the job has a very high requirement.

Caution: No job requires a 5 on every factor, nor will there be many jobs that have only a 1 requirement for very many. Most of your judgments should be in the 2, 3, or 4 category.

By now, you have probably guessed that each factor you were rating represents a behavior representative of one of the four major communications styles. For example, the first behavior, *accepting challenge*, is a High D characteristic. A score of five on that factor would indicate that you're looking for a position that's High D at least on that one characteristic. A rating of one would show a low D requirement.

Six of the factors are High D behaviors, 6 are High I, 6 High S, and 6 High C. Turn now to Figure 6.3 for a listing of each factor's style identification.

Figure 6.2

Position Concept

JOB TITLE: _____

EXAMINED BY: _____

DATE: _____

INSTRUCTIONS

Examine the "job" factors listed below and their relative importance to the job being examined. Using the scale below, give each factor a numerical rating.

1 · Very Low	3 · Average
2 · Low	4 · High
	5 · Very High

THIS JOB REQUIRES THAT I, (he, she):

	ACCEPT CHALLENGE		PERSUADE AND MOTIVATE OTHERS
	WORK MORE WITH PEOPLE THAN THINGS		BE CONTENT WITH REPETITIVE WORK
	MAKE MANY CONTACTS		WORK PRIMARILY IN ONE PLACE
	ACT WITHOUT PRECEDENT		OVERCOME RESISTANCE
	VERBALIZE FLUENTLY		BE GENUINELY OPTIMISTIC AND ENTHUSIASTIC
	INITIATE ACTION		PAY ATTENTION TO DETAIL
	BE RESPONSIBLE FOR QUALITY AND ACCURACY		SERVE OTHERS
	TAKE RISKS		AVOID UNNECESSARY RISK OR TROUBLE
	MAKE A FAVORABLE FIRST IMPRESSION		DRIVE FOR TANGIBLE RESULTS
	EXERCISE SELF-CONTROL		PERFORM WITHOUT ERROR
	COMPLY WITH INSTRUCTIONS		BE A SUPPORTIVE TEAM PLAYER
	BE CAUTIOUS IN MAKING COMMITMENTS		ACCEPT THINGS THE WAY THEY ARE

Figure 6.3. Position Concept Grid and Profile

Position Concept

JOB TITLE: _____

EXAMINED BY: _____

DATE: _____

	TOT - AVG DIF X 5 - 50 - %						PC
	TOTAL	AVERAGE	DIFFERENCE	MUTLIPLE	PERCENTAGE		D I S C
DOMINANCE						99	
INFLUENCE						95 / 90 / 84 / 80 / 70 / 60 / 50 / 40 / 30 / 20 / 16 / 10 / 5 / 1	
STEADINESS							
COMPLIANCE							

THIS JOB REQUIRES THAT I, (he, she):

D	ACCEPT CHALLENGE	**I**	PERSUADE AND MOTIVATE OTHERS
I	WORK MORE WITH PEOPLE THAN THINGS	**S**	BE CONTENT WITH REPETITIVE WORK
I	MAKE MANY CONTACTS	**S**	WORK PRIMARILY IN ONE PLACE
D	ACT WITHOUT PRECEDENT	**D**	OVERCOME RESISTANCE
I	VERBALIZE FLUENTLY	**I**	BE GENUINELY OPTIMISTIC AND ENTHUSIASTIC
D	INITIATE ACTION	**C**	PAY ATTENTION TO DETAIL
C	BE RESPONSIBLE FOR QUALITY AND ACCURACY	**S**	SERVE OTHERS
D	TAKE RISKS	**C**	AVOID UNNECESSARY RISK OR TROUBLE
I	MAKE A FAVORABLE FIRST IMPRESSION	**D**	DRIVE FOR TANGIBLE RESULTS
S	EXERCISE SELF CONTROL	**C**	PERFORM WITHOUT ERROR
C	COMPLY WITH INSTRUCTIONS	**S**	BE A SUPPORTIVE TEAM PLAYER
C	BE CAUTIOUS IN MAKING COMMITMENTS	**S**	ACCEPT THINGS THE WAY THEY ARE

Write the identifying style letter (D, I, S, or C) beside each of your responses in Figure 6.2. Add all of your D scores together. (Be sure that you had 6 D responses.) Your total should be somewhere between 6 and 30. Write the total in the box at the top of Figure 6.3 after the word Dominance. Repeat your scoring for the I factors and write them after the word Influence; then continue for the S factors (Steadiness) and the C factors (Compliance).

Changing these raw scores to percentiles takes a bit of doing. Pay attention now!

Add the totals of your four scores. You'll probably have a sum that's somewhere between 70 and 90 (it will be different for almost every position). Divide your sum by 4 to get your average score. Write the average in each box under the "Average" heading.[3]

Next, subtract your average score from the total for each characteristic. Place your answer in the column under the "Difference" heading. Example: If your dominance score was 22 and your average was 19.5, the difference is +2.5; if your influence score was 15 and your average was 19.5, the difference is −4.5, and so on. To check: add the differences together. You'll get a zero if you have no remainders; you'll get a plus or minus 1 if you had a remainder that you discarded or rounded up.

Now multiply each score in the difference boxes time 5, and place in the boxes under the "Multiple" heading. To continue with the preceding example, the D score would be $+2.5 \times 5 = +12.5$; the I score would be $-4.5 \times 5 = -22.5$

Then, add 50 to these scores to get the percentile ranking, and place your answers in the last column. In the example, the D score would be $+12.5 + 50 = 62.5$; the I score, $-22.5 + 50 = 27.5$.

Finally, transfer the percentage scores onto the respective D, I, S and C positions on the graph, and connect the scores with lines to form the profile of the position. You can read this profile for the position in much the same way that your personal communication profile can be read.

On the profile, circle the job style(s) that have high scores (well above the 50th percentile) and those for those style(s) that are low (well below the 50th percentile). Usually, you'll have ranked one or two styles high and the others midrange or low. Now, look at Figure 6.4 below, and read off the job characteristics for the one or two sets of behaviors you've marked as high requirements for the job. Then, repeat for the behaviors

---

[3] If you have a remainder on your average, drop it if that remainder is 1. If the remainder is 2, retain it as .5 in the rest of the calculations. If the remainder is 3, round up your average to the next highest number.

you've marked as being low requirements. This will give you a word picture of the position you're looking for and its demands. For the job we've been using as an example, the requirements demand High D and Low I behaviors.

Figure 6.4. Position Communications Demands

High D positions demand:
1) Getting results
2) Accepting challenges
3) Making decisions
4) Expediting action
5) Reducing costs
6) Solving problems

Low D positions demand:
1) A protected environment
2) Direction
3) Exercising caution
4) Working predictably
5) Deliberating before deciding
6) Weighing pros and cons

High I positions demand:
1) Contacting people
2) Motivating others
3) Helping people
4) Exhibiting poise
5) Generating enthusiasm
6) Speaking well

Low I positions demand:
1) Concentration
2) Sincerity
3) Reflection
4) Working alone
5) Preference for "things"
6) Thinking logically

High S positions demand:
1) Performing to standards
2) Exhibiting patience
3) Developing special skills
4) Concentration
5) Staying in one place
6) Loyalty

Low S positions demand:
1) Keeping many projects going
2) Seeking variety
3) Dissatisfied with status-quo
4) Reacting quickly to change
5) Applying pressure
6) Being flexible

High C positions demand:
1) Following directions
2) Concentrating on details
3) Being diplomatic
4) Adhering to procedures
5) Avoiding trouble
6) Controlling quality

Low C positions demand:
1) Assuming authority
2) Acting independently
3) Facing up to problems
4) Stating unpopular positions
5) Delegating
6) Acting without precedent

Generally speaking, the D scale measures authority. If the position is rated high on the D scale, you'll have a lot of authority. The higher the score, the more the authority. And conversely, the lower the D score, the less authority you'll have.

The I score measures the requirement to work with and influence people. A high I score indicates the need to be outgoing and to persuade others to do what you want them to do. A low I score indicates that the job is more concerned with things than with people.

The S score can reflect the time requirements of the job. If the score is high on S behaviors, the job doesn't have much time pressure, and the person in the job doesn't have to move quickly on decisions. If the S score is very low, however, the job may have a great deal of pressure, require that you make decisions quickly and take actions immediately.

The C score generally measures two things: first, the requirement for attention to detail and accuracy; and second, the degree of independence the person in the position will have. A high C requirement indicates that the position requires extreme accuracy and grants almost no independence. The person in the position must follow policy and procedures, and work from precedents. A low C score, on the other hand, indicates that the person in the position would be able to act independently.

Scores around the midpoint on a set of behaviors indicate that the position requires an average amount of that type of communication behavior. For D, this would mean the person has an average amount of authority, but must go to someone else for the big decisions. For I, the person is expected to be moderately outgoing and able to work with people. The middle score on the S factors means that the person in that position is expected to be supportive and must have some concern for time. A C score at the midpoint means the position requires some attention to detail and accuracy and provides some independence.

Making Adaptations in Style to Match
Job Requirements

The profile of the position you want and the profile of your personal style may be similar. In this case, you match closely the requirements of the position and should have little difficulty understanding how to communicate on the job.

On the other hand, your profile and the job profile may be quite different. Does this mean that you can't perform the job? No. But you do want to look carefully at those differences. Does your ideal job require that you be a High D, and you're a low D? That can be tough. Still, you would only have to act like a High D once in a while.

It boils down to this: If the job requires a certain style of performance, it doesn't require it all the time, only situationally. You don't have to place undue stress on yourself by trying to maintain that style constantly.

Instead, identify the times when that style is required and sustain it only long enough to get done what has to be done.

How Far Should You Step?

At this point in your life, the degree of risk you're willing to accept is different from that of your youth. Positions are available for people who relish the challenge of a "turnaround" or "startup" situation. If you know you would find these exhilarating and fun, then look for work in these kinds of firms. They will have openings in almost all work areas. But for your own future security, you should investigate the circumstances completely; that is, the company's financing, the personalities involved and likelihood of replacement for top management personnel (your future bosses or subordinates?), the degree of both autonomy and support you would have, the marketability of the company's products or services, the pensions and other benefits, and so on.

Your evaluation of the firm's potential would have to include best-case, worst-case, and mid-range possibilities. Could you survive, economically and emotionally, the worst-case scenario? (In such high-risk situations, the reasons for failure will most likely be due to circumstances beyond your control rather than your own shortcomings.) If your answer is "No, I could not survive," then *don't do it*.

Should You Go into Business for Yourself?

Another high-risk situation taken by more and more older executives is going into business for themselves. One option is to become a consultant to other businesses and business executives. The market for consultants, however, is only for those older executives who are truly skilled specialists, which companies need but would not, or could not, afford to hire on a permanent or in-house basis. In fact, an entire consulting industry has grown up that hires executives and professionals who are then "farmed out" for short-term assignments with companies who need their high-level skills for a specific project or projects, and for which they are willing to pay premium prices.

To make consultancy work, you must have marketable skills; know how and be able to sell yourself and your services; have enough financial reserves to get through the tough beginning states; and produce the results you clients desire when they purchase your services.

Consultancy can be a feast or famine proposition. Even long-established consultants with excellent reputations sometimes have difficulty selling their services. In fact, you must constantly sell yourself. You must be looking for the next contract while continuing to fulfill the current contract. There can be long dry spells between contracts, known affectionately in the trade as being "on the beach." You have to save and allocate funds in expectation of these dry spells.

Still, consultancy—if you are emotionally constituted for the financial ups and downs—can be challenging, exciting and rewarding, especially if you have an opportunity to work with a top-notch consultancy group. Check out the opportunities thoroughly, though, before choosing this as your full-time profession. Talk to other people who are trying to make a living as consultants. Contact consulting groups and ask to talk to one of the consultants about the problems associated with their work. Another line of work may suddenly be more attractive to you.

You might want to consider a retail business—perhaps turning what was formerly an avocation into an occupation. Let's say that when you reviewed the things that give you the most pleasure in life, your woodworking hobby was high on the list. Do your hobbies or favorite pastimes have a business in there somewhere? A surprising number of former executives are making very good livings out of the things they most like to do.

Were you a successful sales representative or sales manager for a major firm? How about becoming a manufacturer's representative for several small manufacturers making compatible lines? If you choose high-quality offerings targeted for the markets with which you are already familiar, you could be off and running in a short period of time, and end up with far greater financial rewards with little in the way of up up-front expenditures. This is one of the fastest-growing segments in the sales area. Currently, many small manufacturing and importing firms are finding that they have larger sales at less cost by using knowledgeable manufacturer's representatives rather than on-staff salespeople. The firms can pay higher commissions because they're not stuck with the fixed costs of benefits or payroll for nonproducing sales staff. But the risk is, of course, greater for you. You have no benefits, other than those you provide yourself. And you have to pay all of the selling costs. There are no nice company expense accounts, company cars or travel and entertainment allowances. On the other hand, you do get to write off most of those costs on your income tax.

Other possible career switches to think about: Do you understand personal computers? Can you install software? Can you train others to use software? Businesses that are going to survive to the 21st century must use computers for more than accounting (payroll, accounts payable, accounts receivable, etc.) But only 30 to 35 percent of older executives are computer literate. The others need to develop computer skills. You might fill a possible niche bringing innovative computer applications to small businesses. This would involve recommending hardware and software purchases, setting up the hardware, installing the software, providing a few days of initial training, then monitoring progress and supplying help only when requested.

What about a totally different second career, one for which you may have to do additional study and preparation? If you're still not sure after going through all of the self-study and introspection suggested so far, it's time to contact a professional. Take the battery of interest, aptitude and skills tests a professional can provide, then make your choice and set your path. In any event, take advantage of the time you have to learn a new set of skills. And whatever your ultimate decision, make a considered, rational change—not just one because you're sick of your life the way it is. You might not like your new life and career, either.

What about Legal Action to Get Back Your Old Job?

A few years ago, contemplating legal action to regain your job would have been ridiculous. Companies and bosses had almost complete freedom to fire at will, regardless of cause. But recent court cases have made this a whole new ball game, though most of the cases have not been based on age discrimination, but on other factors. Still, if you were with your company more than 20 years and are at least 55 years old —unless you were caught "stealing, coming in late or drunk, or raping the boss's wife,"[4] then your chances to win a suit against your company may be good. Sometimes, just threatening such a suit, especially if all of your evaluations were positive, might be good enough to get reinstated.

If you still retain a copy of your company's employee handbook, you may want to check to see what it says about employment and about terminations. It may have been written in such a way that it implies an employment contract (although many companies have recently rewritten theirs because of the rash of wrongful firing suits). If you feel strongly about your situation, at least discuss it with a lawyer to determine whether you might have grounds for a suit. You might also check out your rights in the new *Employee Rights Handbook* (Facts On File) by Steven Mitchell Sack.

The federal Age Discrimination in Employment Act (ADEA), covers both working people and those seeking employment who are age 40 to 70. A brief summary of its provisions:

---

[4] Kelvin Grove, a partner in the labor law firm of Fox & Grove, quoted in *Forbes*, August 29, 1983, p. 122.

It protects you from discrimination in hiring, in holding on to a job, in wages and salaries, and in fringe benefits and perquisites.

It prohibits advertising that excludes women and older workers.

It doesn't protect you if you've reached the stage where age is a bona fide condition for employment, usually because of public safety (firefighters, police, air traffic controllers, airline pilots, etc.).

It doesn't prevent employers from offering incentives for early retirement. But it does prevent them from forcing you to retire against your will. However, employers can observe the terms of a seniority system so long as it isn't used to evade the purpose of the ADEA.

It applies to organizations that employ more than 20 workers. (About 70 percent of all workers are covered by ADEA.)

It permits the mandatory retirement of executives and policy makers at age 65.

If you are disabled, an employer can't force you to retire before age 70 so long as you are able to do the work.

Is it worth it to sue? Maybe, if your suit is not based solely on age discrimination. If you win, the company will have to pay back wages, reinstate you, pay your legal fees and otherwise settle. If the company wins, however (and major companies, at least, consider very carefully every discharge of an older worker to determine if their position will stand up in court), you will still be unemployed and have a big legal fee to pay besides. And should the judge consider your case "frivolous," you may also have to pay a large fine.

Groups and agencies exist who can help you determine whether you have a legitimate case or not. These are the same organizations that help older people who are discriminated against in hiring (See pages 240-242.) Talking to them before you see your lawyer might save you a bundle.

But will the government help you prosecute your company if you have been discriminated against? Not very likely. The government's record on age discrimination prosecution is dismal. In the Reagan administration, and in the Bush administration as well, age discrimination has had a very low priority. Frankly, you would be wasting time and effort, which could better be used looking for a new position in which you would be happier.

In finding a new job, you will ultimately have to answer the major questions—what kind of job to look for, whether to change careers or not, where to look for a new position, whether to try to regain your old job or not—yourself. If you've considered your ego ideal, determined the communications profile of the job you're looking for and compared it with your own profile, and investigated your answers to some of the other questions raised in this chapter, you should at least be ready to make some of these basic determinations now. And you'll be able to engage in a more focused and productive job search.

Part 4

Positioning Yourself in the Market

Resumes That Sell, Part I

A resume will not get you a job. It's a door opener—a sales promotion piece for you. In it, you present information about yourself that will open doors. You include nothing that might keep them closed.

As an older executive you've probably looked at hundreds of resumes over the years. You've used them yourself as screening devices before you interviewed applicants. You identified almost at a glance the people you'd like to see and those you didn't. But did you actually analyze the characteristics that the good resumes had that the bad ones didn't? And how long has it been since you tried to write one? It's a lot harder to write one yourself than it is to evaluate the resumes of others. Also, resume writing has changed, and you don't want to date yourself by using the same form you used when you were younger.

Why do you need a resume? Because a well-written resume is one of your strongest job-hunting tools. Well done, a resume is a marketing piece that says, "Look at this person. See what he/she did for others and can do for you. Isn't he/she great!" It forces you to organize what you've done with your life so that you can give the strongest possible message about your background and experience. It helps you to sell yourself. It's a solid "leave-behind" or "go-before" message. It's like a product brochure that demonstrates your competence. It tells about your "features" and indicates the "benefits" of hiring you.

A resume should be easy to understand, dramatically worded and appealing to potential employers. In it, you present a word picture of your abilities. Make it concise—don't try to cover your entire experience and all of your abilities. Target it to your potential employer, position and industry.

Employers frequently receive hundreds of resumes for positions they have open. (You may have faced a foot-high stack of resumes yourself!)

When employers are deluged by that kind of response, they may look at an individual resume for only a second or two. They look to see: 1) if the resume writer has the qualifications, background and experience for the position; and 2) if there's anything about the resume that suggests they should investigate its writer more closely. They sort the resumes into piles of "probably interested," "possibly interested," and "not interested." If your resume lands in the "possibly interested" or "not interested" piles, it will be filed in that round mailbox on the floor, and will never see the light of day again. You probably won't hear that your resume was received, let alone that the firm isn't interested in you.

When you send letters and resumes as a prospecting device, the screening process is likely to be a little different. The person who receives the resume considers: 1) do I have a need for someone with these qualifications; and 2) is the person worth spending my time interviewing?

How do potential employers read resumes? The same way you read a newspaper story or a lightweight novel. You look at the headline or title, and the beginning paragraph or paragraphs. If this looks interesting, you may read the rest of the article or story. If it's not interesting, you don't continue. Resumes are read the same way. The reader looks at the job title, the job objective or job summary, then skims briefly over the rest of the resume to get an overall impression of the applicant. If the impression is a poor one—the resume isn't well prepared, is poorly typed, has glaring spelling errors or is ungrammatical (these have a way of jumping off the page and hitting the looker in the eye!), or shows obvious lack of organizational skill—the resume is not read further. But if the initial impression is good, the reader goes back to the beginning and reads the resume more carefully. Point: Your resume must make a strong initial impression.

You may want to write several kinds of resumes, each of which has a specific usage. The main types of resumes are:

☐ *Accomplishment or achievement resumes.* These are short resumes in which you give only a tantalizing look at your achievements, your work experience, your education and the most important of your skills. The accomplishments are not arranged chronologically, but according to importance. An accomplishment resume is essentially a "broadside," or ad. It should be restricted to one page, or at most two. Accomplishment resumes are most useful as inserts in letters and should go to people and/or industries which you have identified as having either High D or High I characteristics.

☐ *Chronological resumes.* In these resumes, you arrange your jobs in declining time order, most recent to most distant. For each position, you summarize the duties and responsibilities (or provide a thumbnail job description). Also included is information about your education, honors, professional memberships, a minimal amount of personal information, and either a job objective or brief summary statement about your strengths. You *must* send a chronological resume (or a combination chronological/accomplishment resume) to executive recruiters, human resources departments and when responding to any ads that detail the minimum requirements for the position. Use one when applying for a position requiring technical skill such as an accountant, physicist, chemist, financial analyst, mathematician, statistician or engineer. Also, give chronological resumes to people you think exhibit High S or High C communications styles. Chronological resumes might also be best if you have a strong record of achievement and job advancement in a single field.

❐ *Functional resumes.* In these, you arrange your experience in terms of the kinds of job functions you performed. For each major function, you describe what you actually did, regardless of when you did it. Functional resumes are especially valuable if you've had several kinds of job experiences, although if they're not done carefully, they can give the impression that you're a job jumper. Functional resumes are also good for generalists and when you're applying for a position in a small company in which you might have to wear several hats. Also included in the resume are listings of employers, education, honors, personal information and a job objective or summary statement about your strengths.

❐ *Combination chronological achievement resumes.* These resumes list each job you had, in descending chronological order. For each position, a short summary of the duties and responsibilities is written, then under each job summary are listed the notable achievements which set apart your performance on that job from what others might have done. Also included: education, honors, professional affiliations and some personal information. The combination resume can be given to a person with any communication style, since it provides information in the right form for every style. However, this resume is difficult to keep under control in terms of length and can get too long to be effective.

❐ *Professional/technical resumes.* Professional resumes may be used effectively by engineers, scientists of all kinds, computer analysts and programmers, consultants, construction workers, and anyone else who works on a project basis. It is similar in feel to the achievement resume, but the information is placed in a different order: name and address;

a brief summary or thumbnail description of your strengths; a full listing of professional skills and special professional abilities; and a listing of projects you have worked on that required your special contributions, education, professional affiliations and licenses. No personal information is given. If you have a number of publications and patents, these may be listed before the projects.

❑ *Curriculum vitae.* This is a special kind of resume used primarily by educators and research scientists. The usual name, address and a brief description of your strengths come first; next is listed your education, with any honors included; then a brief listing of jobs held—employer, job title (which in education tells what the job is), and the courses taught or type of research; next are listed publications (if any); important presentations before professional groups; membership in professional organizations and offices held; certifications; and brief personal information. Extracurricular activities which relate to the position desired or show your versatility should be included (almost the only kinds of resume where this type of information is included).

❑ *Letter resumes.* These are resumes in letter format tailored to answer specific needs or to fit the special requirements of a particular job.

❑ *Biography.* This is technically not a resume, but a selling document used almost exclusively by consultants. It is a one-page summary of your special qualifications, written in narrative style. It describes your background briefly, your education, major consulting achievements, and the names of a few clients who can be counted on to give you a good recommendation.

Will you need to write all of these resumes? Perhaps. You'll certainly need more than one if you are looking for and would accept more than one kind of job. Begin by learning how to write the different kinds of statements and resume sections that you will need to use to put together any resume. Let's begin with achievement statements. Writing them will force you to take a hard look at what you really accomplished. These will help you to see that yes, you really did do some valuable work in your previous work life. For some, writing these statements, then putting them into the achievement resume format is the start back from depression and doubt.

Getting Ready to Write

By completing the exercises in the earlier chapters of this book, you've already gathered most of the information about yourself that's essential to writing a good resume. If you didn't do those exercises, you can start with the next step, and still come out with a pretty good, "selling" resume.

To begin constructing your resume, rule several pieces of 8½ x 14-inch paper into four columns. From left to right, place the following headings on the columns (see Figure 7.1): Position Held, Company, Job Title, Superior, Dates; Duties, Responsibilities, Functions; Accomplishments; and Results.

If you have a personal computer and are comfortable with it, this information can be readily input directly into a spreadsheet, or if your word processing has a table function (Word Perfect 5.1 has a dandy one), use that to start collecting your information. This information is the raw material from which you will be able to construct any kind of resume you need. You will want to keep this file or the worksheets you prepare and add to your categories as you think of information. When you do begin to write your actual resume, you'll find that much of the writing is already done. You'll mostly edit, cut and paste, or otherwise clean up the information you've already written.

Step 1. List all of the jobs you've had in the first column, one per page. If you have to make more pages, do so. Include beginning and ending dates for each, the names of your immediate superiors and the location. If you're not sure of the dates, look them up. Employment dates are one of the few legally verifiable bits of information human resources departments can check, so you'd better get them right.

Step 2. List the duties and responsibilities for each of those positions in the second column. What were your functions? Take as much space as you need so that you can go back and include other duties and responsibilities as you think of them. Write mini–job descriptions in this column. Don't attempt to polish. This is a working document, so jot down the information as you think of it. It will be easier later on if you list each duty and responsibility separately, instead of grouping them in one description.

Step 3. Describe what you accomplished. How did you solve problems; what were your sales successes; how did you save the company money; what did you do on that job that set you apart from what somebody else might have done? List each accomplishment separately, even though individual accomplishments were sometimes a part of a larger project. Line up the accomplishments next to the related duty or responsibility which legitimized your accomplishment.

Step 4. List the results of each accomplishment. What did it actually do for your company? Results should generally be quantifiable, unless it

Figure 7.1. Sample Resume Worksheet

Position Held, Company, Job Title, Superior, Dates	Duties, Responsibilities, Functions	Accomplishments	Results

was an absolute, or the first time something was done. Express results in terms of time saved; money saved or earned; product or services sold; or improvement of some kind. Results should be concrete, not abstract. Use numbers, percentages, actual dollars, not vague terms such as "improved company profitability." If you actually did improve company profitability, state how much or by what percentage. For each accomplishment you listed in Step 3, you should write a matching result in this step.

Figure 7.2 illustrates how a worksheet might appear.

When you've completed the initial part of this task, write down the colleges and universities you attended, in reverse chronological order, by date of attendance. Indicate the degrees you received. If part of your professional competence was learned in short courses and seminars, list those, too. (You'll seldom list all of these on a resume, but you might want to mention them in a cover letter if they were essential to performance on the jobs for which you were applying.)

On another page, note memberships or affiliations with professional organizations and associations. Include any licenses you may hold. Also note any offices you held, and the dates.

If you've published or received any honors, list these on another sheet or two of paper. (Some prolific writers may need several pages for this.) List any patents you have been granted. (You may have to do some real personal research to organize all this, complete with dates, journals in which published, patent numbers, etc.)

Don't spend time gathering information on your social or personal life. Most of this information comes under the heading of "illegal" information, and shouldn't be used in a resume. However, if you have some specific skills or accomplishments that might be of value to an employer, you might want to list those: for instance, any languages you speak or write, if you were an officer in a community organization of interest to the business community such as the chamber of commerce or the United Way.

You now have the raw materials you'll need to write your resume. Suggestion: if you have collected them in a computer file, print out the information and keep it in a notebook. Ditto, if you were hand-writing on paper. These are the resources you'll use to write your stand-alone resumes, cover letters and tailored letter resumes.

What about Ages and Dates?
The 1975 Age Discrimination Employment Act did away with the requirement that job applicants give their birthdates and/or ages on job

Figure 7.2. Sample Resume Worksheet

Position Held, Company, Job Title, Superior, Dates	Duties, Responsibilities, Functions	Accomplishments	Results
1981 to Present - AT&T 1989 - Systems Manager, Direct Marketing Services, Parsippany, NJ, Reported to xxxxxxxxx	Manage voice and data systems to ensure that these essential tools operate with minimum down time. Interacts with outside vendors and data centers to solve any serious systems problems Responsible for design, development and implementation of state-of-the-art network, computer and telephone hardware and software used by 150 telemarketing employees and 30 headquarters staff members Direct work of 16 systems staff members, including analysts, programmers, systems consultants, project managers, a systems administrator and a technical writer Must keep abreast of current improvements in direct marketing technology Responsible for seeing that data and systems standards are adhered to Budget, select and purchase capital equipment (budget during installation of new system is $1.1 million) Responsible for ensuring that no unpurchased, unauthorized or "bootleg" software is operating on any computer within the division	Developed standard maintenance procedures followed by the Systems Administrator that reduced system downtime Analyzed three systems, working with vendors, and located serious interface problem related to operational procedures Negotiated shared development costs with another organization Developed system on time, including complete user documentation Made numerous suggestions for operational improvements; implemented many Cut down on time administrators and data center personnel spent trouble-shooting to determine problems caused by non-standard software Obtained three 3B UNIX computers without cost from another organization Set up hardware/software inventory system with employee sign-off	Cut system down time to less than 10 minutes a week from an average of 35 minutes per week Captured an additional $1.1 million in net revenue for the division in 1989 Saved $225,000 in development costs, cut development time by an estimated three months because of combined staff effort Improved representative's efficiency in responding to customer concerns; representatives were able to respond to an average of six more customers each per day Problem incidence reduced by 45% Saved $150 thousand in capital outlay Division passed company software audit for the first time

applications and in interviews. (Check the list of illegal questions in the Interview III chapter for a fuller explanation.) You absolutely *do not* include your age or birth date on a resume. You don't include the dates you attended or graduated from high school or college—which also tell your age. (You will have to provide this information after you have been hired, for insurance purposes, but not before.) Don't even go back to the beginning of your employment career to list every job you ever held. For most older job seekers, showing the last 15 to 20 years of employment is plenty. Those were the years, anyway, when you most likely accomplished the tasks you want to stress on your resume.

The breadth and depth of your accomplishments is one argument against using a functional resume. Detailing all of the functions you've mastered can reveal your general age because no one could have done that much without living and working quite a few years!

General Suggestions for Resume Writing

The following "Do's and Don'ts" might be considered to be the "Ten Commandments" of resume-writing.

1. *Use short statements and abbreviated sentence structure.* Don't use the words "I," "you," "we," "our." The sentences should have no subjects, or have descriptive subjects; i.e., accountant, administrator, manager, communicator. You should be pungent, not poetic; express ideas powerfully and actively, not passively.

2. *Use brevity, not verbiage.* If one word will tell the important point, use it. Write *directed* or *managed* rather than *controlled* or *supervised*, for example, to show the level of your work.

3. *Include only one thing in each statement.* Do not combine unrelated functions, tasks or accomplishments. Keep them separate so that the reader can understand them. Don't mistake economy of words with combining unrelated tasks or accomplishments. For instance, market research and sales are both in the general field of marketing. But each should stand alone.

4. *Begin each sentence with action.* Start as many sentences as you can with a strong verb. "Increased sales 15% as a result of identifying untapped niche market" is much more impressive than "After study, research, investigation and analysis, was able to increase sales."

5. *Clarity.* Use the word that is most precise and informative. Gear your choice of words to the audience you intend for your resume. For example, you would write the same achievement in general terms for a marketing audience, a general manager or a human resources department; you would use technically precise words and more detail if the resume is going to a technical manager. Use industry-specific words only if the majority of the people who might receive your resume would understand them. If you'll be sending resumes to several kinds of audiences, you should write several versions of the same achievement. The rule of thumb: the simpler, the better.

6. *Avoid gobbledygook.* Don't leave it to your reader to guess what you mean or what you intended to say. Don't say that you "coordinated the inside sales function" when you actually "started a telemarketing operation which increased after market sales by 75%" in your role as national sales manager. Also, don't write ambiguous statements. If you don't know if the statement is clear or not, ask someone to explain what you meant in your statement. If they can't, you're probably being ambiguous.

7. *Use language appropriate to the position for which you're looking.* The words a chief executive normally uses are quite different from those employed by a factory supervisor. Target what you write to the audience for which it's intended. Use language that expresses your level of authority and scope of responsibility.

8. *Narration and reader appeal.* Don't sacrifice the continuity of the story you're telling. Be dynamic. Connect statements to prevent your resume from being a collection of disjointed statements and paragraphs. The resume should reflect some underlying theme or unifying principle.

9. *Illustrate.* Point out specifically what you did, how well you did it and how your employer benefitted. Use the illustrations with discretion. Don't overpower your readers with so many examples that they can't understand what you really did and what your responsibilities were. Include some measurement: time, money, number of employees managed, reduction in complaints or problems, significant effect on work of others. Virtually anything is quantifiable if you look deeply enough. Quantify, quantify, quantify.

10. *Sell yourself.* To paraphrase Mae West's famous line, "Modesty has nothing to do with it."

One of the commandments suggested that you choose the strongest verbs you can to explain what you did. Use power words. The words in Exhibit 7.1 are just that. Refer to it when you're looking for the right word. A further suggestion: if you are working on a full service word processing system, try using the thesaurus function as an aid to more powerful writing.

Exhibit 7.1

abolished	audited	combined	demonstrated
achieved	augmented	commenced	designed
acquired	authorized	commended	described
acted	averted	communicate	destroyed
activated	avoided	compared	detected
adapted	awarded	compiled	determined
added		completed	developed
addressed	backed	composed	devised
adjusted	based	conceived	diminished
administered	bought	concluded	directed
advanced	broadened	condensed	disapproved
advertised	brought	conducted	discarded
advised	budgeted	conferred	discovered
advocated	built	confirmed	dismissed
affected		considered	displayed
affirmed	calculated	constructed	disseminated
agree	called	contacted	distributed
alleviated	calmed	contracted	divided
allocated	campaigned	contributed	documented
allotted	canceled	converted	donated
altered	captured	conveyed	doubled
amended	caught	coordinated	drafted
analyzed	caused	corrected	drove
announced	centralized	corresponded	
anticipated	challenged	counseled	earned
appointed	changed	created	eased
apportioned	charged	cultivated	edited
appraised	checked		effected
approved	chose		elected
arranged	claimed	dared	eliminated
assembled	clarified	dealt	employed
assessed	closed	decided	encouraged
assisted	collaborated	decreased	ended
assumed	collated	defined	endorsed
assured	collected	demanded	enforced

engineered	granted	instructed	mobilized
enhanced	gratified	insured	moderated
enlarged	grew	interpreted	modernize
erected	gripped	interviewed	modified
established	grouped	introduced	monitored
estimated	guarded	invented	motivated
evaluated	guided	investigate	mounted
examined		invited	
exceeded	halted	invoked	named
excelled	handed	involved	narrated
executed	handled	isolated	negotiated
exercised	harmonized	issued	nominated
exhibited	hastened		nullified
expanded	headed	joined	
expected	healed	judged	observed
expedited	heightened	jumped	obtained
expelled	held	justified	offered
experimented	helped		opened
explained	hired	key	operated
exposed		knit	opposed
extended	identified		organized
extracted	ignored	laid	originated
	ignited	launched	overcame
faced	imparted	led	oversaw
facilitated	impelled	left	
fashioned	implemented	lessened	passed
finished	imposed	levelled	patched
firmed	improved	lightened	paid
foresaw	improvised	limited	perceived
forestalled	inaugurated	linked	perfected
formed	increased	liquidated	performed
formulate	incurred	localized	permitted
fortified	indicated	located	persuaded
fought	influenced	locked	pledged
found	informed		pleased
framed	initiated	maintain	polished
freed	innovated	managed	possessed
fulfilled	inquired	mapped	predicted
	insisted	marketed	prepared
gained	inspected	matched	presented
gathered	inspired	measured	presided
gave	installed	merged	pressed
generated	instigated	met	probed
governed	instituted	mitigated	processed

proclaimed
procured
produced
programmed
projected
promoted
prompted
proposed
proved
provided
pruned
published
publicized
purchased
pursued

quelled
questioned
quickened
quieted

raided
rallied
razed
reacted
received
recommended
recorded
recruited
rectified
redesigned
reduced
referred
reformed
refuted
regulated
rejected

related
relieved
remedied
renegotiated
reorganized
repaired
replaced
replied
reported
represented
researched
rescued
reshaped
resolved
responded
restrained
restricted
retarded
revealed
reviewed
revised
revitalized
rid
risked
routed

sanctioned
saved
scanned
scheduled
screened
scrutinized
searched
secured
selected
settled
separated

served
serviced
set up
settled
shaped
shaved
sifted
simplified
singled out
slashed
slowed
sold
solved
sought
sparked
specified
spelled
split
spoke
spurred
staffed
stalled
standardized
stated
stimulated
stood
stopped
streamlined
strengthened
struggled
studied
submitted
suggested
supervised
supplied
supported
surpassed

surveyed
sustained
swept
systemized

talked
taught
terminated
tested
thwarted
tracked
traded
trained
transferred
tripled
triumphed

uncovered
undertook
unearthed
unravelled
upgraded
upheld
upset
urged
used
utilized

vanquished
vindicated
vitalized

warned
withheld
won
wrote

Words used in ads and in job descriptions are frequently unsuitable for resumes. They may be weak, ambiguous or misleading. The same is generally true for job titles—Administrative Office and Management Executive are redundant and don't describe any known job. The title you had in your last job may have had meaning only in your company. For instance, in one company, a Controller might work in Marketing and purchase vehicles, oversee sales expense accounts, convention and meeting expenses, and commissions; in another company, Controller is a highest echelon title equivalent to Vice President of Finance.

So, be sure that in addition to job title, you explain what you're looking for and what you did with that title.

Other words may not be effective. Look at the words below. They are weak, nonspecific, vague or tricky. They don't add much to your resume, and may detract seriously from your meaning.

extensive	vague	implies incomplete coverage
considerable	weak	more than a little, but not much
executive	vague	implied random responsibilities
administrative	weak	clerical side of the job
diversified	nonspecific	jack of all trades
assisted	weak	in charge of nothing
participated	weak	can't accept much credit
inaugurated	weak	implies only that something started while you were there
competent	weak	no great shakes in own opinion
qualified	weak	can, but never had the chance to
assigned to	weak	you were an appendage to someone else
handled	vague	can mean almost anything
coordinated	tricky	means whatever you mean it to mean
general	vague	has no meaning whatever

Writing Achievement Statements

The key to selling yourself is to show that you've accomplished—if not miracles—at least solid worthwhile achievements. For each job you've had, you should have already listed both major and minor accomplishments. (Your chart should be similar in format to that shown in Figure 7.2). For each job, you should also determine the achievements you think are most marketable for the positions(s) you're seeking. Select about 12 to 15 of your most important achievements to polish.

What is the most effective way to present these accomplishments? Good accomplishment/achievement statements follow the PAR formula: P = Problem, A = Accomplishment, R = Result. For each accomplishment chosen, ask yourself, "What was the problem I was solving when I accomplished this? What actions did I take? What results did I get and what did it do for my employer?" Stating the problem does not necessarily mean that something was wrong. In the sense used here, a problem can be a specific condition that needs to be corrected or worked around; it can be a situation that needed to be changed or taken advantage of; it could be an assignment you received and made work for you; or it could be something that was working, but could be improved.

For the sake of argument, let's say you managed a purchasing department. You were very concerned with the efficiency of the department. It took your purchasing agents too long (an average of one week) to issue their purchase orders from the time they received a requisition, which ultimately delayed deliveries. A statement of the problem: You needed to reduce the time between receiving the requisition and issuing the purchase order.

Write down the action you took first. What did you do? Example: (*Action*) Revamped purchasing procedures.

What were the results? Example: (*Action*) Revamped purchasing procedures, (*Result*) cutting department costs by 15 percent and the error rate by 5 percent.

Put these items together, and you have the accomplishment. Example: (Action) Revamped purchasing procedures, (result) cutting department costs by 15 percent and the error rate by 5 percent, and (corrected problem) reducing the average time between receipt of requisition and purchase order issuance from one week to two days.

Note that in this, concrete and measurable figures are given. Reduced costs 15 percent, error rate by 5 percent, time from one week to two days.

For clarity, you may want to edit this statement in several different formats. You may want to put the results first, the problem first or the action first. As you rewrite each statement, continue to ask yourself, "What action did I take? What were the results? What did the action change and by how much did it change?"

If in correcting a problem, you accomplished several things, you might use a slightly different format to express problem, action and result(s). In the statement that follows, one problem solution spawned several accomplishments and results.

Developed and installed new purchasing procedures which

❏ Shortened processing time for purchase orders from one week to two days
❏ Cut department costs 15 percent
❏ Reduced error rate 5 percent
❏ Improved order follow-up procedures ensured on-time delivery

❐ Measured for the first time the purchasing effectiveness of individual purchasing agents.

Don't shortchange yourself in writing and editing your achievement statements. Writing them is a learning process—and it will help heal your battered psyche. You *did* accomplish something on the previous jobs. Your employers would not have kept you on board for as long as they did if you hadn't earned your salary. Writing down your achievements enables you to work through your negative feelings and put your career into proper perspective. Take the time to do yourself justice.

Exhibit 7.2 contains additional acceptable achievement statements.

Exhibit 7.2. Sample Achievement Statements

❐ Planned and directed all phases of a company turnaround which:

1. Achieved an 84% increase in sales, included the introduction of new products, and eliminated losses of $2.5 million within a three-year period.

2. Reduced selling and administrative expenses from 21% to 15% of sales.

❐ Pioneered instruction systems development in the Tactical Air Command and subsequent complete restructuring of all major training programs. In one program alone, saved $3.7 million.
❐ Developed new product delivery and pricing strategies which increased profits by over $2 million.
❐ Negotiated contracts and established U.S. sources for electronics components for 25% less than the Japanese component costs.
❐ Prepared and directed two direct mail fund-raising campaigns that generated in excess of $800,000 for a nonprofit agency within a six-month period.
❐ Successfully completed an OEM computer-tape transport project whose compatibility requirements were so rigid that the previous management team left the company. Turned a potential

lawsuit into repeat orders and a profitable $500 thousand OEM business.

Writing Statements Showing Duties, Responsibilities, Functions

In the chronological, functional, combination and letter resumes, you will tell the reader about the kind of work that you did—your duties, responsibilities, job functions, while still keeping in mind that you accomplished something doing those things. That doesn't mean that you necessarily use dollars, time, percentages or words that indicate accomplishment. But you do show that your actions did something for the company.

For instance, a Systems Staff Manager for a major communications company wrote on her worksheet that she:

❐ Managed voice and data systems to ensure that these essential tools operated with minimum "down time"

❐ Was responsible for the security, repair and operating integrity of $5 million worth of capital computer and telephone hardware, software, wiring and interconnections

❐ Interacted with outside vendors and data centers to solve any serious systems problems

❐ Was responsible for design, development and implementation of state-of-the art network, computer and telephone hardware and software used by 150 telemarketing employees and 30 headquarters staff members

❐ Directed work of 16 systems staff members, including analysts, programmers, systems consultants, project managers, a systems administrator and a technical writer

❐ Remained abreast of current improvements in direct marketing technology

❐ Budgeted, selected and purchased capital equipment (budget during installation was $1.1 million)

❐ Was responsible for ensuring that no unpurchased, unauthorized or "bootleg" software was operating on any computer within the division.

How can these be condensed and capsulized for the greatest impact? First, analyze the activities for those with a similar theme. For instance, the manager listed a number of items related to the management of the sizable investment in computers, telephone equipment, network installation and software. These should be joined together in as direct a statement as possible. The budget and purchase decision power is another item of importance. The number of staff members she managed should be included as well as the kind of work they did. An acceptable paragraph of duties and responsibilities statements for a chronological resume might look something like:

> Managed voice and data systems for a direct marketing division of 150 telemarketing and inside sales employees and 30 headquarters staff members. Responsible for design, development, budget, purchase and implementation of state-of-the-art computer and telephone network, hardware and software with budget of $1.1 million. Directed work of systems staff of 15, which included analysts, programmers, systems administrators, a project hardware manager and a technical writer.

For a combination chronological/achievement resume, these statements would have to be condensed. She would integrate some of her functions into achievement statements, and highlight them under the "job description" paragraph.

Job Objectives or Thumbnail Sketches?

Most of the books on resume writing emphasize the importance of writing good job objectives for your resumes. These are the second item on standard resumes after the name, address and telephone numbers. Job objectives are fine for young applicants looking for their first positions. However, for the older executive or professional, including the term "job objective" doesn't do justice to that person's status, background and experience.

Instead, head the first section after your name and address with the job title that you are pursuing. Then under that heading, write a "thumbnail sketch" or word picture that illustrates the strengths and abilities you bring to that job title. The sketch could also give some idea of the background, industry or areas in which you have already performed. The thumbnail is more powerful than a job objective. By describing what you can do, you are essentially describing the kind of job you want. The thumbnail sketch is both a good advertisement and a superb job-objective statement.

How do you write a thumbnail? Don't begin writing your resume by writing the thumbnail sketch. Choose the job title first, or at least the general area (say marketing) toward which you're going to pitch your resume. Then write the entire body of the resume. After you've written that in a draft form that you can live with, write your thumbnail.

Guidelines for Writing the Thumbnail Sketch

1. Choose an accurate job title for the position you're pursuing.

2. Tie each statement in the thumbnail to the job title. The statement should describe some ability or characteristic that would enable you to do that job better.

3. Keep the thumbnail sketch short (somewhere between 30 and 55 words, with an ideal length being around 40 words). You don't have to write complete sentences. Use descriptive phrases or telegraphed sentences.

4. Use highly descriptive verbs or nouns to describe what you can do. Use modifiers only when they add to the concrete impression. Don't use any of the weak modifiers mentioned earlier in the chapter.

Remember that you're writing an "ad" when you're preparing a thumbnail. Does what you've written sell? This is a case where the sizzle sells the steak.

Sample thumbnail sketches are shown in exhibit 7.3. The people who wrote these sweat blood over them. These few words are probably the most important part of your resume. This is the one thing that people screening resumes will read. If your thumbnail grabs them, they will read the rest of your resume, and you'll at least have had an initial chance.

Exhibit 7.3. Sample Thumbnail Sketches

Advertising Director/Manager. Originator of proven creative advertising and marketing concepts. Manages, directs and motivates team in fast-turnaround environment. Plans and implements successful direct-mail campaigns, sales promotions, public relations programs and trade shows. Experienced in estimating, creating deadlines and overseeing vendors throughout production process.

Healthcare Professional. Experienced professional with comprehensive background in healthcare administration. Proven record of reducing operational costs, improving profit margin, controlling finances and increasing staff productivity. Strong leader, communicator and problem-solver. Accomplished in operational analysis, strategic planning, budgeting, contract negotiations, project development, medical-office leasing and marketing.

General Manager. A results-oriented General Manager with exceptional business skills in marketing, manufacturing and financial control. Demonstrated ability in managing manufacturing companies and subsidiaries for publicly owned corporations. Successful record of improving profits, increasing market share, reducing costs and managing assets. An action-oriented and creative problem-solver with excellent people skills.

Project Engineer. Hands-on engineer skilled in designing and installing electro-mechanical products and systems. Practical troubleshooter. Knows how to design a product that can be manufactured efficiently and cost-effectively. Builds good working relationships with vendors and outside contractors. Innovative user of technology to solve problems. Experienced planner. Superior motivator with strong interpersonal skills.

Other Sections of the Resume

You can include a number of different sections in your resume. Several of them are almost mandatory: your education and your business affiliations. You'll include a personal section only when it provides personal skills or achievements which can be related to the job.

Education. In every resume, you should include a section on your education. Young people are advised to include their dates of attendance or the date they received their degrees. You'll have to give this information when you make a formal application so that the potential employer can check on your credentials. But you don't have to put dates on a resume, and you shouldn't. Unless you earned some spectacular kind of honor in college, say Phi Beta Kappa, simply list the universities and colleges you attended, in most recent to most distant order, along with any certificates or degrees you earned. If you've had short courses and seminars, list them if they're important to the job title shown on your resume. Otherwise, omit them entirely or provide a summary statement, as in the example below.

Education

University of Illinois	MS in Biochemistry
DePaul University	BS
Belleville Community College	AA

Numerous short courses and seminars on various phases of general management and biochemical laboratory procedures.

Business Affiliations. This section is included when you write an achievement or professional resume. It is placed immediately after the education section. In it, you simply list the companies you worked for and your job title. (In the professional resume, if you have been working as a consultant, you may head this section "Clients.") Don't state the dates worked. You can include some identifier, such as "a division of ————" when you worked for a subsidiary of a major corporation, and give some idea about the line of business and its location. But if you're trying to get a resume on a single page, then the following format (most recent to distant) will suffice:

Business Affiliations

Omni/Penthouse Publications, Ltd.	Director Financial Planning
Schatz Bearing Co., Inc.	Director Finance/Administration
Dutchess County Government	Budget Director/Controller
Savin Corporation	Assistant Controller
RCA Corporation	Cost & Budget Supervisor

Professional Affiliations. For jobs in which professional certification or membership in professional or trade organizations is a must, this heading should be included. Or you can use a heading called "Other Affiliations," and include business and community organization memberships that show your competence—for instance, president of the chamber of commerce, chairperson of fund raising for the alumni association of your college chairperson of a major committee. The following example shows how these might be listed.

Professional Affiliations

New York State Society of Certified Public Accountants
National Association of Accountants

Military Experience. You may choose to include this or not, depending upon your rank and whether or not the experience your military service provided is transferable to civilian life. Ability to bomb the enemy is not necessarily a transferable skill. Ability to fly might be.

Honors, Publications, Presentations, Patents. This heading (or it can be more than one heading) should be included in any resume *if it adds to your hireability.* If you're listed in any of the *Who's Who* books, it's nice to include it. Briefly identify any other honors. Published papers and books also add to stature as do patents granted. Use a telegraphed format for these. List only the names of articles or books, not the dates, the publications or the publisher. (Note: If you include publications, you should also prepare a complete list of these in standard bibliographic form to leave behind with the interviewer if you are asked to do so.) Describe patents in some way (but don't give them esoteric titles). List the organizations before which you made major presentations and include a brief title of your topic.

Technical Expertise or *Area of Specialization.* This section is always included in a Professional resume. In it are listed the skills and knowledge areas in which you are an expert; you may also include areas in which you have a working knowledge, if you think that would be advantageous. The example below, prepared by a former AT&T Systems Manager, gives an idea of the detail you might include under this heading:

Technical Expertise

In-depth knowledge of:
- AT&T 3B/300, 310, 400, 600 (UNIX 5.2/3) Processors
- AT&T Terminals, Modems and Printers
- AT&T 6500 Series Synchronous Controllers
- AT&T Network Software
- UNIX Operating System and SHELL
- Personal Computers: IBM compatibles (MS-DOS), AT&T 6300 series, Apple and Franklin computers, numerous PC software packages.

Non-AT&T work experience with:
- IBM 4331 (RJE Batch)
- IBM 370/155, 158, 168 (OS/MVS JCL)
- Honeywell 66/60

❏ AMDAHL 470 V6/V7
❏ Burroughs 3500
❏ Data 100 V5.1

Working knowledge of:
❏ Structured BASIC, COBOL, FORTRAN, INFORMIX

Personal. Most personal questions are no longer the legally valid concern of an employer. You can put a minimum amount of information in this section—or leave it out altogether. Prospective employers don't need to know if you're married, divorced or single (unless being single is a requirement, as it is in some international work where housing isn't available for married employees). How many children you have is none of their concern either, and should not be included, no matter how proud you are of your children. You might want to mention that you're active in civic and community affairs, although mentioning that you're active in your religion can be a deselector. You have to use discretion. You don't want your citations to sound as though you spend too much time away from work on these activities. However, if you are considering a position in education at the secondary or college level, the decision-makers want to know about your extracurricular activities in college. These are still of interest even these long years after the fact, as a pseudo-measure of your participation in the functioning of the system.

If you include a personal section, you should include the phrase "Willing to relocate/travel" or something similar, even if you really don't want a job that will require you to relocate. You don't want to be deselected on the basis of its omission.

Resumes That Sell, Part II

As mentioned in the preceding chapter, you'll write different resumes for different purposes. For some of you, the only resume you'll ever need is either the Chronological or the combination Chronological/Achievement resume. In fact, if you're only going to write one resume, the best format is probably the Achievement/Chronological Resume. However, to write that one correctly, you'd have to do all of the work it would take to write both an Achievement and a Chronological resume first, so you can't do that one resume just to save time and effort.

Interim or Temporary Resume

Putting together a good resume takes time. Give yourself the time you need to do it right. In the interim, put together a temporary resume to use until your good ones are ready.

At the top of a single page, place your name, then your address and telephone number. List your education next (most recent first), and military service, if you were in the military. Follow that with your business affiliations (most recent first). List the employer you worked for, your job title and a brief explanation (a short paragraph) of what you did for that employer. Include a short personal section that mostly says you'll "travel and relocate." You should be able to get this on a page to a page and a half. Take the time to make the resume look good, even though you'll be using it for only a short time. Be sure you have no misspelled words or typographical errors. Print the resume out on good paper—even this summary resume has to reflect class. Your resume is not a place to economize.

Achievement Resume

Learning to write achievement statements that legitimately tell your story is the hardest part of writing resumes. You learned how to do that in the last chapter, so the rest of writing an achievement resume should be a snap.

Begin by typing your name, address and telephone numbers. If you don't have an office or an answering service, don't include a business number. Give an alternate number—say that of a friend who's generally available—where the telephone will be answered. If you are using a word processor and a printer with fancy type fonts, Times Roman Bold is a nice font for your name and address. Use bold type on your resume only on the headings—and your name is your most important heading.

Next, write your job title as a heading, then place your thumbnail sketch, in indented paragraph form, under the heading. The job title should be in bold print, the thumbnail sketch should be the plain font.

Your next heading should read *Selected Achievements*. Under that heading, choose five to eight of your significant achievements. These must illustrate the accomplishments you've made in jobs that relate to the job title you've used to head the thumbnail sketch. Put the best achievement first, the next-best second, the third-best last, and spread the others out in between. If you keep a file of achievement statements, either on paper on in a word processing file, you can prepare a number of slightly different Achievement Resumes with achievements specifically tailored to a job title or industry.

Follow the selected achievements with an *Education* section, follow that by the *Business Affiliations* section, then any of the optional sections which you feel should be included. Place the personal section last or omit it altogether. In an Achievement Resume, you are trying for a one-page "flyer" that titillates the reader, leaving him or her to know more. You really have to hone your statements to get rid of unnecessary words and include only the essentials.

Figure 8.1 illustrates the way one executive completed his Achievement Resume.

Even after you have finished an Achievement Resume you can stomach, continue to rework and polish your achievement statements. No resume has ever been written that couldn't be improved by a little judicious editing. You will find that you think of better ways to express your achievements as you go along.

Chronological Resume

The Chronological Resume begins exactly like the Achievement Resume. You list your name, address and telephone numbers, then the job title and thumbnail sketch follow.

Figure 8.1   Achievement Resume

David G. (Greg) Sloan

9563 Willowpond Road   Office (214) 555-4781
Dallas, TX 75238   Home (214) 555-6678

Senior Engineering Manager

Innovative, practical Senior Engineering Manager skilled in the planning
and execution of technical programs in both the product development
and research environments. Exceptional background in analog and
digital circuits, magnetics, physics, mechanics and electro-optics.
Demonstrated skill hiring and developing key contributors.

Selected Achievements

o   Successfully completed an OEM computer tape transport project whose compatibility
      requirements were so rigid that the previous management team left the company.
      Turned a potential lawsuit into repeat orders and a profitable $500 K OEM business.

o   Personally developed PC-based technical software to reduce electronics and
      electromechanical design time by 15%. Developed expense forecasting programs that
      reduce monthly forecasting time by 80% with improved accuracy.

o   Developed needs-driven market analysis that points to important future products with
      large revenue potential. Identified digital keyboards (music), cordless keyboards
      (computers), consumer freeze-frame video device and optical disk data storage before
      first introduction of these products by competitors.

o   Developed the first $900 disk-based, video freeze-frame device.   Prototype was
      extremely well received at 1981 broadcaster's convention with offers from ABC to share
      production design and tooling costs. $15 million potential over two years.

o   Personally developed magnetics algorithm for the world's fastest print solenoid.
      Resulted in a $12 (cost) calculator printer and a $50 (cost) 80-column printer design.

o   Successfully completed the first Bernoulli disk drive four months after taking over
      project that was five years behind schedule. Spawned the 3.5 inch floppy disk market.

o   Personally developed industry standard analog/digital bubble memory drive technique
      used by TI, IBM, Rockwell, Intel and others.

o   Published numerous technical articles in *Electronics, Popular Electronics* and *Electronic
      Design News.*

o   Received special award in 1981 from TI's President, J. Fred Bucy, for "Outstanding
      Technical Contributions to Texas Instruments."

o   Received "Key Personnel" awards and stock gifts in 12 out of last 15 years with TI.

Education

University of Houston   B.S. Mathematics
(Additional course work in Electronics Engineering and Physics)

Your next heading can be *Background and Experience, Business Affiliations, Experience, Relevant Experience, Employment History* or *Business Record*. For each position you've held, give your job title, your employer, and some identifier about the employers' business, if you feel that it's necessary. Then fill in the duties, responsibilities and functions statements for the position that you wrote earlier.

The next section should list your education, followed by any of the other resume sections you think would be helpful. You may want to include some narrative in an honors or patents section, and you may increase the amount of information in the business and community organizations and personal section. You may want to detail your military service. You write a Chronological Resume for people who are concerned with detail, and you should supply that detail without becoming verbose.

Figure 8.2 is an example of a Chronological Resume.

Functional Resume

When you're applying for a position that incorporates several different functions, and you've had experience in each and possibly in other related areas, the Functional Resume is called for. You can write the statements you plan to include in the achievement format. Or you can use the duties and responsibilities function-statements if they're more illustrative of your competencies.

This resume also begins as do the Achievement and Chronological ones. You list your name, address, telephone numbers, the job title you're looking for and the thumbnail sketch.

The next heading you'd list as *Selected Achievements, Related Experience* or simply *Experience*. Then you place subheadings, such as "Management," "Planning," "Manufacturing" and "Technical." After each subheading, you list the achievement or duties, and responsibilities functional statements that are illustrative of the subheading.

The rest of the resume is completed much as are the other resumes: the education section, a business affiliation section (just a listing of employers you worked for and your job titles) and then add any of the other sections you think are needed to best carry your message.

Figure 8.3 is an example of a Functional Resume.

Combination Chronological/Achievement Resume

A Chronological/Achievement Resume is easy to develop if you've already written your Achievement and Chronological resumes. The section of the resume where you detail your work experience is generally headed *Experience and Selected Accomplishments*. You can use the

Figure 8.2   Chronological Resume

Yvonne Morris

1685 Jackson Square, Somerset, NJ 08873
(201) 888-3355 (Office) (201) 555-3656 (Home)

Management Information Systems Manager

A bottom-line, results-oriented manager with an outstanding record of accomplishments in MIS, telecommunications and marketing management. Expertise in project planning and management, technical sales management, budget control, standards and documentation development, applications definition and specification, contract negotiations, and training curriculum specification.

Professional Experience

1981-Present   AMERICAN TELEPHONE AND TELEGRAPH (AT&T)

1989-   **Direct Marketing Systems Manager**, Parsippany, NJ

Manage all MIS communications, voice/data hardware and software, for a direct marketing division. Direct design, development and implementation of state-of-the-art network, hardware and software. Ultimately responsible for special systems projects as well as day-to-day systems operations and problem resolution. Staff includes analysts, programmers, systems consultants, project managers, assistant systems manager, and technical writer.

1987-89   **Business Automation Project Manager**, Basking Ridge, NJ

Responsible for the standards for and security of a $200 million nationally distributed data processing project incorporating UNIX and MS-DOS hardware, software and network products, and affecting 22,000 marketing employees at 300 plus sites. Designed and oversaw development of an automated (i.e., electronic library) technical documentation source which saved hundreds of thousands of dollars of paper and printing costs, and ensured that each of the branches had immediate access to the most current application documentation. Developed requirements and negotiated contract for systems administration to be provided by an external AT&T group

1986-87   **Sales Operations Support Staff Manager**, Basking Ridge, NJ

Responsible for defining UNIX business automation standards for programming development, documentation and implementation. Determined systems administration needs, including span of control, training requirements, asset management and trouble-shooting requirements. Defined training requirements, then worked with AT&T training to set up a specialized program that provided 114 new systems administrators with one month's intensive hands-on training for a shared cost of only $500 K.

1985-1986   **Marketing Area Staff Manager**, Denver, CO

Managed $8 million office automation project for an eight-state area. Project included electronic mail functions, word processing, spread sheets, centralized message center with electronic messages, status reports, scheduling and booking of executive briefing center and conference rooms. Responsible for training end-users and systems administrators. Set up automated inventory program and procedures. Requested by headquarters to work on national Business Automation Project.

1983-1985　**Branch Systems Manager,** Wyoming and Colorado

Managed 22 systems consultants for Wyoming and Colorado, working out of three offices. This group provided technical sales support on all sales within Wyoming and Colorado. For 1984 and 1985, the branch exceeded quota objectives by more than 30%. The systems consultants sold and implemented the first two ISN networks in the Western Region, as well as making numerous telephone and computer sales.

1982-1983　**Systems Consultant,** Denver, CO

Responsible for complex data equipment and network sales to utility and computer companies. Placed in charge of a complex project managing four other systems consultants to design, develop, present and implement the move of a 2000-plus employee company to a new building. The project included voice, data and network sales, and required the evaluation of company needs, conceptualization of these needs and our solution in terms that nontechnical users could understand.

1981-1982　**Systems Consultant,** Atlanta, GA

Responsible for complex telephone PBX sales to military installations within the Southern Bell region. Implemented strategies for replacing an antiquated system with a modern state-of-the-art system without requiring the military to put the job out for bid. Identified numerous sales opportunities that were untapped, and worked directly with customers to obtain numerous small sales.

1977-1981　**GEORGIA POWER,** Atlanta, GA

Manager, MIS System Support and Documentation

Managed group of methods analysts supporting all Georgia Power systems. Analysts performed control, problem resolution, documentation review, training of systems technicians. Set up a special group to evaluate inefficient programs and identify corrective action, and obtained approval to implement changes. Changes increased operating efficiency, reducing execution time for some programs from four weeks to one hour.

Honors and Awards

o　Consistently evaluated as "Outstanding" or "Consistently Exceeds," resulting in monetary and promotional awards.

o　Received "Best of the Area" and "Best of the Region" awards when sales exceeded annual quotas (130% plus) in two consecutive years.

o　Received multiple nominations from both peers and management for quarterly "Excellence" awards. Selected "First" for two quarters and "Second" for two quarters out of 33 nominated individuals.

o　Received monetary award and recognition for benefits derived from billing system software.

o　Recognized for both the quality and the quantity of work produced on or before target dates.

Education

Georgia State University　　　　　　BBA. Major:Accounting/Minor:Information Systems

University of Wyoming　　　　　　　　　Began work on degree in business

Numerous management and technical courses presented by AT&T, Georgia Power, the Air Force and outside seminar providers.

Figure 8.3   Functional Resume

John Daly

116 Walnut Street, Montvale, NJ 07645   (201) 555-7891 Home   (212) 999-9054 Office

Writer/Editor

Strong writer/editor with solid background in financial analysis,
business operations and administration. Skilled at clarifying
complex subject matter, persuasively and with style. A seasoned
problem-solver who works well with people at all levels.

Selected Accomplishments

Writing

o   Planned and wrote definitive *Financial Brochure* that explained
intricate, multi-industry company to financial community and
resulted in critical support during liquidity crisis.

o   Conceived and promoted financial public relations campaign to
reposition corporate image through brochures, press releases,
improved stockholder communications, speeches and
correspondence.

o   Motivated nationwide field staff and enhanced public support of
prominent voluntary health foundation through monthly
newsletter, feature articles and news stories.

o   Created marketing/promotion materials and sales display aids
used to successfully position new product line in competitive
national market.

**Financial
Relations**

o   Led key Wall Street analysts to follow corporate progress by
fundamentally changing traditional annual report presentation
and following up with personal contacts.

o   Satisfied institutional and individual stockholder inquiries
concerning sensitive information reported in the press.

o   Successfully negotiated $385 million credit arrangement by
traveling extensively and maintaining communications with some
350 bank and institutional lenders.

**Analysis/
Research**

o   Conducted in-depth analyses and prepared report leading to
acquisition and merger forming nation's third largest consumer
finance company.

o   Researched and wrote exhaustive market and economic reports on
various industries to support major long-term loan commitments
of leading bank.

Administration

o   Instituted and supervised centralized office responsible for
financial administration, planning and relations with the
lender/investor communities for multi-industry company.

o   Oversaw advertising/promotion activities, government agency
relations, credit, personnel and other staff functions for
privately-held company dealing in food commodities.

o   Headed operational and training unit responsible for national and
international credit relationships of New York bank.

John Daly	Page 2

Affiliations

Daily and Associates	Editor/Writer/Consultant
March of Dimes	Editor/Writer/Publicity Manager
Spice Market, Inc.	General Manager
Avco Corporation	Second Vice President Vice President, Avco Financial Services, Inc.
Chase Manhattan Bank	Senior Credit Supervisor - Domestic/International

Education

NYU Graduate School of Business Administration	Finance/Accounting/Financial Public Relations
Brown University	B.A. Political Science
Chase Manhattan Bank	Special Development Program

Personal

Willing to travel/relocate	Fluent speaker of French, German and Spanish Can read Portuguese and Italian

material you prepared for the other two resumes plus your resume worksheets to put this one together. Begin the usual way: name, address, telephone numbers. Next comes your old friend, the job title and the thumbnail sketch. Third is the *Experience and Selected Accomplishments*. The positions are listed in the same order as on a Chronological Resume—most recent to those in the past. List the company, your position, then the description of your duties, responsibilities and/or functions (from the Chronological Resume). Tighten this section as much as you can—you shouldn't have more than four or five lines of text. Indented underneath the job description, arrange three or four of your achievements at that position. Place the most important accomplishment first and the second most important one last. Your most recent position should have the longest description and the most accomplishments. Decrease the job description and the number of accomplishments as you go back in time.

Complete the rest of the resume exactly as you would any other resume. Include education, honors, awards, patents and publications (if these were not included as accomplishments), professional and business affiliations, military service, and personal information (if desired). You do not need the business affiliation heading (see the Achievement Resume in Figure 8.1 for an example), because this heading is covered in your *Experience and Selected Achievements* heading.

Figure 8.4 illustrates a combination Chronological/Achievement resume.

Professional or Technical Resume

A professional or technical resume is used in three instances: (1) If you are a professional (engineer, researcher, computer analyst, etc.) who has been working on a project basis, or in an area where you must have a high degree of specific job related skills; (2) If you are a consultant who has worked on a large number of projects for a variety of clients; or (3) If you are highly skilled in a particular area, but have had a number of employers. The purpose of this type of resume is to highlight your professional or technical skills, while showing the range of your ability to apply those skills.

You describe these skills slightly differently, depending upon whether you were a consultant, or whether you worked on staff for the particular firm. In each instance, begin with the job title and thumbnail sketch. Follow these with a section titled *Areas of Expertise, Professional Skills, Special Skills, Skills Areas, Special Competencies*, or some other title that highlights the special knowledge which you possess. This section is a list, not an explanation, unless your special skill requires that. You would also include any licenses in this section. The next section is a variation on the Achievement Resume. It is titled *Projects Completed, Selected Projects, Major Projects, Projects Completed for Clients* or *Major Project Participation*. (Note: In many technical fields, individuals participate collegially on a project, and unless you were the general manager for the project and could take full credit, you are stuck describing the project and your contribution to it. Employers looking for your special kind of expertise are fully aware of this. You simply have to make the project sound interesting.) If you received patent(s) or are published, include these in a small section titled *Special Accomplishments and Awards*. A section on education follows, including any educational honors. The resume can end with a heading titled *Selected List of Clients, Company Affiliations*, or a similar title which is illustrative of the information contained in the section. You do not list any job titles in conjunction with this listing. You do not include any personal information in a professional resume.

Curriculum Vitae

The Curriculum Vitae is a special resume used only by professional educators of all levels, and by researchers working in an environment in which achievement is measured by your educational attainments, what

Figure 8.4 Combination Chronological/Achievement Resume

Ronald LeBow

4071 Greenville Road   Office: (609) 555-9054
Princeton, NJ 08540   Home: (609) 555-7844

Marketing Manager

Innovative, practical manager skilled in developing marketing strategies, solving problems and training sales and customer service personnel. Experienced writer, editor, platform speaker and presenter.

Experience and Selected Achievements

C AND S ASSOCIATES   Princeton, NJ
1978 - present: Consultant

Consult with clients on problems in sales, marketing and customer service; prepare and present seminars for client companies; write books and training courses for publication.

o   Authored comprehensive state-of-the-art books and manuals on customer service management and operations.

o   Developed and conducted on-site seminars to help clients solve specific marketing problems.

o   Directed publication of unique middle-management training programs incorporating multi-media techniques for a major publisher. Sales of the programs exceeded projections.

o   Prepared and conducted over three hundred thirty seminars for managers of customer service departments. Instructed more than 3500 managers representing more than 2100 companies.

McGRAW-HILL BOOK COMPANY   New York, NY
1975-1979: Marketing Manager

Managed activities of the department and department staff, including planning and budgeting, staff assignments and scheduling of exhibits and promotions. Planned catalogs, estimated development time and costs, assigned advertising and promotional projects. Evaluated potential acquisitions and conducted feasibility studies. Worked with editorial department on packaging. Made presentations at national conventions and for major accounts. Directed development of sales training materials and made arrangements for sales training sessions.

o   Developed campaign for winning state adoption of textbooks, resulting in sales of over $25 million.

o   Instituted standardized cost analysis procedures for determining project feasibility, cutting by 30% the non-productive time and costs charged against the project.

o   Instituted new procedure mandating yearly evaluation of existing product lines. Removing unprofitable books from list cut warehouse and other carrying charged by $155,000 the first year.

o   Produced award-winning catalog cited for excellence of both graphics and copy.

1973-1975: Product Manager   New York, NY

Managed advertising and promotion for secondary reading product. Developed sales strategies and related materials. Prepared sales demonstration kits. Determined economic stocking levels. Presented sales training and educational seminars. Devised product packaging. Planned and staffed displays for national conventions.

o   Increased market share and doubled product line sales to $5,000,000 by selling instructional systems rather than books.

Ronald LeBow

o   Conceived and installed a system for writing sales proposals, dramatically cutting preparation time and resulting in increased big-ticket sales.

o   Executed low-cost crash development of product line, saving estimated $95,000 in development costs and increasing potential sales by getting product out by the beginning of the school selling year.

1970-1973: Educational Consultant   Houston, TX

Conducted seminars, developed training materials and sales proposals, made high-level sales presentations, managed free-lance consulting staff.

HOUSTON AUDIO-VISUAL SERVICES   Houston, TX
1962-1970: Sales Manager

Sold and serviced audio-visual equipment and related filmstrips, cassettes and books. Managed warehouse and repair staff as well as hiring and training sales staff.

o   Originated profitable training seminars leading to improved customer relations and increased sales.

o   Recruited, trained and directed a professional consulting staff which charged to conduct workshops and seminars, enabling the company to turn a required activity from a loss into a profit.

o   Exceeded area market projections with new product line, earning company national "Top Ten" sales status.

1959-1962: Sales Representative   Houston, TX

Introduced audio-visual product line to the educational market in southeast Texas. Won national sales recognition award.

Education

North Texas State University   M.A. in Education
University of Illinois   B.A. in Liberal Arts

Numerous business and management short courses and seminars

you have published, and the number of presentations you have made. (These are usually the first three headings.) After these attainments, the jobs are usually dispensed of in a section titled Positions Held, which is a listing of the schools or places you worked, and the job title, in descending chronological order (most recent to least recent). The job titles in education generally tell exactly what you did. However, you can add to this section if you did anything unusual in that position, or received a special honor. If you are trying to make a career transition from business to education, this is the format you must use.

Typically, the thumbnail sketch is not included. Do keep in mind, though, that you should not down-rate your accomplishments. For executives who happen to be working in education, the Curriculum Vitae format, which is expected by boards of education, can be

138

Figure 8.5 Professional or Technical Resume

Ellen Fisher

40 West Village Lane   (512) 347-7555
Browns Lake, TX 77828

Summary:

> Senior Business Writer/Analyst with over fifteen years
> experience in writing and editing data entry standards, methods
> and procedures, user's guides, management training programs
> and instructional materials.

Experience:

Published author and writer. Wrote or co-authored 12 business-related books on data accuracy, professional selling, customer service, telemarketing, job hunting, problem solving and listening. Wrote and/or edited 85 educational publications. List on request.

1. As a Writer/Consultant for a mid-size ethical pharmaceutical company:

    o   Developed corporate human resources policies and procedures, interviewing responsible staff members for information and researching applicable legal aspects of each policy.
    o   Wrote Employee Handbook containing information about company policies and benefits.
    o   Prepared desk manuals documenting key positions within the Sales and Human Resources Departments, including user computer interactions which had been previously undocumented.
    o   Revised Human Resources Department forms to make them easier to use and to comply fully with current legal requirements.
    o   Wrote an employee guidebook for new employees.

2. As a Technical Writer for a major telecommunications company:

    o   Documented both major and minor computer systems.
    o   Prepared user's manuals, staff and management systems guides, position papers, proposals and reports.
    o   Planned and wrote an initial training program for new technical staff members and contractors.
    o   Documented the hardware/network for the site.
    o   Developed portions of the on-line documentation for a major hardware/software network system used at more than 300 locations.

3. As a Writer/Consultant for a major food product company:

    o   Prepared user's guides for a Head Count System used to analyze corporate staffing levels and a Purchasing Control System which allowed the MIS Department to track computer hardware and software purchases.

4. As a Marketing Consultant/Writer for a major telecommunications research organization:

    o   Researched industry standards, then wrote data entry standards, initiated and monitored data cleanup, instituted changes in procedures, wrote user's guide, prepared a catalog for a Distribution List DataBase housed on a UNIX system, and trained staff members.
    o   Worked directly with programmers to troubleshoot, write user documentation and implement a non-affiliate Order Entry System using PC's and Local Area Network (LAN)
    o   Prepared summaries of company publications for inclusion in a computer library information service.
    o   Wrote executive summaries of technical and non-technical publications.
    o   Coordinated presentations and wrote books for a series of familiarization workshops.

Ellen Fisher   Page 2

o   Conducted planning sessions for the Customer Service and Distribution
     groups, editing the plans before presentation to management.
o   Wrote general policies, procedures and training guides.
o   Planned, developed, wrote and managed promotional campaigns and materials
     for highly technical telecommunications systems and network documents.

5.   As an Analyst for a management consulting firm:

o   Interviewed clients and analyzed interviews conducted by others to determine
     client needs.
o   Wrote and edited training materials based on assessed needs.
o   Managed projects undertaken by the firm on behalf of clients.
o   Conducted competitive technology assessments in which library and field
     research were utilized to determine the probable state of competitor's
     technologies in specific product areas.
o   Managed the development of a productive relationships pilot training course
     for sales managers.

6.   As a Consultant/Analyst/Writer for own firm:

o   Prepared and presented seminars for client companies and the American
     Management Association.
o   Edited business and educational materials for clients.
o   Wrote comprehensive books and manuals on customer service management and
     operations for client-specific applications.
o   Developed and conducted on-site seminars to help clients solve specific
     customer service and marketing problems.
o   Wrote policy and procedures manuals, job descriptions, and job standards for
     clients.
o   For a major publisher, directed development and participated in the writing
     of two middle-management training programs incorporating multi-media
     techniques.
o   Wrote instructional materials and conducted seminars for customer service
     and telemarketing managers representing more than 1,500 companies.

7.   As a Senior Editor for a major publishing company:

o   Planned content and managed schedule, budgeting, and staff for major
     editorial projects.
o   Edited and/or wrote significant portions of major editorial projects.
o   Estimated production time and costs for new product development.
o   Worked closely with the Marketing Department on product packaging and the
     development of marketing strategies.
o   Made presentations at national conventions and for major accounts.
o   Conducted training sessions for sales staff and educational seminars
     explaining product use.

Software:

Word Perfect 5.1, DisplayWrite 4, Multimate Advantage, Samna, Wang Word
Processing Programs (dedicated and PC versions), Perfect Writer, Wordstar, First
Choice, Word, Freelance Plus, Harvard Graphics, Lotus 1-2-3, 20/20, several UNIX
based editors and applications, PC Paintbrush. Familiar with dBase applications.

Hardware:

Personal computers; HP and IBM mainframe experience as a program user

Education:

Texas Women's University   M.A., Education
University of Illinois   B.A., Biology

Numerous short courses in writing, management, customer service, sales and
marketing

restrictive. You might want to prepare the Curriculum Vitae and expand the Positions Held section with accomplishments. For further help with this kind of resume, check in the education section of the library for assistance.

Letter Resume

Each letter resume is prepared individually for a specific target. This is a good resume to use in response to an advertisement or to send to someone referred to you by a networking contact. Use the list of achievements you have in your achievements file or notebook to write the resume. You can write it in standard letter paragraph form, or use the structured pattern presented in Chapter 9, "Using Letters Effectively." In the regular letter form, you begin with a statement expressing interest in the job and a reason why you're a good candidate for the position. Continue with the accomplishments, background and experience you have that meets or exceeds the requirements for the position. Figure 8.6 illustrates a letter resume put together this way.

As an alternative, write your letter resume in much the same form as you would a standard resume, but with a letter heading, a subject line indicating the job you're applying for, a summary statement (like a thumbnail) specifically mentioning the background, strengths or experiences asked for in the advertisement, plus other strengths you possess that might be valuable to them. Then, list your accomplishments, work experience and education much as you would in a regular resume. End with a paragraph expressing interest in the position and asking for an interview. Finish with a standard closing ("Yours truly" works just fine), and your signature.

Biography

A biography is not strictly a resume. However, if you are looking for work as a consultant, or have decided to try short-term projects on your own, a biography is an extremely useful leave-behind document.

In a biography, you refer to yourself in the third person. You write the biography as though you had interviewed yourself and wrote it for publication in a newspaper or magazine. The biography begins with your name, in large print and centered, as a title.

Figure 8.7 illustrates how one consultant wrote his biography.

Testing and Revising Your Resume

A resume is ineffective unless it's well presented. It should be imaginatively conceived. It should advertise what you have to sell. Put yourself

Figure 8.6 Letter Resume

Dear Mr. Pickard:

Dr. James Field told me of your current search for an experienced Chemical Engineer, and suggested that I contact you. He felt that my background and experience matched the requirements for the position you have open.

I have a strong technical and business background in the engineering and chemical industries with an emphasis on process technology planning, industrial economics, and research and development.

The scope of my work was primarily related to petrochemical, chemical and synfuels industries, and centered around the following activities:

o   Planning of overall facilities for monomer and polymer processing complexes
o   Preparation of economic evaluations, feasibility studies and processing schemes
o   Participation in economic and business strategy reviews related to projects and long-range planning. This involved interfacing with the Corporate Planning, Project Management, Marketing, Sales and Research and Development departments as well as interactions with research institutions and universities.
o   Coordination of patent review activities
o   Preparation of budget estimates, technical reports, proposals and publications
o   Identification of future technological and economic trends
o   Support of technical sales and business development
o   Planning, directing and technical and economic evaluation of proprietary chemical research and process development projects.

My responsibilities included official contacts with many top management clients, high-ranking government officials (both U.S. and foreign), the press and academic faculty members.

My education includes a PhD in chemical engineering, an MBA in general business and a BS and MS in chemistry.

My salary requirements are subject to negotiation, but have always been competitive with those of others in the industries in which I have worked.

I am looking forward to meeting with you at your convenience. At that time, I can provide a more detailed resume as well as any other information, such as references, that you might need.

Sincerely,

in your prospective employers' shoes and test your completed resume to see if it meets their standards. Will they want to see you after they read it?

Put your emotions to bed. Look at your resume with fresh eyes:

1.   Does the thumbnail sketch mirror the experience shown in the rest of the resume? Do the achievements or experience substantiate each assertion included in the thumbnail?

Figure 8.7 Biography

Frank J. Solveig & Associates

15422 Hempstead Road
Charlotte, NC 28205
(704) 555-5587

Biography of Frank J. Solveig

Frank Solveig is President of a consulting and training firm that consults widely in general management, marketing management, sales management, corporate communications, customer service, and telemarketing, both in the United States and overseas.

Dr. Solveig was formerly Dean of the Business School at Dixon University in Dixon, North Carolina, where he designed and directed innovative graduate programs in management for local area businesses and industries. Other academic positions include chairs as Professor of Marketing and Management at Dixon and Professor of Sales and Marketing at Old Dominion in Norfolk, Virginia. He has also been an officer and director of a Richmond, Virginia-based management consulting firm. Dr. Solveig holds a PhD and an MBA with honors from the University of Pittsburgh, and a Bachelor of Business degree from the University of Texas.

Dr. Solveig has published extensively in all the human dimensions of management, as well as contributing articles to the widely read *Sales and Marketing Management* magazine.

In workshops with all levels of management from first-line supervisor to top executive, Dr. Solveig is recognized as a skilled motivator, especially adept at instilling the human dimensions of management and sales-connected activities.

Clients include business, manufacturing, banking and telecommunications companies, petrochemical companies, educational institutions and retail operations. Recent clients include AMOCO Oil Company, Swift and Company, R.J.R. Nabisco, North Carolina Bancorp, Norfolk Public Schools, Bell South and Coca Cola.

Dr. Solveig is also active in government and community affairs. He has been a City Council member, a State Representative, a director of the Charlotte Chamber of Commerce, and the United Way. Dr. Solveig is also a member of a number of professional associations, including the American Marketing Association, the American Management Association, the Academy of Management and the American Institute of Decision Sciences. He has been listed in *Outstanding Educators in America* and *Who's Who in the South*.

---

2. Does the experience section read smoothly, continuously and logically? Or do some of the statements seem

❏ Out of context, as though they belong some other place?
❏ Irrelevant to the theme of the resume as a whole?
❏ Too technical, too precise or, conversely, too general and imprecise?

3. Does the person behind the resume become increasingly clear as you read? Or is the image blurred from time to time by statements that don't seem to fit the rest of the picture?

4. After you read the resume, do you have a single, clear picture of you as a person? Is this the image of someone you'd like to meet?

Did your resume meet the acid test? Is it apt to open doors?

Evaluating Different Parts of the Resume

Now, come back and look at each part of your resume by itself. Leave the beginning—the thumbnail sketch—until after you've evaluated the other sections of the resume.

Achievement Resume. Begin by reviewing the *Selected Achievements* section. Evaluate each statement in the section, using the following criteria as a checklist:

1. Do your accomplishment statements begin with action words? Does each statement include the result? Do the results include measurements of success (dollars, time, qualifying adjectives, percentages, other numerical values)?

2. Does each statement list only an accomplishment and a related result? If you've included more than one accomplishment in a statement, consider splitting it into two or more accomplishments. Or use subdivisions under the main statement to show that a single activity resulted in multiple accomplishments and results.

3. Have you written the statements in forceful, simple language? Or do they contain jargon, technical words or abbreviations that might not be universally understood?

4. What about the order of the accomplishments? Do you have a strong accomplishment at the end of the section as well as at the beginning? (Some knowledgeable recruiters read achievement resumes from bottom to top because they believe applicants put their lesser achievements at the end.) The usual order is to put the best achievement first, the next-best second, the third-best last and distribute the others evenly in between.

5. Do you have too many or too few accomplishments? Somewhere between five and eight is about right. If you have more solid accomplishments than these, you may want to write different resumes emphasizing different aspects of the job. (Whatever you do, don't throw away any good accomplishment statements. Save them in your notebook for possible reuse in writing cover letters or letter resumes.)

6. Do your achievement statements match the type of position and the industry for which you will be applying? Example: A programming achievement is inappropriate if you will be applying to manage an information system. An accomplishment related to installing/directing the operation of a management information system would be appropriate.

After you've finished the Selected Achievements section, go on to review the other sections, which are similar for most kinds of resumes. (Turn forward a couple of pages to find how to evaluate these sections.)

Chronological Resume. Begin by reviewing the section you titled *Background and Experience, Relevant Experience* or *Experience.*

1. Are your positions listed in reverse chronological order?

2. Did you write the descriptions of your duties, responsibilities and functions of your last position in the present tense? (Even when you're not working, you want to imply that you are. Using the present tense is not deceitful. For all practical purposes, that's still what you are.)

3. Have you described the duties, responsibilities and functions for other positions you had in the past tense?

4. Have you described your experience in short sentences? (Please, no more than a line, or at most two for a single sentence.) Have you used simple, forceful language? Does each statement begin with a strong verb? Do the statements show that you managed, delegated, planned, organized, developed or otherwise controlled your job? Or do your statements make your performance sound passive and low level? (You assisted, helped, participated in, represented, handled.) Or worse yet, did you use nouns to describe your duties and responsibilities rather than strong active verbs?

5. Does your record show increasingly higher-level duties and responsibilities?

6. Are the descriptions of the most recent positions longer than those for earlier positions? (Most recent positions could have up to five or six lines of description, although three or four lines is better. Earlier positions should be described in no more than two or three lines of print.)

7. What about the order of the functions, duties or responsibilities within a statement about a position? Did you put the most important aspects of the job first, and the less important or less time-consuming aspects later?

8. Did you include descriptions for only the last 15 or 20 years? (If your entire working life was with one company, you may include it all. Otherwise, if you have worked longer than 20 years or so, only include the earlier years if you did something during those years that is important to explain your qualifications for the current job title.

Evaluating the Remaining Sections of your Resume. Now look at each section you've included in the resume. With an Achievement Resume, especially one you're trying to get on one page, you may have included only *Education* and *Business Affiliations* headings. In a Chronological Resume, you may have included other headings. Consider if the section should even be in this resume. Does it contain enough information to be useful? Does it add to the picture of your competence? Have you listed your business affiliations in reverse order, most recent to most distant? Have you listed too many of these? (Remember, you need only go back 15 to 20 years.) Have you listed your education in reverse order? (Education is something employers will check, so your listings must be correct.) Do you need to include any short courses or seminars to validate some of your claims? (Don't put in too many, as they seem to call attention to shortcomings.) Have you earned any special licenses or registrations?

Do you need all of the information you've put in the *Personal* section? The catchall term "Will travel/relocate" is often enough. Don't restrict your job opportunities by listing "Houston area only," even if that's true. Don't mention marital status unless you're interested in applying for overseas positions which don't have family housing and are available to singles only. If you have any special abilities or skills which might be of value on the job, include them. Example: Speak Italian, Spanish and French; have traveled extensively in Europe, South America and the Far East. Licensed to fly single-engine aircraft. Omit hobbies and membership in social or community organizations—unless you've done something in a community organization that might strengthen your job bid (Chairperson of the United Way Campaign, President of Rotary, President of the Chamber of Commerce).

Should you have included any other section? Have you received business honors or published articles or books? Do you hold any patents? If so, include the most important in a category you call *Honors and Publications, Honors and Awards, Publications, Patents* or whatever fits your situation. Don't cover any of these achievements under the heading *Selected Achievements*. Do it one place or the other, not both. Don't list all of your publications by name and journal or publisher. Give titles only, on those most relevant to the job you're looking for, and include the others in a catchall statement such as "numerous others in the area of_____."

Do you have any professional affiliations (job-related organizations only) which add to your stature? Do you have an office in the organization or have you held one? If you do, consider adding a Professional Affiliations heading.

The Thumbnail Sketch. The thumbnail sketch is the first thing a recruiter or potential employer will read after your name and address. It may be the first thing, since many don't bother with names and addresses unless they're really interested. Check the following:

1. Does your job title match the content of the thumbnail sketch? Does it fit the information—the accomplishments and/or achievements—given in the rest of the resume? Is it too broad or too specific?

2. Does the content in the sketch give the reader a good summary of your skills and abilities?

3. Would it make a good advertisement?

4. Does it fit with the rest of the resume? Is each statement substantiated by a related achievement or experience?

5. Are the statements in the sketch concrete and descriptive? Or are some of them flowery and abstract? Do they seem like puffery?

6. Are the different statements in the sketch written in parallel form? Or have you used verbs to describe your abilities in some statements and nouns in others? (This is a technical point, but can contribute to a lesser impression if you've mixed your nouns and verbs incorrectly. The person who's reading your resume may not know what's wrong, but does know that something about it doesn't sound quite right.) If you're not sure, ask someone whose knowledge of grammar you trust to review your resume for just this point.

7. Is your sketch longer than 40 words? What can you leave out? How can you condense?

8.   Are related skills and abilities tied together? Does the writing carry you along from one set of skills to the next or does something feel jarring or out of place?

Think of your resume as a dynamic document. Constantly reword, rework and improve it.

Group Critiques of Your Resume

In job search clubs and organizations, one of the really helpful activities is what is known as a "Job Jury." Essentially, this is a small-group critique of your nearly finished resume by people with similar backgrounds and experience. The purpose of this critique is to improve your resume, to polish the wording, and to help you be sure you've included the most important aspects of your work life in your resume—that you've "put your best foot forward." If you don't belong to a job search group, you can still get the benefits of group thinking by setting up your own job jury.

Ask four to six friends, former associates or people you know who have jobs that are similar to yours if they'd be willing to meet with you and help critique your resume. Invite them to your home, or to a semi-public place where you can have some privacy. You may want to include a meal or some other social event as part of your invitation. Send each person who agrees to help a photocopy of the draft of your resume. You may also want to photocopy the brief checklist below and include it with the resume.

After your friends or associates arrive, begin by summarizing your experience and accomplishments verbally. Tell them what kind of position you would like to obtain. Then, ask them to evaluate the resume on the basis of whether the individual statements further your job search objective. Tell them to make notes on their copies of the resume and to give them to you when you're finished so you can have the full benefit of their thinking. Take full and complete notes on your copy as you talk.

Regardless of the kind of resume you're having critiqued, hold the thumbnail sketch for last. Begin with the accomplishments or the experience section, depending upon the resume format. As the group works, you may want to bring out some of the points you learned for self-critique, as well as the questions in the following checklist.

❏ Have I presented each one of my accomplishments effectively?

❏ Have I put the statements in the right order?

❏ Have I included the key functions of the jobs I had? Have I included some which are of minor importance and should be omitted? Have I given them the proper priority? What should I have included that I didn't?

❏ Have my principle liabilities or weaknesses been played down?

❏ Is it clear what kind of job I'm pursuing?

Go over each accomplishment or experience by itself. Read the first achievement or job description. Ask if it is all right as it stands. Is the statement reasonable and believable? What could be better, what should be deleted or omitted? How could the statement be presented more strongly? If it should be reworded, how do they say it should read? Work toward consensus. If they agree, be sure you get the reworded statement written down. If they don't reach a consensus, note the most important things that were said, and rework the statement later. Don't be touchy. Remember that they are here at your invitation to help you put together the best resume you can. Accept their collective wisdom, even if some of the things they suggest hurt.

Did you leave out an important achievement, or omit some important aspect of your duties and responsibilities? It's especially easy to omit very important functions on Chronological Resumes.

When you're looking at the achievements, either on the Achievement Resume, or on the Combination Resume, ask about the order of the statements. Do they present the strongest statement in the existing order, or would they be better ordered in another way? If reordered, what should that order be?

Next, ask them to look at the education section. This should take just moments, since the education section should be a simple listing of colleges and degrees. Follow this with each of the other sections. Ask them what you have inadvertently left out, what you should add, what you should take away. If you've considered adding another heading with additional information, explain your thinking and ask for their advice on whether to include it or not.

Finally, ask them to go back and look at the thumbnail sketch. Explain why you used a thumbnail instead of a job objective. (If you can't remember, go back and read why in the preceding chapter.) Do they think the thumbnail is descriptive of the person you've described in the achievements or experience? What's missing, and what should be left out? How could you change the thumbnail to make it stronger? Also ask about the job title. Is it the right one to fit the resume and thumbnail? Take notes on their comments. If they want to help you rewrite the thumbnail, do so. Otherwise, work on it later, using your notes and the ones they give you to polish your text.

Discuss appearance. Does the resume seem cluttered? Is there enough "white space?" Can you easily scan it?

Final Copy
After you've finished with your personal and group evaluation, your next step is to revise and rewrite. Then after each section is polished to your satisfaction, put the various sections together in usable form.

Suggestions:

1. Each of your resumes must be as perfect as you can possibly make it. No typos, erasures or smudges. Pay someone to prepare it perfectly on a word processor if you can't type well or don't have access to a computer. Or better yet, prepare it yourself on a word processor or computer and rework and correct it until the grammar and format are exactly the way you want them. (The ideal is to use a computer and to print a fresh resume for every application, to go with every letter, or to take to every interview.) As mentioned several times, you may need several different kinds and styles of resumes so that you can match your resume to the recipient.

2. If you're planning a large mailing for a mail campaign (see the next chapter), you may want to have your resume typeset and printed on an offset press. Don't assume that typeset resumes will be without error. Proofread your resume carefully before paying for the service. Don't photocopy your resume unless the copy machine achieves quality near that of print (no dark lines or blurs) and can copy on good quality paper. Fortunately, some of the newer copiers can produce acceptable photocopies on good paper.

3. Paper suggestions:
   - ❏ Good quality bond paper in white, off white, ivory, eggshell, gray, pale yellow or soft gold. Blues, greens and pinks don't project an executive image and are an absolute "no- no."
   - ❏ 8 1/2–by–11–inch standard paper is fine, although executive size paper (6 1/2 by 11 1/2) is a nice touch, and the resume stands out from the pack.

❏ Consider printing longer two-to-four–page resumes on both sides of 11 by 18 inch paper, and fold it instead of printing on two to four separate pieces and stapling. The folded resume looks like a brochure and gives a nice, not overpowering appearance. If you use the folded format, you might want to consider using your name, the job title, the thumbnail sketch and a "Career Summary" on the first page, then begin the Chronology/Achievements, etc. on the next page.

Other Documents You Should Prepare

Before you begin interviewing, you need to prepare back-up documents and other information sheets or exhibits to take along. Of the following list, the first three you must prepare, the others you may or may not prepare, depending upon your area of work.

1. A list of the organizations you worked for, including names, addresses, telephone numbers and the name of the person you reported to, if you have all of this information or can obtain it.

2. A list, in descending order, of all of your job titles, and the salary ranges you earned for each. (This information is often checked. You do, however, have to give a potential employer written permission to do this.)

3. A list of your references. Include names, job titles, organizational affiliation, address and telephone number.

4. If you have listed publications in your resume, prepare a full bibliography which a potential employer may use to substantiate your claims, including coauthors, article or book name, publication or publisher (and city of publication), date of publication and page numbers or number of pages. (Incidentally, if this is an important part of your usefulness to an employer, plan to take along several examples to an interview as well as this "leave-behind" list of achievements.)

5. If you have listed presentations in your resume, prepare a full listing of these, including dates, locations, the organization before which the presentation was made, and approximate number of attendees. If the presentation was summarized in a conference book or journal, include this information.

6. A portfolio of representative work. You would need to prepare a portfolio if you are looking for a position in marketing, advertising, publishing, or in any other type of work where there is a visible work product. You might include copies of advertising campaigns, brochures, catalogs, sample plans, books, magazine and journal articles, etc. **Do not include anything which might be proprietary.**

Using Letters Effectively

Often a letter is your first contact with a company. It carries the weight of your hopes and dreams. You are trying to sell whoever will read your letter on your capabilities—that you're someone to consider further. The operative word here is *sell*. You're trying to persuade, to convince—but without a hard sell. During your job campaign, you'll write cover letters for your resumes, letters trying to find out if employers have jobs in your area, letters asking for appointments for interviews, networking letters asking people for help or to touch base on a referral, follow-up letters and thank-you letters.

But these letters, even though they are a major part of positioning your "product" in the market segment you've chosen, can carry the seeds of deselection. How? If they sound stilted, if you use archaic expressions or out-of-date business expressions. And they may be a dead giveaway to your age. Why? Because current business writing is informal and conversational. But back in the "good old days," business letters were taught as formal communications. You were taught an entire set of business expressions that may be ingrained in your writing style. Or, you may have been in the military, which requires a very "stiff" style. Now, this formalistic style is no longer considered the best way to write. It's difficult to understand. It's too wordy, impersonal and uninteresting. You want to avoid these "age-related" writing characteristics primarily to show that you've kept up and remained current.

So, how do you make changes, and what are they?

Hints to Remove Age Indicators from Letters

Let's start with ways to remove age from your letters first, then look at some general hints for better letter writing.

Archaic, outmoded business expressions. Traditionally, business writers used a number of utilitarian phrases which sound stilted and unfriendly today. They also sound as though you failed to stay current. In short, they tell your readers that you're not up-to-date. The quickest way to put distance between you and your reader is to fill your correspondence with these phrases. Writing in a more conversational style eliminates this distance and brings you closer to your reader, without being too familiar.

Change this	*to this*
As per your letter	Your letter
In reference to your letter	This letter or your letter
Subsequent to this letter	After you get this letter, or later
Please advise me	Please tell me
For your convenience, I have enclosed	Enclosed
Under separate cover, please find	I am sending
Propose alternatives	Suggest alternatives
Attached hereto	Attached
If you desire	If you want
It is the hope of the undersigned	I hope (this may sound obsequious. If so, try "I trust," or "I think")
May I take the opportunity to tell you	*Leave this out*
Enclosed herewith is	Enclosed
Per your request	As you asked
If you utilize	If you use
If you require	If you need
I would like to thank you	Thank you
If I can be of further service please don't hesitate to call me	Please call
I would like to thank you	Thank you

Use of slang, buzz words, jargon, technical words. Certain words become fashionable in business for periods of time and writers become attached to them. They continue to use them to show they're current with the latest trends. The words are stylish for a time, but quickly become passe. The problem: When you continue to use them long after they've gone out of general usage, you're dated. And, of course, using industry-specific jargon and technical words can be a big turnoff to people in other industries or to people who don't understand the technical side (people in the human resources department, for instance).

Word choice. Use the *right* word to express what you mean. Choose the simple word instead of the complex, the concrete word instead of the abstract, the single word instead of the phrase. Writing styles of older executives often contain the following flaws:

1. Using abstract words instead of concrete words. Abstract words deal with concepts; concrete words deal with reality—they represent something that can be seen, felt, touched or heard. Abstractions such as good, bad, nice, fine, moderate, conservative, liberal are imprecise, and really don't tell anything. Instead of *bad*, why not use *defective, flawed* or *spoiled.* Instead of *good*, how about *competent, skillful, able, capable, efficient, fit, qualified*? But many writers also clutter their letters with multisyllabic words that are less vivid and concrete than short, plain words. This also cuts down on the readability of what you write. It takes more time to recognize multisyllabic words than it does one- and two-syllable words.

Change this	*to this*
demonstrate	show
utilize	use
sufficient	enough
initiate	start
remunerate	pay
facility	plant, headquarters, branch
substantial	large, sturdy
subsequent	next
terminate	end
anticipate	expect
ascertain	find out, discover, determine
consolidate	combine, merge, meld

2. Using a noun form of a word when a verb form would be better. This is the bane of executive writing in general. Many executives, who should know better, will change a perfectly good and useful verb into a noun by adding *-tion, -ation, - ion, -sion, -ance, -ence*, and *-ment.* Then they'll use the resulting word in a phrase and use a weak verb such as *is, are, was, were, will, took, get, come, have, give, provide* to show action.

For instance, "We took the cost into consideration before we made a decision," is not nearly as strong as, "We considered the cost before we decided."

Change this	to this
take into consideration	consider
make a decision	decide
take action on	act
give assistance to	assist
make an investigation	investigate
have an achievement	achieve
develop a formulation	formulate
make a classification	classify
come to an agreement	agree

3. Similarly, a word that can be used as either a noun or a verb can weaken the sentence when it's used as a noun and another verb does the action. This makes the sentence longer and wordier, too. Example: "The accomplishment of our cost reduction was made by March 25, at which time the implementation of the revised procedures was plant-wide," is very wordy and not too understandable. Simplified, it reads: "We reduced our costs by March 25 and implemented the revised procedures throughout the plant."

Change this	to this
make a study	study
make a purchase	purchase
effect or undertake change	change
make an increase	increase
make a decrease	decrease

4. Making verbs out of nouns, adjectives and adverbs by adding -ize or -ate to the end of a word is equally bad. For instance: collective + ize = collectivize. Others: legitimize, randomize, systematize, incentivize, methodize, interpretate (instead of interpret) or effectuate (instead of effect). These sound smart-aleck, trendy or, in the case of the words with ate endings, uneducated. A related mistake is adding -wise to the end of a word to attempt to condense a complex idea into a single word. "Profit-wise, I made the decision to phase out that product line." "By purchasing

the chemical feedstocks in advance of the price increase, I put the company in an enviable position, *material- wise.*" These sound pompous and cause readers to feel the writers have an overinflated sense of their own importance.

5. Using incorrect or imprecise words. Sometimes even well-educated executives will choose an incorrect or imprecise word because it sounds like the one they mean. The following words are often used in letters and in resumes during job hunting. Use the dictionary to be sure you've chosen the right one to express your meaning.

Examples:

cite/sight/site	accept/except
adapt/adept/adopt	credible/creditable/credulous
allude/elude/refer	continual/continuous
compose/comprise	complement/compliment
defective/deficient	definite/definitive
attribute/contribute	diagnosis/prognosis
biannual/biennial	canvas/canvass
despite/in spite of	discreet/discrete
economic/economical	average/mean/median
explicit/implicit	forceful/forcible
fortuitous/fortunate	insoluble/unsolvable
libel/liable/likely	equal/unique/perfect
insure/ensure/assure	*irregardless/regardless
ingenious/ingenuous	healthful/healthy
observance/observation	phenomenon/phenomenal

* *Note*: This is *not* a word.

Active Writing

Use colorful, active verbs. Another practice which dates letter writers is the form of their sentences. Writers actually make two different kinds of mistakes here. First, they use colorless and imprecise verbs. They write the verb *think* when they could use a meaty and more interesting verb such as *confirm, verify, conceive, judge, corroborate, decide, settle, resolve, surmise, discover* or *determine.* Using any of the other words would have shaded the meaning of the sentence and given a much clearer picture of their intent. If you are using a computer with a word processing program that has a thesaurus function, use it to find the better, more precise word. If you don't, purchase a paperback thesaurus and use that. Your writing will be much more interesting. Some common examples of overused words and clearer, more precise substitutes:

Change this	*to one of these*
pass	proceed, stream, circulate, occur, judge
feel	believe, consider, grope, probe, touch, think
make	form, build, construct, fabricate, create, devise, formulate, establish, perform, force, cause
have	hold, control, own, possess, experience, undergo, master
get	adopt, seize, bring, catch, capture, cause to be
give	deliver, impart, surrender, yield
tell	inform, notify, appraise, acquaint, familiarize
try	tempt, persuade, urge, test, rouse, provoke

Second, older writers use too many passive verbs and passive sentences. When you're looking for a job, you're trying to tell what *you* can do. *You* should be the subject of your writing, even if *you* is implied. By using passive verbs and sentences, you lose your personal claim on the action and remove yourself from the arena. For instance:

The defective design of the pulverizer was corrected before installation by the contractor, saving $10,000.

You aren't even in the preceding sentence. The reader is left to wonder *who* corrected the design. The contractor? Notice how much clearer the meaning is in the rewritten sentence:

I corrected the defective design of a pulverizer before the contractor installed it, saving $10,000.

But the real problem with passive verbs is deeper than this. Letters filled with passive verbs may give the reader the impression that:

1. The writer is not accepting responsibility.

2. The writer is dull and long-winded.

3. The writer doesn't have anything important to say and/or is uninteresting.

4. The writer was not involved and doesn't care.

Why do people continue to write with passive verbs? They confuse passive writing with objective, businesslike writing. Or somewhere along the line, they were brainwashed into thinking that using themselves as the subject of a sentence is bragging.

General Letter-Writing Hints

Every letter should be grammatical. It must be free of typographical, spelling and punctuation errors. This may be the toughest part of letter writing if you no longer have a secretary and are having to rely on your own skills. Using the spelling check on your computer will help some, but it won't catch problems with your grammar, some typos (your error still looked like a word, so the machine didn't catch it), and incorrect punctuation. Proofread each letter carefully to be sure no gremlin stepped on your keyboard. Errors cost—they make you appear careless.

The letter should be clean. If you're sending out copies of the same letter to many different people, you may photocopy or offset-print your letter. But be sure the copies are clear, with no smudges or "edges" and no faint print (or print that squiggles).

The Salutation. Even if you're answering a blind ad, don't *ever* write: "Dear Sir or Madam," or "To whom it may concern." Use the person's name in the salutation: "Dear President_____," "Dear Chair-man_____," "Dear Mr._____," "Dear Mrs._____," "Dear Miss_____," or "Dear Ms._____," (when you have a woman's name without a Miss or Mrs.) If you have a job title, you can use that, "Dear Department Head," "Dear Recruiter," etc. Use a colon after the person's name, not a comma. If you don't have any idea whom to address, you can leave out the salutation entirely and use a subject line. "Subject: Marketing Director position advertised in the Chicago Tribune June 15, 1990."

Tone of the letter. Be friendly—almost the same as you would be when writing to someone you know well. The letter should sound conversational when you read it out loud and give that feeling. Project enthusiasm. Let the letter recipients feel your confidence. You *can* do the job for them.

Even if you feel desperate about getting the job, you shouldn't *sound* or read as though you are. Don't mention any outside factors that don't bear directly on the topic. Get directly to the points you want to make and leave everything else out.

Length. Keep your letters from one to one-and-one-half pages long. Write short paragraphs. (If a paragraph is much longer than six or seven lines, see if you can break it into two paragraphs.) Set up the letter so that it has a lot of "white space." You know from your own experience that busy executives tend not to read anything longer than one or two pages. If the letter is longer, they either put it aside or skim it quickly, reading the first paragraph, the first sentence of subsequent paragraphs and maybe looking at the signature. They put it aside, and may never look at letters that look dense and complicated. Increase your readership by using little words, short sentences and short paragraphs.

Readability

Readability, or how easily a reader can read something, is made up of several factors, including sentence complexity and length, vocabulary level, style and tone. The average business communication should be written at about the level of a *Reader's Digest* article—i.e., seventh to ninth grade level. One of the easiest ways to check your personal level is to use the Gunning Fog Index. This index considers sentence length as a measure of sentence complexity and the number of multisyllabic words as a measure of vocabulary level.[1] Neither is absolutely true. But a high Fog index is more likely to indicate a difficult select than a low fog Index. And it's easy to do. Here's how:

1. Choose several of your writing samples—about 100 words each. Count the total number of words, then count the number of sentences. Divide the number of words by the number of sentences to find the average sentence length.

2. Count the number of words containing three or more syllables. Don't count proper names, compound words formed by combining short easy words (overcome, grandfather), or words which become three syllables because *-ed, -es or -ing* have been added. Then calculate the

---

[1] Adapted from Robert Gunning, *The Techniques of Clear Writing*, rev. ed. (New York: McGraw Hill, 1968), p. 38

percentage of difficult words by dividing the number of difficult words by the total number of words and multiplying by 100.

3. Add the average sentence length (calculation 1) to the percent of difficult words (calculation 2) and multiply this by the constant 0.4. The result is the Fog Index or approximate reading level.

Example: If you had three passages totalling 316 words, with 21 sentences and 42 multisyllabic words, your calculations for the Fog Index would be:

1. $\dfrac{316 \text{ words}}{21 \text{ sentences}}$ = 15 average words per sentence

2. $\dfrac{42 \text{ multisyllabic words}}{316 \text{ words}}$ x 100 = 13 percent difficult words

3. $(15 + 13)$ x 0.4 = 11.2, the Fog Index.

This is about the top level for letters. Above that, the letters are too hard to read and end up in the file on the floor or in the "to be read" pile on some manager's desk.

A few simple ways to check for readability without using the Fog Index.

❏ Rewrite any sentence that goes over two or three lines. It's too long. Try to keep sentences under 14 words, if you can.
❏ Keep sentences simple: no more than 20 percent compound (two sentences joined by *and* or another conjunction), 40 percent complex sentences (these are the tricky ones with clauses).
❏ Check for overuse of multisyllabic words and excess words and phrases. Get rid of those that aren't essential.
❏ Use the other suggestions in this section to edit your writing.

Using Letters in Your Marketing Effort

You can often accomplish things with letters that you can't do on the telephone or with a personal visit. As you well know, managers are programmed to respond to print. They'll answer a letter where they'd simply be unavailable otherwise. The following types of letters are those which you'll find most useful in marketing yourself.

"Fishing Expeditions"—Prospecting for Jobs

You can write two kinds of "fishing" letters. In the *prospecting letter*, you write to people you already know—friends, acquaintances, former colleagues or members of your industry—asking for suggestions which might help in your job search. Often they'll refer you to people they know or possibly even tell you about others in their industry who are hiring. These letters should be short, friendly, direct and to the point. You don't beg for help or in any way "put the arm on them." Prospecting letters are a part of your networking efforts. (See Exhibit 9.1.)

Follow up the prospecting letter with a phone call at the time and on the date you mentioned in your letter.

The second kind of prospecting letter is the *referral*. You write these to take advantage of leads you get from personal contacts (such as the one you asked for above), or from other correspondence. Exhibit 9.2 is a good example of a referral letter. In the first paragraph, you mention the person who suggested the contact and why, along with a brief description of what you hope to gain. You're not *asking* for a job, but for assistance or suggestions of ways you might go ahead with your job campaign. Ask if they have time to see you or to talk to you on the telephone. These letters are still a part of the first two marketing activities, Surveying the Market in General, and Segmenting the Market. If you're

Exhibit 9.1. Prospecting Letter

```
Dear Alan:

Recent cutbacks in our industry caused the XYZ Company to eliminate
the department where I've worked the past ten years.  While I had
several possibilities for further employment within the company, none
of them had the future I would prefer.  Therefore, I will soon be
leaving the company.

Alan, I'm writing to you for advice.  I don't expect that you
presently know of anything that might be suitable for me--but I do
want you to know that I'm available.  You know my general background
and experience.  The attached resume gives more details.

I'm open to suggestions that might help me as I begin my campaign.
Perhaps you know people in other companies who might be able to give
me some assistance, or who know of possible openings in my area of
expertise.

If you have time next Wednesday or Thursday, I'd like to come in and
chat with you for no longer than 15 to 20 minutes to get your
thoughts on my job search.  I'll call on Monday to find out if that's
convenient for you.

I look forward to seeing you.

Sincerely,
```

lucky in your contacts, they may lead you directly into the third and fourth part of your campaign, but not necessarily.

Follow up by making the phone call at the time you said you would.

Letter Campaigns

A few years ago, letter campaigns—contacting a number of firms which might have openings for someone of your caliber and qualifications— were very popular and productive. But times are different now. It's still an employer's market, and many of the managerial and professional categories may be in oversupply. For example: in the early 1990s, oil, real estate and financial people are in oversupply. Technical, research and development, and accounting executives are in short supply. But if you've been looking quite a while, a letter campaign might prove productive with potential employers in small- and medium- size companies, and in the non–public sector. Below are the two major types of campaigns and a variation.

1. *Broadcast or "shotgun" campaigns.* In this campaign, you send out a minimum of 100 letters (500 to 600 is a better number) to a variety of companies in the geographical area or industry where you'd like to work. Address the letter to the president or C.E.O. of the company in entrepreneurial or privately held firms, a vice president or a division manager in mid-size to larger companies. In a major corporation, a letter to the chairman of the board or the president will probably not be read,

Exhibit 9.2. Referral Letter

Dear Ms. Roberts:

A mutual acquaintance, Alan White of Johnson and Brown, suggested that I contact you for advice. I am presently facing an important decision about my career and am looking for a very special kind of situation in electronics, specifically chip design. Alan tells me that you have special expertise in this area and could guide me in the right direction.

The enclosed resume details my background and experience. I realize that it's unlikely that you'd have a suitable position for me in your company. However, you know the industry and the opportunities in this area. For that reason, I would be very interested in hearing your thoughts about ways to conduct my job search. I would appreciate it very much if you could arrange to see me for no longer than 15 to 20 minutes to discuss this.

I'll call you next Monday to see if we can arrange a mutually convenient meeting.

Sincerely,

except by a secretary—or at least, will not be answered. Write instead to a vice president (by name) in your area of specialization, a division or department manager or an officer one or two ranks above the position to which you might aspire.

Write a fairly general letter listing several of your accomplishments and give a brief overview of your background, as in Exhibit 9.3. This letter is a sales letter (selling you) and should have some kind of "grabber" that makes you stand out from the crowd as someone to consider further. Since you'll be sending out so many of them, you might consider putting together a mailing list, then using the merge feature of your word processor to "personalize" the letters. If you don't have this feature on your computer, then use a generic salutation, ignore the inside address, and have the letter printed. Then, precisely address the envelope individually. Don't use the labels feature of your word processor or purchase labels from a mailing company. If you do this, your letter goes into the "junk mail" category, and is guaranteed to land in the file on the floor.

Disadvantages: A broadcast campaign is expensive, both in time and in postage, duplication and stationery costs. It's seldom very effective. You'd need a really dynamite letter to draw more than a one or two percent response (a six percent response would be almost unbelievable). The lack of feedback relative to the amount of effort expended can also be depressing.

2. *Targeted* or *"rifle" campaign.* This letter campaign is similar to the broadcast campaign except that you send your letter to specific people in specific industries. Your letter is much less general and is not "canned." You research the companies to whom you will address the letters (see the reference sources in Chapter 6, "What Kind of Job Should You Search For?") so that you can mention something about the company and its products or services and tie that directly to your abilities, background and accomplishments. The letters are selling letters, much as they are in a broadcast campaign. (See Exhibit 9.4.)

Disadvantage: These campaigns are time-consuming and require a great deal of effort. Each letter is tailored to fit the situation, although a substantial portion of each can be "boiler plate" (canned information). The response rate is better than that of a broadcast campaign, but is still low. A ten percent response would be exceptional.

3. *Letters used as part of a combination campaign.* The response rate on a combination campaign is better than for either a broadcast or

Exhibit 9.3   Letter Campaign—Broadcast Letter

Dear Mr. Anderson:

In today's world, using information systems to gain a competitive edge is no longer an option - it is an imperative. Information systems executives must lead their companies in applying technology to business opportunities.

To earn the credibility needed to take on this leadership role, the information systems function must first effectively and efficiently support current operations. To achieve this objective, I have:

o   Improved responsiveness of the systems department to user needs by fostering a service-oriented attitude and producing results

o   Improved system quality and speeded the development process by implementing and using advance systems design and development tools

o   Replaced the "us vs. them" attitude common between end-users and systems personnel with a team approach.

Once credibility is established, information systems executives must have the vision and skills to participate with senior management in rethinking how the business will operate in the future. To prepare organizations for the years ahead, I have:

o   Worked with senior management to develop a blueprint for the future and implemented a tactical plan to accomplish it.

o   Helped executives become comfortable with technology so that they can spot strategic opportunities for using it.

I am a skilled, results-oriented manager who can help your organization overcome existing problems as well as prepare for the challenging decade ahead. If you need a proven information systems executive with those attributes, I can be reached during business hours at (212) 555-2088 or at my home in the evening.

Sincerely,

---

targeted campaign. You send a letter much like what you'd send in a broadcast campaign, but you end the letter with a paragraph saying something like: "I'll call you next week to discuss this further with you." Exhibit 9.5 is a good example of a letter used in a combination campaign. Then, next week, you telephone and ask to talk with that person. Your chances of at least getting to talk are substantially better than if you try to call the person cold. Should a receptionist or secretary answer when you call, you might say, "This is in reference to the letter I sent Mr. or Ms._____ last week." You will almost always be put through.

Responding to Advertisements

In the employer's market of the past few years, advertisements in a major newspaper like the *Wall Street Journal* draw as many as 500 to 1,000

Exhibit 9.4 Letter Campaign—Targeted Letter

Dear Mr. Monroe:

Your organization is one of only a handful of companies in the
Northeastern United States that could benefit from the services of a
Technical Advisor on Corporate Investment Planning. Because your
company's manufacturing processes are energy intensive, you have the
reputation for being constantly on the lookout for ways to cut costs
and increase efficiency.

Some time ago, I performed a careful analysis of the benefits to my
company of building a cogeneration plant. The plant was built and
paid for itself in only 2 1/2 years. It has saved the company in
excess of $1 million per year in energy costs.

This was only one of many feasibility studies I conducted. Some of
my other accomplishments are in similar areas that your company
might find of value:

o   I improved the cooling of high-voltage cables by burying a
      small-size water pipe alongside the cables. This innovation
      enabled four cables to do the work that previously required six.
      Savings amounted to $2 million in capital expenditures.

o   A utility project budgeted $500,000 for a capacitor bank. I
      changed some key points in the specifications and tested the
      modifications in a pilot project. The modifications worked, and
      the bank was built for half the allocated costs.

o   I carried out a complete development study for a new plant site
      in Latin America. The development opened the way for 2,000 new
      jobs, brought an income of U.S. $12 million into the country and
      provided major sales of hardware by U.S. suppliers.

In planning new projects, I generally consider the following: how to
reduce the technical and management factors to common terms that
everyone involved can understand. During the planning stages, I also
consider possible intangibles, human factors and vested interests
that might affect the project. Then, I perform pilot plan
experiments before asking the company to commit major funding.

I have a broad education with degrees in electrical engineering and
physics and a doctorate in nuclear engineering. I speak Spanish,
German, French, Italian and Portuguese. I have worked 10 years in
Europe and Canada. In addition, I've had extensive business dealings
in Brazil, Argentina, Venezuela and Colombia.

I look forward to discussing my experience with you further in a
personal interview.

Sincerely,

---

responses. Depending upon the general state of the economy, ads will
continue to draw sizable responses. Should you ignore the ads and not
respond? No. Most of the job offers are legitimate. But this depth of
response does mean that your letters and resumes must be outstanding
just to survive the selection process and be read by the people who will
be doing the hiring. Begin by analyzing the advertisement for communication style, then write the kind of letter that matches the style exhibited
by the ad.

Exhibit 9.5 Letter for a Combination Campaign

Dear Mr. Garagiolo:

Recent announcements in the local and national press highlighted the expansion efforts planned by Madison Electronics in the Southwestern U.S. All of the articles specifically mentioned your intent to source components for manufacturing in the U.S. instead of overseas. This aspect of your corporate philosophy is especially interesting to me because it matches my own philosophy. I think I could help you implement your plans.

My entire career has been focused on managing and improving the productivity of industrial operations for well-known U.S. corporations. I have been particularly successful in planning, organizing, and staffing new manufacturing facilities to assure minimum production and overhead costs, with a maximum return on investment. I have achieved these results with a minimum of labor problems and unrest along with a maximum of "human productivity" through careful inclusion of human factors in the planning process and in all later management decisions. Notable successes include:

o   Planning and start-up of two manufacturing plants within budget and timetable requirements

o   Established U.S. sources for components at 25 percent less than the costs for their Japanese counterparts

o   Increased an installation's efficiency by 20 percent with a concurrent reduction in overtime costs of 20 percent

o   Mechanized scheduling procedures to decrease lead time by 50 percent and work-in-progress by 30 percent

o   Increased final assembly by 20 percent with no increase in labor or machine retooling costs

o   Coordinated plant relocation without disrupting schedules or billing productivity.

I have held positions as a General Manager for an electronics and components manufacturing complex in Juarez, Mexico; as a Production Control Manager planning and scheduling all aspects of production in a 670,000 square-foot manufacturing facility with more than 2,500 employees; and as a consultant working with manufacturing facilities in California, Arkansas and Maryland that wanted to optimize their utilization of people, equipment and material.

I would appreciate an opportunity to meet with you personally to discuss how my experience and background could assist Madison Electronics during its exciting growth period. I will telephone you next Wednesday morning to discuss this further.

Sincerely,

Letter resume. When the advertisement is very specific and gives exact job requirements, you are looking at a High S or High C ad. A letter resume is generally the best response. Analyze the ad, underlining each requirement. For each requirement, write a statement detailing how your background meets that requirement. If you don't match on a requirement, show how your abilities and experience would equal or exceed that stated need. Follow the requirements/background experience section with a paragraph of additional information, which gives a larger picture of your strength. End by asking for an interview. Tell them that you'll bring a complete resume of your background and experience to the interview.

You can write the resume in standard paragraph form. Or you can make a chart, listing the requirements in the left-hand column and matching them to your background and experience, shown in the right-hand column. The following examples show how you might do this. Figure 9.1 shows how to do the ad analysis. Exhibits 9.6 and 9.7 show the two different ways to respond to the ad.

Figure 9.1. Analyzing an Advertisement for Requirements

Summary of Requirements

Familiar with statutory, GAAP and investment accounting

Able to scope out a project, develop an action plan and prepare concise summaries

Analyze investment laws and/or proposals and their impact on C& F portfolios as well as calculate dividend-paying ability

Perform treasury-related projects as assigned

A minimum of 5 years experience in treasury, operations or accounting, preferably research related

Strong analytical interpersonal and communications skills

Understanding of automated financial systems, including General Ledger

Capable of working independently

College degree in accounting, finance, economics or equivalent.

Exhibit 9.6. Letter Resume Response to an Advertisement,

Standard Paragraph Format

Dear Ms. Maynor:

Subject: Senior Treasury Analyst Position advertised in the May 7 Star Ledger

My background and experience fully match the requirements listed in your advertisement. After you read my qualifications, you'll agree that I'm well qualified for your Senior Treasury Analyst position.

As a Treasury Analyst with a major financial organization the past five years, I have successfully managed an investment portfolio in excess of $250 million. This position required that I be:

o   Familiar with the statutory, GAAP and investment accounting required to legally comply with regulations of the financial industry.

o   Able to scope out a project, develop an action plan and prepare concise summaries. I received top management commendation for the comprehensive, yet concise nature of my communications.

o   Able to analyze investment laws and/or proposals and their impact on the company's portfolios as well as calculate dividend-paying ability. My position papers on these topics were also well received by senior management.

o   Able to perform treasury related projects as assigned. One assignment I undertook uncovered a problem investment, which I recommended we sell. The company agreed and sold our holdings in the problem company just three months prior to that company's Chapter 11 bankruptcy.

I have ten years total experience in various treasury positions, three years experience in operations and five years experience in accounting. Almost all of my treasury experience was research related. My analytical, interpersonal and communications skills are my greatest strengths. In addition, I fulfill the other requirements mentioned in your ad. To perform the duties I held during my career, I had to understand and use automated financial systems, including General Ledger and be capable of working independently. I graduated from Boston University with a degree in finance, and a second major in accounting.

I'd like to discuss my background with you further in a personal interview at your convenience. I have enclosed is a chronological resume which details my experience further. As for a salary history, my salaries have always been competitive with those in other, similar companies here in New Jersey. I will bring a full salary history, including bonuses, to an interview, along with further details about my background and accomplishments.

Sincerely,

Selling letter. Many ads don't give much information about the job in the advertisement. They may list only the job title and a little bit about the company. (This might be a High D ad.) They may spend the entire ad selling you on the company. (These are High I ads.) Or, all you get in the ad is the job title. (Ads placed by executive recruiters are often like this. See the section on writing letters to headhunters

Exhibit 9.7. Letter Resume Response to an Advertisement,
Chart Format

Dear Ms. Maynor:

My background and experience fully match the requirements listed in your advertisement for a Senior Treasury Analyst in the May 7 <u>Star Ledger</u>. After you read my qualifications, you'll agree that I'm well qualified for this position.

<u>Job Requirements</u>	<u>My Qualifications</u>
Familiar with statutory, GAAP and investment accounting	Five years recent experience as a Treasury Analyst with J and C Investments, successfully managing an investment portfolio in excess of $250 million required that I have this familiarity.
Able to scope out a project, develop an action plan and prepare concise summaries	Received commendation from senior management for the comprehensive, yet concise nature of my analysis of the various projects that we were considering for investment.
Analyze investment laws and/or proposals and their impact on J and C portfolios as well as calculation of dividend paying ability	About 20% of my time during the last two years was spent analyzing the impact of the massive changes in investment laws resulting from the October 1987 stock market sell-off and subsequent financial industry problems.
Perform treasury-related projects as assigned.	I have successfully completed numerous special assignments. One uncovered a problem investment, which we were able to sell just three months prior to that company declaring Chapter 11.

In addition to ten years total experience in treasury positions, I worked three years in operations, and five years in accounting. Most of my treasury experience was research related. My analytical, interpersonal and communications skills are my greatest strengths. I also fulfill the other requirements mentioned in your ad. I understand and use automated financial systems, including General Ledger. I can work independently. I have a degree from Boston University in finance, with a second major in accounting.

I'd like to discuss my background with you further in a personal interview at your convenience. You asked for a salary history. My salaries have always been competitive with those in other, similar companies here in New Jersey. I will bring full details on my career, including salary history and bonuses, to an interview.

Sincerely,

and employment agencies.) Write a letter which presents yourself in the best light, giving a few of your major accomplishments, a brief description of your strengths, along with a couple of reasons why the company should consider you. Exhibit 9.7 shows a letter resume in chart format. You can include an accomplishment resume with your letter or you can omit it. In either event, mention that you'll bring a

Exhibit 9.8. Response to Nonspecific Ad

```
Dear Sr. Vice President:

Subject:   Opening for a National Sales Director, Communications
Division

During the past three years, I have been Northwest Regional Sales
Manager for Trefoil, a rapidly growing consulting firm specializing
in data processing and management consulting.  My sales background
includes awards for best performing salesperson, presented for $1.5
million sales of program analyst and programmer consultancy to
Pacific Bell and Mountain States Bell for major projects.   I was
promoted to the Seattle District Sales Manager, and in that
position I trained and supervised a group that produced the best
district sales record for the company for all five years I was the
Manager.  This record of accomplishment led to my promotion to the
Regional Manager's position.

I understand fully the communications business and the kinds of
sales opportunities within the industry.  I am an excellent trainer
and motivator of sales personnel.  The groups I have managed have
been exceptional producers, have been loyal to their company and
have had a very low turnover rate, which is relatively unusual in
this business.

I look forward to discussing my qualifications in more detail
during an interview at your convenience.   I know that I can help
your company experience the growth in the industry that you desire.


Sincerely,
```

detailed resume with you when you have your interview (which you request strongly).

Sometimes, the ads are vague and include only some "insinuations," or include phrases or suggested requirements that are ridiculous. One ad for an accountant, for instance, asked that the applicant be a CPA and have a sense of humor!

If you're interested—and many of these ads are titillating—go ahead. The author of the letter in Exhibit 9.9 responded to one such vague ad. He felt the ad called for a tongue-in-cheek sense of humor, so responded in kind.

Cover Letter for a resume. Many ads ask that you send a detailed resume. When the ad asks for a resume, send your Chronological Resume or a combination Chronological/Achievement Resume, if the ad seemed to be a High S or High C communication. If the ad was terse and to the point (High D), or a "selling" ad (High I), send an Achievement resume and write a cover letter addressing any points mentioned in the ad that aren't in the resume. And, of course, ask for an interview.

Ads now frequently ask for a salary history. Some ads even say that no one will be considered for an interview if that information isn't

Exhibit 9.9. Response to Nonspecific Ad

Dear Advertiser:

After looking at my enclosed resume, you'll probably agree that I have a most dynamic and productive background in sales and sales management. However, that background does not appear to be in the industry which you represent. But a resume cannot show the real person. Your ad describes an adventurer -- one who has had experience in selling exciting venues and putting together one-of-a-kind experiences.

What you are describing has been my avocation. On vacations, I have always searched out the novel, the unusual. I went around the world on a tramp steamer. I climbed mountains, went on rafting expeditions on white water, traveled to the steamy jungles of Brazil, even went to the Antarctic with the first commercial travel group to do so.

I have used my avocation on a "not for pay" basis for groups, too. I organized memorable special occasions as events chairperson for national Ccnventions of three different groups of which I am a member. I made all arrangements for a white water rafting experience for a local fraternal organization. I belong to the Sierra Club and to a regional archaeology association, for both of which I have organized one to three week study tours of interesting, out-of-the-way places. In all of these instances, I also prepared copy and made printing arrangements for brochures, program copy, and other "sales type" literature.

These are the kinds of experiences and the background you need for the advertised position. Putting my avocation, and my very real and solid sales management accomplishments together would give you the best of both worlds--what your company needs to develop and sell the kind of travel and adventure programs that will make your company the best in the business.

I think I'm the right person for your job. After you meet me in a personal interview, I'm sure you'll agree. I'll look forward to hearing from you.

Sincerely,

included. Most employment experts say that you can omit this information; but cover yourself by saying that you'll bring your salary history to an interview, or that your past salaries were competitive with those generally paid in the industry. You may even combine the two by saying: "My past salaries were competitive with those generally paid in the industry. I'll bring a complete salary history to an interview."

Put together as good a cover letter as you can, as fast as you can. Be very direct and straightforward—and watch the "weasel" words—the words you might use to denigrate yourself. Do not be self-effacing, and include no negatives. The cover letter has to be positive and upbeat.

Letters of Application. The Letter of Application and the Cover Letter or the Letter Resume in response to an ad are very similar in appearance. If you are writing a letter to cover your resume as your first correspondence with a potential employer, use a letter of application instead of a

Exhibit 9.10. Cover Letter for a Resume

Dear Mr. Malpass:

Subject: Director of Training Position

As indicated in the enclosed resume, I have an extensive background
in writing, preparing and presenting training programs for both
management and nonexempt personnel, both as an in-house trainer and
as a consultant. During the past five years, I also managed a group
of independent consultants who developed, prepared and presented
upwards of twenty-five seminars a month on topics varying from time
management to Advanced Lotus 1-2-3 and word processing.

As an independent consultant, I conducted training needs appraisals
for several companies, and later directed company in-house trainers
in the preparation and initial presentation of courses designed to
meet those determined needs. I know how to schedule a mix of in-
house trainers and outside consultants so that training is most cost-
effective. I have also worked with technical staff members to
develop technical training courses involving such areas as sterile
laboratory techniques and the use of quality control instrumentation
not otherwise available outside the company.

I know that Berlex would be very pleased with the contribution I
could make as Director of Training. I look forward to meeting with
you at your convenience. At that time, I can bring samples of some
of the training courses I have overseen so that you can see for
yourself the quality of the work.

Sincerely,

letter of transmittal (see the next item) because of its sales possibilities. In a letter of application, you write a detailed letter which signals that you are genuinely interested in working for the company. You explain how your qualifications meet their company's employment needs. This shows them that their company is not just one of many organizations on your potential employment scorecard. Finally, a well-written application letter enables a prospective employer to begin judging how well you might mesh with the company's work force. The letter gives you an opportunity to allow your personality to come through, which the resume, in its third-person style, does not.

Ronald E. Dulek and James A. Suchan, writing in the November-December 1988 *Business Horizons* suggest four credos to follow in writing application letters:

"1. I will always keep in mind that employers want to examine my credentials and get a sense of the kind of business person I am. I will therefore avoid manipulative organizational strategies such as gimmicky opening paragraphs and the transparent hype that characterizes many application letters. Instead, I will stick to clearly and precisely presenting my qualifications.

Exhibit 9.11. Letter Resume Sent in Response to an Agency Ad

```
Dear Executive Recruiter:

Subject:  Advertisement for Corporate Treasurer in June 20 Daily
Record

The position for which you are recruiting is of great interest to
me.   My hands-on skills in forecasting and managing cash flows
(accounts receivable, collections, disbursements, investments and
bank balances) would be of real value to you.

I have been a pioneer in cash management in Northern Illinois, and
have shared my expertise in this area as a consultant to the
largest multi-location corporations, government agencies, hospitals
and health-care organizations.  Both as chairman and a member of my
bank's product and pricing policy committees, and as head of
strategic planning, I worked with the executive management team to
produce top cash management results.

As you can see from the enclosed resume, I left banking last year
to pursue personal investment interests which I thought would fill
my interests.     I find, however, that I miss the day-to-day
interactions and mental stimulation that go with a corporate
position.   I am most eager to use my broad financial experience to
cross over into the corporate treasury area.  The opportunity your
search presents seems custom tailored to my skills.

Please telephone so that we can arrange an appointment to discuss
this opportunity further.  Thank you.

Sincerely,
```

2. I will remember that employers are busy readers who don't have time to leisurely peruse my letter. I will therefore state in the first paragraph why I am writing and what my major qualifications are. Also, I will do everything I can to make the letter as easy to read as possible.

3. I will remember that employers are intelligent, shrewd readers of application letters and not easily susceptible to insincere flattery. I will therefore not patronize them or massage their egos.

4. I will have confidence in my own qualifications; consequently, I will not feel compelled to rely on exaggerated language and complex sentences to showcase my talents."

Letter to headhunters and employment agencies. Most of these advertisements list only the job title or give little information about a position. Read the ad for whatever information you can get, then write the agency exactly as you would a potential employer. However, always include your Chronological or combination Chronological/Achievement Resume. Don't send an Achievement Resume. Your response is guaranteed to hit the wastebasket or be ignored. It doesn't have the detail these

Exhibit 9.12. Thank-You Letter (Networking)

```
Dear Alan:

Thank you for seeing me and giving me such constructive help and
advice on my job search.  At your suggestion, I contacted both Mr.
Adams and Ms. Johanssen.  Mr. Adams saw me last week, and Ms.
Johanssen today.  They were most gracious, as you said they would be,
and extremely helpful.  Mr. Adams gave me an excellent lead on a job
he knew was available in another company.  Ms. Johanssen helped me
improve the effectiveness of my resume by pointing out that I hadn't
included an important achievement related to a currently saleable
part of my experience.  She also gave me several other people to
contact for possible job leads.

I'll let you know when I get a new position.  In the meantime, I hope
to see you again at the regular association meeting.

Thanks,
```

people want and need to even consider you. Employment agencies and headhunters, because they are providing a service, are almost by definition High S.

Other Uses of Letters in Your Job Search

Letter of transmittal. Sometimes after your initial contact, potential employers contact you asking for more information or for a more detailed resume. They may send a company application, a survey or a test of some kind for you to complete and return. Write a letter stating simply what you are sending. Include other information in the letter only if it's germane to what you're sending. Restrain your fingers. The letter of transmittal could be as simple as: "Enclosed is the application for employment you asked me to complete. I have listed all my past employers and included the references you asked me to supply. If you need any further information, I'll be happy to send it."

Thank-you letters. Job-hunters all too often fail to thank those who have helped them. Resolve not to fall into this category. Write thank-you letters in the following instances:

1. To people who have helped you. Send them to friends who have given you leads; to executives who have been willing to give you suggestions for your job campaign; and to receptionists, secretaries and/or assistants who were especially nice or helpful to you when you went on an interview. These letters should be short, should mention what they did that you appreciated, and should be sincere.

2. To interviewers after an interview (especially if you had a good interview and you really want the job). Thank them for their consider-

Exhibit 9.13. Thank-You Letter to an Interviewer

```
Dear Ms. French:

Thank you for considering me for your sales engineer position.  I
came away from our meeting with a very positive feeling about your
company and my ability to contribute to your goals and objectives.
My seven years' experience as a sales engineer selling and
overseeing the installation of stainless steel sterile production
equipment for the Babcock organization highly qualifies me for the
kinds of sales and installations your company will be making.

My other qualifications would also enable me to make a significant
contribution:

o     Your sales engineers prepare and submit detailed process and
      equipment proposals.  I had a very high 78 percent close
      record on the proposals I submitted to customers during the
      past five years.

o     Your sales engineers oversee equipment installation.  My
      record here is excellent.

o     Testing after process start-ups on my installations were
      uniformly acceptable.

o     Manufacturing and maintenance staff members were able to
      operate and maintain the lines without callback because of the
      effectiveness of the training I provided.

You indicated that your hiring decision would be made by September
second.  I'll look forward to hearing from you.

Yours truly,
```

ation, summarize the main points you made during the interview. If you thought of something that you should have covered during the interview, but didn't, include that. Close the letter with a positive statement that you would really enjoy doing the particular job for them, and look forward to hearing from them soon.

If you don't want to be considered further, write the interviewer and thank him or her for interviewing you, and graciously remove yourself from contention for the position.

3. If you felt your interviewer didn't think you were qualified for the job, or the interview was generally unfavorable, you may not want to spend the time to write the interviewer. However, if you are still interested in the position, take advantage of a thank-you note to say you're still interested in the job and bring out additional reasons why you could provide the kind of services the company wants and should be considered. In the following letter, a human resources manager made several points which she felt might gain her further consideration, even though the interviewer had obviously been looking for someone with a very narrow and focused experience.

Exhibit 9.14. Thank-You Letter Sent after an Unsuccessful Interview

---

Dear Mr. Anderson:

Thank you for interviewing me on Wednesday, November 30. You're right, my experience in labor relations is limited. However, I am wholeheartedly committed to employee/company relations, and believe that I could perform the duties of the position to your satisfaction.

I'm a quick study, an avid learner, and eager to work with managers and other staff members to resolve problems. My experience with both the Wire Service Guild and the United Telegraph Workers' unions has given me great exposure to resolving grievances in a practical way.

We did have the advantage of solving problems occasionally by transferring staff members. However, transferring employees is costly, not always workable, and certainly not the only or the best way to resolve an issue. We all work within the structure that exists in our organization, whatever it is. Your company has options available to it that United Press International did not have.

Having a staff completely devoted to employee relations tells the world that you are sincere about your company's relationship with its employees. I admire your sincerity. I would bring to your Employee Relations Representative position a commitment to excellence. I believe that I could further improve your employee relations program and deal with your employees in a positive, practical and open way.

I look forward to hearing from you.

Sincerely,

Letters of acceptance. You've received a job offer. A formal notice of acceptance simply states your willingness to accept the position at the salary offered, and lists what that amount is as well as what other perquisites were offered. It should also state when you can begin work. If you have negotiated the job contractually (see Chapter 13, "Evaluating the Job Offer, Making the Decision and Beginning Work"), the letter of acceptance should include the signed contract.

Letters of rejection. Write these when you can't or don't want to accept a job offer. The key is to refuse the position graciously so that you don't antagonize the person who made the job offer. Things might change in the future, and you might want them to consider you again at a later date.

Informational letters. These run the gamut from letters giving names and addresses of references to information on your plane schedule when you're flying in for an interview. Keep the letters short and courteous; include only necessary information; and don't try to write an omnibus letter.

The Interview, Part I

You've gotten a positive response from your telephone call, your letter or your resume—you've been asked to come for an interview. The ball is in your court. Unless the job is totally different from what you want, accept the interview. You have a golden opportunity—if not for employment, then at least to practice your interview skills and learn from the experience.

When you were in the catbird seat—doing the interviewing instead of being the interviewee—you probably used interviews as much for deselection as for selection. You were literally looking to see whether a job candidate was a member of the "to be considered" or "not to be considered" group before you even thought about anything else. So, your primary goal now as an interviewee is to make it into the "to be considered" group on your initial interview. A job offer is seldom tendered on the first interview, so if you make it into the "to be considered" group, you have other opportunities to impress.

Your key to ultimate success is to show not only that you're looking for a position, but that you're ready and prepared to perform in that position. Sell yourself. Project energy, enthusiasm, interest in the interviewer, the company and the position. Remember: An interview is a deck stacked in the interviewer's favor. You are an actor walking onto a set stage. You must be positive and alert. You must be sensitive to your audience—the interviewer—and play to him or her.

General Tips on Interviewing

In planning for an interview, think about the things you looked for when you were interviewing prospective employees yourself. What did you want to know about the candidates? What characteristics did you look for in them? You wanted to know what they'd done and how they'd done it. You were vitally interested in how they'd perform for you and you wanted to know something about them as individuals.

How did you feel as the interviewer—were you nervous, or were you able to interview the candidates without stress? The shoe's on the other foot now. You're the person looking for the job. But the interviewers on the other side of the desk are not so different from you. They're looking for the same things you looked for. They want to know *what* you've done, *how well* you'll perform, *why* you're a good prospect for their company and *who* you are as an individual.

The most common interview process within medium- and large-size firms is the following: 1) an interview in the human resources department; 2) another interview by the hiring manager (the manager usually interviews only those applicants who "passed" the first interview and are recommended for further investigation by the human resources department); and 3) subsequent interviews with other members of management. The third step may be repeated several different times with different management groups, especially when the job to be filled is a key position.

In smaller firms, and most particularly in single proprietorships, partnerships and entrepreneurial firms, the interviewing process may begin at the top, and the owner, the president or vice president, the partners, or some other high-level official does the initial screening and involves other management members only on subsequent interviews, if at all. You must be prepared on your initial interview for the whole ball of wax. If you get in to see this person, you are having an interview, whether the meeting started out that way or not.

Government positions require the most interviewing. You must go through channels, not always clearly specified, to obtain an interview. At the local, state and federal level, civil service jobs almost always start with a human resources professional; and you have to fill out forms, take tests and otherwise demonstrate certain proficiencies before you ever get to interview. Then, the interview process is a two- or three-step process much like that for large companies. However, another entire level of local, state and federal level jobs is related to the political party that is in power, who you know, and sometimes, how active you've been in someone's campaign. This type of government job is filled exclusively through networking.

Interviews at not-for-profit associations are generally conducted by nonprofessionals, very often a committee composed of volunteers. The committee may be poorly organized, and have a hard time finding their focus. In this kind of interview by committee, emphasize tactics (nuts and bolts stuff) rather than strategy. Concentrate on the mission and focus of the organization. Sometimes, the interview process begins with a search firm. In this case, you must "pass" an interview with the recruiter before you can actually interview for this position.

Making Arrangements

You have an opportunity to prepare for most interviews, and you can at least partially control a number of factors related to the interview.

Timing. You can usually influence the day and time of the interview. Think back to your active employment. What days were the least hectic? Which the most? Don't set up interviews on days when interviewers are likely to be harassed. That knocks out Mondays and Fridays as interview days. Set up your interviews, then, on Tuesday, Wednesday or Thursday, if you can. Try for an appointment early in the morning, between 9 and 10 or early in the afternoon, just after lunch. If those times are out, at least ask for an appointment that is not too late in the afternoon so that the interviewers won't be too immersed in their job activities, too tired to conduct a fair interview or resentful because they have to interview you after normal working hours.

Research the Organization. Your next move is to prepare for the interview. You may already know a great deal about the prospective employer because you researched the organization early in your job campaign. Or you may know next to nothing about it. To present yourself in the best light, and to make your self-marketing strategy work, you *must* be informed about the company so that you can show your understanding of the organization's situation, and can make the necessary tie- ins between your abilities and the potential employer's needs.

Go back to some of the same sources you checked when you were preparing your marketing campaign. Look for information in the library, the various directories, and the information sources mentioned in Chapter 4.

If it's a small company, you may want to telephone the librarian at the newspaper in the town closest to the interview location. Or an equally good, and easier, method is to consult a computer data base. You have several choices here. One option is to contact a company whose sole purpose is to research companies for prospective job candidates. For a relatively small fee, you will get a complete printout on whatever information has been printed about the firm in business publications, technical journals and other media. This service can include information about competitors, what the company said in its press releases, security analysts' published information about the company's potential, information about key executives, stock ownership data, etc.

A second way to manage a computer search is through your local library. Most local libraries now subscribe to various informational data bases. (More than 700 public data bases are accessible, although most libraries only use a few.) If you go this route, you're charged only for the computer search time, the telephone call and the printout. A third method, if you have a home computer and a modem, is to contact one of the public data base services such as Dialog or CompuServ, and conduct your own search.

If you still don't have the information you'd like, you have a few more options. Call your interviewer's secretary or the company's public relations department and ask for information or brochures on the company. At least, find out what the company or organization does. Should this be unproductive, then ask the secretary or receptionist some questions about the company while you wait for your interview. If all else fails, ask for information during the interview. Say something like, "I tried to locate information about your company. I couldn't find out anything in public sources. But the position sounded so interesting, I felt that I just had to find out about it." Or, you can ask them very early on, "Exactly what does your company do? I tried to research the company, but couldn't find any information in public sources."

Ready for the Road

You're ready to leave for the interview. You've made the necessary changes in your wardrobe and appearance (see Chapter 2) and you'll make the best impression you can. But just to be sure, run through the following checklist:

Personal Appearance

❐ Dress neatly. Be sure your shoes are polished and heeled and that your clothing matches the industry style, and is in quiet, conservative colors.
❐ Hair. Men, you've had a recent haircut; women, your hair is clean and attractively styled in a current business style.
❐ Women: take special care with your makeup. Wear eye makeup and blush, but toned down. Wear tasteful, "quiet" jewelry, or no jewelry. Men: no chains (and no earrings!)
❐ Hands: Prior to the interview, check to be sure you don't have ink on your hands from reading a paper or magazine in the waiting room. If your hands are clammy, wash them just before going in. If your hands perspire, use an antiperspirant or spritz a mild, alcohol-based cologne

on your hands to remove moisture. Women can wear nail polish, but men shouldn't even wear clear polish.

Briefcase

☐ Carry one if you will be taking work samples or a portfolio.

☐ Don't leave a copy or sample if it contains important information which could be of value to the interviewer. The company might think it doesn't need you since they've already picked your brains.

☐ If you're interviewing for a position where you normally wouldn't need work samples or a portfolio, don't carry them along in your briefcase. If the interviewer is interested, you'll have an "in" for another interview, where you can show what you've done.

☐ Resumes. Always carry copies of each of your different styles of resume. But don't offer one unless the interviewer asks for it. Reread all resumes in advance of the interview.

☐ Salary history. Bring a list summarizing your salary history. You may need this for filling out applications or to answer very specific money-related questions. (Try to hold this for the second or third interview, if possible. Sometimes the interviewer insists on exact salary figures; and if you're interested in the job, you'd better be prepared to answer accurately.)

☐ References. Carry a list of business references, complete with correct addresses and telephone numbers. You will also need this information if you are asked to fill out an application. However, as a general rule of thumb, don't give references unless you are seriously being considered for the position. You don't want to bother your references unnecessarily.

Travel

An obvious, but important point. Leave early enough to get to the interview on or before time. If you're driving, check the route on your map the evening before. If you've flown into an area the night before the interview, check at the hotel for some idea of the driving time (if you've rented a car) and best route, or arrange for a taxi to pick you up early enough to get to the interview on time. Of course, some companies arrange beautifully for the "care and feeding" of their management-level interviewees. In this case, you'll be picked up by someone from the company and driven to the interview in plenty of time.

The Preliminaries

Too often, you feel as though you are running a gauntlet just to get in to see the interviewer. At a factory or a research site, you may have to check in with the guard at the gate, sign in and go through a pass or badge routine, undergo a search-and-find mission to locate the office and so on. Especially when you're already nervous, these delays may seem interminable—but they're just part of the drill. And you have to allow for them.

OK. You're now into the sanctum sanctorum where the interview will occur. You're ready. What other barriers do you have to hurdle?

The secretary, receptionist, "assistant to" or other staff member. Be as polite and cordial to staff members as you will be to the actual interviewer. Accord them status. Don't talk down to them or treat them as lesser beings.

Don't tell the secretary or staff members what position you will be interviewing for. Respond with something like, "I'm here to interview with Mr. (or Ms.) X. He (or she) is expecting me."

Filling out the application forms. Many companies have become shrewd about the use of resumes as hiring devices. Resumes are not legal documents, and don't have the force of the law behind them. They're generally not signed and don't have a notarized statement testifying to their veracity. Therefore, many companies require that even candidates for top executive positions complete a company employment application *before* they will begin an interview.

A reminder: Don't give wrong schooling information. This is now one of the few permissible and checkable sets of information which companies are allowed to get before you're hired. Yet a nationwide survey a few years ago showed that education was also the most lied-about item on resumes and applications. An application is a legal document—if you lie on it and are found out, it's a fireable offense. Use your chronological resume to fill out the application accurately. Be especially neat and be careful to answer all the questions. Occasionally an application form will contain illegal questions. (See the list of questions that are illegal to use on applications and interviews in the next chapter, The Interview, Part II.) You can choose to answer the question if you want. Or, you can do as most knowledgeable applicants do these days: Fill in these blanks with NA (not applicable) or draw a dash across the response blank.

The wait. Use your waiting time to find out about the company, to check your appearance again, to review the answers you prepared to questions that might be asked, to go over your resume one more time, and to focus in on the place and your purpose for being there. If any brochures, annual reports or advertising pieces on the company products or services are in the waiting area, look them over for additional background information.

Talk pleasantly to the secretary or receptionist. You can often pick up useful information without being overtly curious. And do ask how your interviewer's name is pronounced if you're not sure.

You have no problem if you're told the interview will be delayed. But when it's more than 20 minutes late, ask how long the delay will be. Say something like, "Is Mr. or Ms. Y aware that I'm here?"

Should the delay run to 45 minutes or more, you run a risk. They've made you wait. Without any kind of rancor, comment something like, "I had an appointment at 10:00. I would like to reschedule the appointment, if possible." However, if you were flown in or drove a long distance for the interview, you must wait, rechecking every 10 minutes or so without appearing nervous. Some companies actually delay interviews as a sort of test to see how you react to and manage stress.

The Actual Interview

The order of events varies with each interview and interviewer. Remember, though, that most interviewers are predisposed in your favor. They want to hire someone—and most of the time, they'd as soon it were you. Most people conducting interviews are not professional interviewers. Interviewing is just a part of their job—and a part they're usually not very good at.

You'll generally see one of three types of interviewers: (1) *Self-made individualists* pride themselves on their ability to size people up. They're sure of themselves and conduct their interviews accordingly; (2) *Inexperienced interviewers* and the kind of interviewers you see far too often in the not-for-profit sector are unsure of themselves and how to begin. These are the most nervous interviewers and may spend too much time on small talk before leading up to ask any of the nitty-gritty questions they feel are essential; (3) *Professional human resources department interviewers* know their business. They may be nondirective and low key, but they will be relevant. They'll also maintain reins on the direction and pace of the interview.

Some general tips for the interview:

Handshake.

❐ Use a strong, firm, "normal" handshake. Slide your hand into the other person's hand to avoid hitting or crunching rings.

☐ If the interviewer offers his or her hand when you meet at the beginning, take it. Otherwise, don't offer to shake hands yourself. These days, both business men and business women routinely shake hands when the interviewer offers.

☐ After the interview is over and rapport is established, you can initiate the handshake.

Eye contact

☐ Look your interviewer straight in the eyes and avoid shifting your eyes away or down.

☐ In a group interview situation, begin by looking at the questioner, then slowly look around to include everyone in the group in your answer.

☐ Wear glasses if you normally do so. That way, you can see properly.

Body language

Yours

☐ Sit comfortably in the chair.

☐ Don't fold your arms over your chest. This is a blocking move, and says something like "show me." For a similar reason, don't put your hands behind your head. That's perceived as an aggressive move.

☐ If you cross your legs, do it toward the interviewer. Keep the contact open. Then, periodically, recross your legs (across the calves or ankles) to avoid having them go to sleep.

☐ Keep your hands away from your mouth and face. This is read as a nervous gesture, indicating you're unsure of yourself. In fact, keep your hands down, preferably in your lap.

☐ Try to avoid making any kind of too quick, nervous movement.

☐ Lean slightly towards the interviewer, if you can. This denotes alertness and paying attention.

Theirs

☐ Watch their position with regard to you. Are they sitting higher than you, or do they keep you standing for what seems a little too long? Both of these are power plays.

☐ Have they placed you in a confrontational position, directly across the desk from them, or have they seated you at a more friendly right angle position?

❏ What about their arms and legs? Have they crossed their arms across their chest or put their arms behind their heads (both blocking or aggressive moves). Are their legs crossed so that the top leg points away from you (they're keeping you out) or crossed toward you (they're interested and open to what you are saying).

❏ What about the position of their hands? Salespeople say that they know they're not making their sell when customers cover their mouths with their hands. On the other hand, if their hands are under their chins, they are seriously considering the points that you are making.

Don't put anything on your interviewer's desk. If you happen to interview with a High S (and human resources departments are full of High S's), remember that they are very possessive—and you would be encroaching on their territory.

Don't chew gum—or anything else.

Don't lose your sense of humor in an interview. If the interviewer says something that is obviously intended to be funny, laugh—or at least smile. However, be very careful using humor yourself. Your interviewer may have a hidden agenda and take great offense at something you think is innocuous and inoffensive.

Formality/Informality

❏ Don't go to a first-name basis unless the interviewer requests that you do so. The interviewer may consider it disrespectful. Age can play a part here. Especially when your first interview is in the human resources department, you may be interviewed by someone who is young enough to be your son or daughter. The temptation is very strong to go directly to a first-name basis just because you're older and have a lifetime of receiving deference from younger people. Resist the temptation.

❏ Avoid using a first name at all if you haven't been given permission. Use the last name of the interviewer with Dr., Mr., Miss, Mrs., or Ms. But be careful with Ms.—some women don't like the term. If you'll be speaking with a woman and don't know her marital status, either ask the receptionist or secretary ahead of time, or ask the interviewer directly, "Is it Miss or Mrs._____?"

❏ When the interviewer has a difficult name, write the name correctly with phonetic respelling so you won't make a mistake.

Identify the interviewer's communication style. Are you faced with a High D, a High I, a High S or a High C? (See Chapter 4.) Make your judgment early in the interview and modify your responses accordingly.

Don't appear to control the interview. Listen carefully, then answer questions thoughtfully. (More on this in the next chapter.)

Chemistry is important in an interview. But even if rapport isn't there, *don't blow the interview.*

❐ The chemistry may be wrong because one or both of you takes an instant dislike to the other.
❐ The interviewer may remind you of someone you don't like.

Don't smoke

❐ Even if the interviewer smokes, don't do it yourself. Smoking is now a deselector in many companies. They're consciously looking for nonsmokers. Research on smoking employees indicates that they are off sick more days from work, have more costly illnesses, and may cost a company several thousand dollars a year more than do non-smoking employees.[1]
❐ Smoking may interfere with your ability to handle the interview, even though it does give you something to do with your hands.
❐ Even if the other person suggests that you smoke if you'd like, you'd be wise to avoid it. Nonsmoking has become a major health and personal preference issue, so you might be playing into the interviewer's personal prejudices.
❐ Absolutely no cigars or pipes. Many managers and employers have a whole set of sterotypes which they falsely apply to cigar and pipe smokers.

Health

If you're asked a question about your health, answer "excellent." If you answer anything else, you can dig yourself a hole. But should you find yourself coming down with a cold or the flu, call ahead of time and tell them you're catching a cold or flu, and ask if they'd prefer to reschedule the interview.

---

[1] A survey conducted by Robert Half International and reported in both the *Wall Street Journal* and *Reader's Digest* (March 1990, p. 17) indicates that one in four employers would reject a smoker competing for a post with an equally qualified nonsmoker.

Interviewing tricks

Some unscrupulous interviewers engage in underhanded tricks to find out your reactions to stress. Some of the tricks that have been reported by interviewees:

❏ Rocking chair. One leg of the chair may actually have been shortened to make it rock. Comment, "There seems to be something wrong with this chair." Change chairs if you can. Don't sit there and accept discomfort.
❏ Don't sit on a low couch if you can avoid it. You may sink into it too far, be unable to maintain alert posture, or be placed at a disadvantage because you are lower and have to look up at the interviewer (you are in a position of subordination).
❏ The interviewer can use distance or height to your disadvantage—can place you too far away or too close for your comfort level.
❏ You may be seated so that the sun or a light shines in your face. Tell the interviewer that you'd like to move so that you can see him or her.

Lunch or other meals

❏ If you are asked to join the interviewer for lunch, by all means, go ahead.
❏ Don't order expensively. And don't order anything that could be messy—no pasta sauces! When you're nervous, as you are bound to be a little, you don't need to decorate your tie or your blouse.
❏ When you are asked if you'd like a cocktail and you either don't drink or don't want to drink, don't say, "I never touch the stuff." Join in by ordering Perrier or club soda with a twist. If the others in the party are having drinks and you choose to join, stay well behind. More than one or two drinks may make you slur your words or make a misstatement. But wait to order a drink until after the interviewer does. Then match the drink type, and preferably have only one. The interviewer may be checking your interest in, capacity for, and tolerance of alcohol.

Follow up after the interview. Write a thank-you note to the interviewer. The letter should be brief, but you can use it to amplify important points not covered to your satisfaction, correct possible misconceptions or transmit supplemental information the interviewer requested. The thank-you letter is a superb place to summarize the interview and strengthen those two or three clincher points you want the interviewer to remember. It's also a good idea to send a thank-you note to an especially helpful secretary, receptionist or other staff member.

Coping with a Stress Interview

Welcome to the stress interview. Instead of an interviewer, you've got an interrogator—you feel as though it'll only be a matter of a few minutes before "they" come and take you to be finger printed and have a mug shot taken.

The stress interview is the one in which you're treated as though you're the enemy. The interviewer asks you a number of offensive questions that are designed to put you on the defensive or to make you blow your cool. The physical setting may also be deliberately uncomfortable—the room is full of smoke, has inadequate lighting, heating or cooling, uncomfortable chairs or too low a couch for you to sit on comfortably, or you may be asked to sit so that you have to face a bright window and can't see the interviewer's face.

In a tight job market, companies tend to use these "grilling" interviews to "separate the men from the boys, the women from the girls." They're a trick—and it's one you can learn to play.

First of all, don't put up with an unpleasant environment. Ask politely to sit elsewhere or to move so that you don't have to face a light or the window. Comment on the lack of heat or cooling in a commiserating fashion. "Gee, it must be tough to have to work when the heating (or cooling) isn't adjusted for your comfort. I hope they get it fixed for you soon."

Second, refuse the invitation to go on the defensive (or the offensive, if you happen to be a High D). Practice responding to tough questions (see the list in the next chapter) so that if you're asked one, your response will be easy and relatively automatic. You want to answer tough questions in a sincere, direct manner. You try to move through the volley of unpleasantness as fast as you can so that you can get on to the meat of the interview.

Also consider your own hot buttons. What kind of comments or questions tend to put you on the defensive? What in your background or experience could be embarrassing? What is on your resume (or isn't on there) that might need some explanation? Prepare these answers in advance, too. People who regularly conduct stress interviews have an absolutely uncanny ability to go for the jugular. And they'll be successful if you're not ready.

But if you've been subjected to a stress interview and handle yourself with confidence and aplomb, you'll find that you've made a conquest. They'll be trying to get you signed, sealed and delivered.

Many people say they don't want to work for a company that would employ stress interviews.

That's unrealistic. As you are fully aware, many jobs out there are full of daily stress. It's not unreasonable for companies to want to know how you react. If you keep your cool and respond well under fire, they'll be more likely to want you. That's the kind of executive timber they must have if they're going to survive in the tough competitive environment of today.

Multiple Interviewers

A relatively new trend in business interviewing is the "interview by committee." You are interviewed by a committee of from three to eight members. It's difficult to identify the one person who is the lead decision-maker—and in fact, there may be several decision-makers, with the person who ultimately gets the job being the one who has made the fewest mistakes with the group as a whole. It is difficult to identify individual personalities early enough in the interview. You may already have done some damage before you have time to sort people out.

When faced with a committee, you do want to try to answer a question in the style of the questioner. You want to look at the person who asked the question, and answer directly to him or her, looking away at the other members of the committee only incidentally during your response. If one person tends to monopolize the questioning, then you should make a concerted effort to bring in the others on the committee, and to include them in your answer by looking at each of them for at least one or two sentences in your response.

Several traps exist for the unwary in the multiple-interviewer situation. First, the contact with several people tends to make you more nervous than interviewing with a single person. These interviews are energy draining, and require you to make a much higher level of personal energy investment. You may be either too laid back or too up-tight. Second, you can easily get caught up in the "good cop, bad cop" routine. You may find yourself being led into areas which you don't want to dwell on, and answering the questions because the person who asked the questions is playing the "good cop."

Third, you may discover yourself empathizing with the person you met or interviewed first, and responding or deferring to him or her and not paying enough attention to others in the group.

The group interview is widely used by nonprofit charitable organizations; the interviewers are generally nonprofessionals and each member tends to have a different and separate agenda. The questions tend to be narrow in focus, and you have to direct the discussion into the more general areas which the interviewers need to consider.

Colleges, universities and many research laboratories are collegial in nature. They use the multiple interview because they want to find out how you would "fit in" with the other members of their group. They also are very concerned about your specific area of expertise, and how it helps make their work unit more complete. The questions in these instances will tend to be much more technical and/or work-oriented. You may also get involved in philosophical discussions, into matters of style, of corporate culture and of specific projects.

The Second, Third and Fourth Interviews
The second interview is really easier than the first. You've already survived the initial screening process. You know more about the company now. And, your first interviewer has a vested interest in you. He or she has essentially said you're all right. So, you may be able to ask and get the ammunition you need to sail safely through the next interview.

With lower-level employees, the job offer is typically made on or after the second interview. But with mid- and top-level executives and managers, four and five interviews before hiring are not uncommon.

If your first interview was with someone in personnel, the second interview will probably be set up with the person to whom the position will report, or if the job is a top-level position, your interview may be with the board of directors or the executive committee. If either of these is the case, you might call the original interviewer and ask if you should know anything specific before you meet with the next interviewer(s). You can also ask if there would be any objections to your making a direct call to the interviewer before you go in for the interview.

Since there will usually be no objection, call the second interviewer. Say something like, "I'm looking forward to meeting with you on (*date*). Would you like me to prepare anything in advance or bring along anything special to our meeting?" If you get specific requests, then collect them and bring them along to the interview. In any case, you've introduced yourself pleasantly to your interviewer, acknowledging that you're ready to do whatever you can to enhance your chances.

A second interview can follow the same track as a first interview—or it can be entirely different. It depends upon who's interviewing you and whether this will be someone to whom you'd be reporting or someone higher up. If it's the person you'd report to, expect the interview to be more direct and job-related. If the meeting is with someone nearer the top, you may have a relatively general interview in which you'll be expected to talk about your personal goals and objectives; about the company's goals and objectives, and bottom line; and about the contribution you would be expected to make.

Ask the first interviewer if he or she is going to introduce you to the second interviewer. If the answer is yes, upon your arrival ask the first interviewer for a briefing on what you can expect. You'll get at least an idea of the timetable and may gain other valuable insights. Also, when you're introduced by someone else in the company, you get a little bit of rub-off halo. The interview will get off to a friendly start, and the second interviewer may be predisposed in your favor.

One other suggestion. Before the second (and subsequent) interviews, ask for annual reports, brochures, descriptive information, catalogs and any other information sources available. Then bone up even more thoroughly on the company before the second interview than you did for the first. You'll give more informed responses. And the interviewers will be impressed by your interest in the company and your attention to detail.

Mock Interviews

Many applicants talk too much during the interview. They're so uncomfortable that they jump in and fill even a moment of silence with words. They offer too much information, not choosing carefully enough what they tell the interviewer. And, they don't ask enough questions themselves, to get the information they need about the position to make a valid judgment.

How do you become better at interviewing? You plan for different types of interviews, then you practice them with friends, relatives or other job-hunters. Start with this technique:

1. Read through the list of questions you may be asked and should be able to answer in the next chapter. Choose 15 or 20 that you think would be representative. Include at least two of the bad ones you hope you won't be asked. Organize your questions and answers on a "crib" sheet. (As you read the next chapter, mark the questions that fit this criteria.)

2. Use the list to prepare yourself for interviews. Read each question to yourself, then formulate what you think would be an appropriate response to make to a High D interviewer. After you've come up with answers for the High D, go through the complete process again for each of the other three communications styles.

3. Ask someone to help you by acting as an interviewer. Explain that you'd like to practice responding to different kinds of interviewers, and

ask them if they're willing to role-play with you. Tell them a little about the way a person who's communicating in a High D style would behave, then ask them to conduct a mock interview using the questions on the crib sheet. You're not trying for a complete interview, just the part where you're called on to respond to information-gathering questions.

4. Go through the question-and-answer procedure for the High D. Listen for feedback on the effect your answers are having. If you think you've fouled up an answer, ask to try it again. Record the interview on a tape recorder.

5. After you've gone through the questions, ask the "interviewer" for feedback. Which answers were good, which needed work, how did you handle the tough ones, what suggestions does he or she have to make? Work together to develop better answers on the ones that weren't so good. Listen to the tape to locate exact responses. (You may choose to listen to the answers alone later, if your time together is limited.)

6. Repeat the interview in High I style, then High S and High C.

After you feel you have your question responses firmly in hand, practice a more free-flowing interview. For this interview, begin with a newspaper advertisement for a position in which you're interested. Glean as much information about the job and the company as you can from the advertisement and the information sources that are readily available to you.

Give the ad to the person who is to conduct your mock interview. Ask that the interview be conducted as though you were actually being interviewed for the position in the ad. The interviewer can act in any style he or she wishes (or use his or her own style). Go through the entire interview process, making it as lifelike as possible. Record the session, on videotape, if that medium is available, or at least tape the session for later playback and review.

What to look for in the critique and playback:

❐ Were you responsive to the clues and cues you got from the interviewer?

❐ Were your answers clear and convincing? Did they give the interviewer a positive picture of you?

❐ What about your voice tone and inflection? Did you show stress in your voice or did you hesitate or stumble unduly when you responded to the difficult questions? (Be sure you include a couple of the really tough ones. A real interviewer will ask at least one, without fail.)

❐ Were you stepping on the interviewer's lines—talking too much, or not giving him or her enough time to react?

❐ Did you understand correctly what the interviewer said to you and make an appropriate response?

❐ What about your appearance? Were you obviously and visibly nervous?

❐ What about your gestures, your posture and facial expressions? Did you look at the interviewer and maintain eye contact? Did you appear alert and interested in what the interviewer said?

❐ When you do begin going on interviews, try these tricks to ward off feelings of rejection: Depersonalize the interview (I'm only one of many trying for this job); don't make it all or nothing (it could be mine—it's not an impossibility); don't blame the interviewers (they don't think and behave your way, but how they do is probably all right for their situation); don't live in the past (don't dredge up past failures prior to your interview—they don't pertain to the here and now); don't get mad at "the system" (follow the rules, everyone else has to and you have to, too); take the spotlight off of yourself (sell your skills and abilities, concentrate on the interviewer's problems and show how you can help solve them); see yourself in the new role (form a positive mental picture of yourself at the interview); and keep your sense of humor.

After each real interview, you should similarly "debrief" yourself. Were you able to evaluate the communications style of the interviewer? Did you feel that most of your responses were on target? What questions should you have answered better? Work on adequate responses. Write them down and practice saying them.

The Interview, Part II

Question and Answer Techniques

Chapter 10 ended with a suggestion that you practice in advance by going through mock interviews with friends, family or other unemployed executives. What you want to develop is your ability to answer the really tough questions (see the last part of this chapter). You also want to hone your ability to parry unwanted questions and to ask yourself for the information necessary to evaluate the company, the position and any offer that is made.

The general purposes of questioning are to collect information, to evaluate how someone thinks or feels, and to confirm facts and attitudes uncovered by other questions or sources.

Both you and the interviewer use questions to build rapport, understand the situation and move the interview along. Questions come in two major forms, open-ended and closed. Open-ended questions allow answerers to give free responses and to direct responses into areas of concern to them. They often begin with who, what, when, where, which, how or why. Either you or the interviewer can direct open-ended questions to a wide variety of uses:

❒ to open conversations and provide background
❒ to ask for information
❒ to follow up, to ask for elaboration
❒ to probe for causes, additional or related information
❒ to check understanding, determine awareness of pros and cons
❒ to ask for reasons why (Why do you suppose...?)
❒ to ask for suggestions
❒ to determine sources
❒ to check knowledge or memory

Closed questions, on the other hand, are questions that have only one or a restricted number of answers. They can usually be answered with a yes or no. You use these to narrow your field of inquiry, to get confirmation and to determine that you're on the right track with your questions.

Closed questions usually begin with some form of the verbs *be, do* or *have*: is, are, were, isn't, aren't, weren't; do, does, don't, doesn't; have, has, haven't and hasn't. Closed questions can also begin with should, would, will, won't and so on.

The examples in Exhibit 11.1 illustrate the difference between open-ended and closed questions:

Exhibit 11.1

Open-ended Questions	**Closed Questions**
What hobbies do you have that might help you perform well in this position?	Do you understand what this job entails? (This is a question calling for a "yes" or "no" response. If you are asked this one, after you say, "yes" or
What can you tell me about yourself that makes you think you're a good salesperson?	"no," continue either with a summary of what you understand or with a question of your own to clarify what they mean.)
Based on what I've told you about this organization, why do you thnk you'd like to work for us?	Did you have enough opportunity for advancement in your last job?
How do you feel about the hours?	Do you think you could work for a younger person?

In addition, you may ask or be asked semi-open questions which have only one answer, such as, "When can you begin work?" or "Which do you prefer, a straight salary or a lesser salary plus a bonus tied to your performance?"

You'll both answer and ask general and specific questions. Interviewers use general questions early in the interview to open topics, to begin exploring areas of common interest and to define areas of concern. They use specific questions later to focus on details, gather specific information and verify their understanding of what you've told them. You will ask the same kinds of questions of your interviewers, although to begin with, you're more likely to be the responder than the asker.

Two kinds of questions are particularly important to you. The first are *strategic questions*. Strategic questions are primarily offensive weapons. You use them to uncover information about the employer's needs and attitudes. For instance, if the interviewer says something like, "I'm afraid you're overqualified for this position," a strategic question for you to ask might be, "The word 'over-qualified' puzzles me. Why do you say that, Mr. Ellis?" You ask a question on the offense, rather than becoming defensive—but without reacting emotionally or negatively. A strategic question, then, keeps you in charge. At the same time, you gain enough information about the needs and attitudes of the employer to deal productively with the situation.

The other kinds of questions you'll use are *tactical questions*. Tactical questions are primarily defensive weapons used to sidestep or parry difficult or nuisance questions and to shift the psychological initiative from the interviewer to yourself. For example, the interviewer asks one of those really tough questions such as, "Why did you leave your last job? In the past 10 years, you've worked for several companies." Rather than answering the question outright, turn the conversation back on the interviewer by asking something like, "You mean you're concerned about the fact that I've held several jobs recently?" After the interviewer responds, you could go into the reasons why you took and left the various jobs, particularly if you took them to learn something new, you lost them through mergers or because you'd finished your assignment. (This last is particularly true for engineers and technical people.)

Both strategic questions and tactical questions can be used at any point in the interview where they seem appropriate. Either type can be open-ended or closed, depending upon how you word the question.

Interviewer: This job requires a real specialist. The right person for the job must have the right kind of training and experience.

Applicant: What kind of training and experience would that be, Mr. Murray? (open-ended, strategic question)

Interviewer: We won't make our final decision until after we've interviewed the two other candidates who fit our initial specifications. It should take us a little while longer.

Applicant: Do you plan to make your final decision by the end of next month? (closed strategic question)

Questions to Answer and Ask

It is a good idea to keep the following guidelines in mind, according to James E. Challenger, the president of Challenger, Gray and Christmas, a national Chicago-based outplacement consulting firm:[1]

> The strategy for success in an employment interview is to be who the interviewer wants you to be. It is done by listening for clues as to what he or she wants and responding with the appropriate answer.
>
> All interviewers are seeking the answer to the basic question of why they should hire you as opposed to at least six other candidates who are equally qualified. How well you address yourself to their image of the ideal candidate will usually determine whether or not you get the job offer.

Questions You Should be Able to Answer

The key to success or failure in a competitive employment interview often hinges on how you answer five questions, says Challenger. Those questions and why your answers are important to the interviewer are shown below.

1. *"Why are you interested in us?"* Most jobs that job-seekers accept have not been publicized and may not even have been created yet when the job-seeker comes to call. Rather than answer how you can fit in, tell the interviewer how good you are at what you do and demonstrate that you are so well qualified that the company cannot do without you. Let them figure out how you can best fit into their plans.

2. *"Tell me about your current and previous employers."* Don't criticize current or former employers because it will reflect unfavorably on you. But don't go to the other extreme and give your superiors all the credit for your professional development. Take as much credit for what you've done as you can. This is what impresses the interviewer.

3. *"Tell me about your strengths and weaknesses."* Concentrate on the strengths and avoid the weaknesses. Even a seemingly harmless statement such as "lack of patience with inefficiency" is dangerous. It

---

[1] From a press release, June 25, 1984. This comment and Challenger's list of the five questions you should be able to answer are still valid today.

can be read as a sign that you have a quick temper, are hard on subordinates or can't handle a difficult situation without losing your cool.

4. *"What are the best and worst aspects of your present (or last) job?"* As far as you are concerned, there are no worst aspects. It is much better to talk in terms of the challenges that confronted you and what you did to meet those challenges.

5. *"Tell me something about yourself."* Responding correctly to this directive is very important to your success. Think in terms of what the interviewer wants to hear. He or she wants to know how good you are, but also if there is anything about you that could cause problems. Tell about all the good stuff, and avoid the latter.

Challenger's questions are the easy ones. As an unemployed older executive, the toughest questions are those that go for the jugular—the questions that show age bias or touch an emotional nerve—say, why you're not currently employed.

The preceding questions are general and could be asked in interviews with applicants for almost any job. You will also be asked questions to elicit more details about the information, achievements, job responsibilities and duties you listed on your resume. Many of these will be strictly job-related questions. A person applying for a sales position, for example, might be asked questions such as:

❑ What kind of products and services have you sold before?
❑ What were your typical customers like?
❑ How would you go about selling our products (or services) to a typical customer?
❑ Which type of selling gives you a greater satisfaction: frequent small successes or many turndowns followed by a really big success?
❑ Do you think selling requires better health than inside work?

Your ground is safer on job-related questions. You can answer the questions in a straightforward manner, without feeling trapped. Answer both the general questions and the specific job-related questions according to your analysis of your interviewer. If you think your interviewer is a High D or High I, use a broad brush in your responses. Offer detail only if you are asked for more. With a High S or High C, respond fully and in detail from the beginning. A High S or High C considers broad brush responses to be dissembling.

Following are questions that you might expect to be asked on an interview. Develop a good answer for each of these questions. Most of them are "loaded," even those that seem straightforward.

Exhibit 11.2

Questions You Might be Asked   Points You Should Make

Related to your last or current job:

1. Why did you decide to leave your present (last) job?

Whatever you do, be positive. Do not bad-mouth the company, your boss or other staff members. Try to have some plausible, positive reason why you left: You were looking for a position with more of a challenge; you were interested in making a career change; the company was in financial difficulties and was reorganizing. *As a highly paid executive, I was expendable.*

2. What are some of the things that your company might have done to be more successful?

You can be very positive about this. You might discuss retargeting your marketing efforts, developing new products, tighten up on purchasing, etc. If asked, why didn't you do these things, your response should be that you did, but not soon enough. *In some of the areas, I did not have responsibilities which would have enabled me to do these things.*

3. Describe a typical day in your last job.

Choose a day where you had a number of high-level, executive actions, with decisions to make.

4. What is (was) your boss's title, and what are (were) his/her functions?

The questioner is trying to find out if you in fact did the job you claimed to have done. If your boss did not have a title that was commensurate with what he or she actually did, give the title one level higher (if you know in detail what they did). This may have been the person you really reported to, anyway.

5. What did you do on your last job (current job) to make yourself more effective?

Describe training, schooling, seminars, the books and journals you regularly read, the professional societies to which you belong.

6. What kind of references do you think your previous employers will give you? Why?

If you don't know, ask someone (Forty Plus does this) to check your references. The desired response: *I expect them to be good because I did a good job for them.*

7. How do you explain the diversity of jobs that you've held? The positions don't seem to be in a logical progression.

The questioner has identified you as a "job-hopper" and legitimately wants to know why your jobs have been so diverse. Be careful to explain why they are, in fact, a logical progression, considering your overall career objectives.

8. How did you like working for your last employer?

This question is really loaded. Be careful. *The boss was wonderful.* End of discussion.

9. Where do you think the power comes from (came from) in your organization? Why?

What the interviewer is looking for is how well you understand the structure of the organization. They also might want to know if you were empowered.

10. How long have you been out of work now?

Answer honestly, without emotion. Don't elaborate unless asked, then do so simply.

11. What suggestions did you make in your last job to cut costs, increase profits, improve morale, increase output, etc.? What results did you get, and how did you go about getting them? What were you proudest of?

Use accomplishment statements from your resume to answer this one. Explain or elaborate as the interviewer shows interest. This gives you a chance to brag without seeming boastful. You can talk about the special skills you have that enabled you to pull off these accomplishments.

12. How did your previous employers treat you?

This is another version of Challenger's question, "Tell me about your current and previous employers." Watch your answer carefully. So far as you're concerned, your other employers treated you fine.

13. What would you like to have done more of on your last job?

Answer honestly, but concisely. Be sure the answer is in keeping with the job you are interviewing for.

14. In your capacity as a_____at X company, what did you actually do? Tell me in detail.

Describe briefly, in terms of duties and responsibilities.

About yourself:

1. Tell me a little about yourself.

Take no more than two minutes to give a summary of who you are: where you came from, where you were educated, where you've worked. Then ask a question related to the company with which you are interviewing.

2. Tell me three (four or more) characteristics about yourself.

Same answer as number one, above. Talk only about work-related characteristics and abilities.

3. What would you consider your most significant (three at the most) accomplishments in your business life?

Lucky you if you are asked this one. Choose the one (or two) best accomplishments from your accomplishment resume and discuss them in a little more detail than they appear on your resume.

4. What specific strengths did you bring to your last job?

This gives you a chance to legitimately brag. Elaborate on your thumbnail sketch.

5. What has been your biggest failure (three biggest failures) or frustrations in your business life? Why?

Be careful. This question is a trap. You don't want to set a trend that makes you sound a failure. Trusting someone who was not trustworthy might be acceptable, but it is not acceptable to blame someone for a failure which you should have prevented.

Not enough capital to complete a project might be acceptable. You might even say that the failures and frustrations you had were not big enough or important enough to become an issue. *I did have some things that I learned lessons from, though.*

6. Think of something (or more than one thing) that you consider a failure in your life and tell me why you think it occurred.

This is a personal question. *Any personal failures I had did not relate to the job. Since they were personal, I would prefer not to discuss them.*

7. Tell me about your hobbies and interests.

The interviewer wants to know if you are well rounded, and if you are involved in your family and community life. Answer briefly, but carefully. Many companies want their executives to be involved in approved community affairs.

8. What specific strengths can you bring to this job?

Describe the match between your skills and the job requirements.

9. What risks did you take in your last few jobs, and what was the result of those risks?

Tie the risks to your accomplishments for the best response to this question.

10. If you were starting your career now, what would you do differently?

This one may be dangerous because it may bring out that you really don't like the kind of work for which you're applying!

About your future work/personal life:

1.   What would you like to be earning two (three-four-five) years from now?

I would like to see a steady progression in my earnings to reflect the contribution I make to the company.

2.   Where do you see yourself three (four-five) years down the road?

Another version of the preceding question. The difference is you may be able to discuss any obstacles or road blocks you see in the way of getting where you'd like to be. It used to be acceptable to say, "I see myself in your job." With the job market what it is today, that would be too threatening.

3.   What would you like to be doing two (three-four-five) years from now?

Your answer had better relate to the job for which you are interviewing. Example: *I'd like to be doing somewhat the same thing, but in a department that is twice as big because the company has grown larger.*

4.   What is your philosophy of life? Of business?

Spend no more than two minutes on this. Give a brief general outline of what you think good business morality is, and leave your life philosophy out of it.

5.   Tell me, would you lie for the company?

Hedge on this one. The best response: *I'd do nothing to hurt the company.*

6.   Do you drink?

Probably the best answer is, *I will occasionally have one or two drinks.*

7.   What is the state of your health?

Frankly, this question is illegal. Your answer would be, "Excellent." The only questions about health or disability that can be asked: Do you have any impairments—physical, mental or medical—which would interfere with your ability to perform the job for which you've applied?

Are there any job duties that you can't perform because of a physical, mental or medical disability? If so, please describe.

8. Would you mind discussing any long-term plans that you have for yourself and your family?

The correct answer is not "No." Try to couch your answer in terms that could include a long-term relationship with the organization with which you are interviewing.

9. What is your net worth?

This is a valid question to ask of a financial person. It probably isn't any of their business if you're looking for some other position.

10. Are you generally lucky?

The interviewer who asks this might be looking for malcontents or someone who's frustrated. If you answer "Yes," explain further. Be upbeat—explain how and with what you've been lucky.

11. We all know that family members tend to be critical of each other. What do your family members criticize you for?

Watch it. This question is a trap. You are probably safe if you answer something like, "They would like for me to spend less time on the job and more time with them."

12. What do people criticize you for?

The interviewer is trying to get you to incriminate yourself. It is used to bring out your personality traits.

13. How do you spend your spare time? What are your hobbies?

Show a variety of interests, if you can.

14. What do you think are your best qualities?

Pick out the two or three qualities that are most needed on the particular job for which you are interviewing, and discuss your strengths in those areas briefly.

15. What is the most difficult thing you've ever tackled? What did you

The answer to these questions show the interviewer the level of your aspido that was most satisfying? What work was the most monotonous?

rations and your ability to handle detail without being bored to tears.

16.   Are you a leader? Do you like to be in a leadership position? If so, why?

Being a leader is not the same as managing. The interviewer may be trying to determine your aggressive tendencies.

Your knowledge/interest in the particular job/company:

1.   Why are you interested in this job?

It is an industry I know; the job is a good match to my skills and experience; the job would be a challenge; your company has a fine reputation for quality in the industry. It is important to me to work for the best.

2.   What do you know about our company?

You really should know something about the company. Do your homework. If the company is not a public company, or has not had any publicity, you can respond, "I tried to find information about your company in the library, but found very little. Would you please tell me what you do?"

3.   Why do you think we should hire you?

Basically the same question as above. Emphasize the match between your skills and the job, and the results you've achieved in your previous assignments.

4.   What do you think differentiates you from other applicants for this job? Why?

Discuss the kind of results you've achieved in other places. Not too many other people will have these kinds of achievements. *My experience directly applies to the position you have open. I can do for you what I have done for others.*

5.   What kind of work do you think you might be expected to do if you come to work for us?

Answer briefly, based on what you've been able to discover about the position, and what a person with that job title generally does.

6. If you've done work along these lines, what in your experience would fit you for this job?

Interviewers frequently tell applicants about the job, then ask this question. They're expecting you to summarize your background and experience and relate it to the position. This is a golden opportunity to do "needs benefits link-ups" to sell yourself. (See Chapter 12.)

7. Why do you think you'd be good in this job?

The interviewer really wants to know what qualities you have that might especially fit you for the position. But he or she might also be trying to determine if you're a braggart.

8. What sort of progress would you expect to be normal in our company?

Answer on the basis of what you know about similar companies. Be careful with this answer in family owned or closely held small companies. There may be no job progression.

9. How does this job compare with others you've applied for?

The interviewer may want to know how much shopping around you've done and what your "luck" was. This is really an unfair question, but should be answered by saying something like, "I can't answer that question comparatively. This job is the only one like it that I've applied for."

Your "style" on the job:

1. What are the most difficult aspects of your current job, and how do you approach them?

If unemployed, talk about your last job. The question can be a trap, or a real god-send. Discuss your interpersonal skills, your ability to negotiate, your personal integrity and how you overcome obstacles.

2. What do you think it takes for a person to be successful in your particular area?

Basic knowledge and expertise. Suitable experience in the field, a desire to succeed, an ability to communicate and to motivate and/or work through others.

3.   What do you do when you are having trouble solving a problem?

The interviewer is looking to see if you use all available resources. You can discuss it with a peer, a superior, or subordinates; consult experts; look for similar problems in trade journals.

4.   Describe the best boss you ever had. What made him (or her) the best?

Be careful. You may step on someone's toes, or reveal something about yourself that may be detrimental. The person was fair, equitable, consistent, treated you (and everyone else) with respect, made you feel competent and valuable.

5.   What did you do day before yesterday—in detail?

The interviewer is looking for organization, ability to recall, and whether you are what you say you are.

6.   Tell me about the people that you hired on your last job. How long did they stay, and how did they work out?

Discuss the level of the people you hired and what they were expected to do. Then respond to the rest of the question.

7.   How do you go about making a decision?

The interviewer wants to see your methodology. What resources do you use? Do you use a problem-solving approach that is acceptable to the situation? Do you realize that every decision is a compromise? Explain that in many situations, almost any decision is better than none. You get as much information as you can within the time constraints, then decide, based on the available facts, your experience and intuition.

8. What type of position are you interested in and would you most like to have?

This question is all right if what you want is on the career ladder from the position for which you're applying,but be careful. Your answer might be threatening to the interviewer.

Your age, self-employment, other toughies:

1. After being in business for yourself, do you think that you can fit into the corporate world again and be happy?

Yes. Or, ask them, "Why did you ask this question? You have the same problems in a small business that you have in a large business, but on a different scale. You have more resources available in a large business. I am interested in working with people."

2. You appear to be over-qualified for this position. Why are you interested in it? Will you be content to work at this level very long?

Why do you think I am overqualified for this position? What is your definition of overqualified? Then discuss the role of technology in a changing work environment, and the necessity for staying current. *How, in light of this, can one be overqualified?* Or you might stress your qualifications against a younger candidate. Point out that experienced executives are at a premium today. And, because you're experienced, it will take you less time to become proficient in the job.

3. This job requires a large amount of travel. Do you think you have the stamina to keep up?

This is an age question. Handle carefully. You always traveled, are in good health and can fulfill the job requirements.

4. How much did you make on your last job?

Answer honestly. If you have earned more previously, say why, without apology.

5. What kind of salary do you expect?

It would be easier to discuss salary needs if I knew more about the job. Could we discuss it in more detail? I would expect a salary commensurate with my experience and appropriate to the duties and responsibilities of the job. I imagine that the company has already established a salary range for that job. What did you have in mind?

6.   Could you work for a younger man (or for a woman)?

I can work for anyone as long as there is mutual respect and the person knows the job.

Your education and training.

1. Why did you decide to go to college?

Answer briefly.

2. What percentage of your college did you pay for and what sort of jobs did you have while you were in school?

Answer briefly. If any of the experience pertained to what you are still doing, bring it up.

3.   Tell me a little about what you did in school.

Discuss briefly—no more than a minute or so.

4.   Why are you working in a field other than the one in which you have your degree?

I recently read that almost everyone has several career changes during their work life. I'm no different. Many companies as a policy move their managerial people into different disciplines, and I found one of them more interesting than what I had trained for.

5.   What were your best and worst subjects in school?

Answer truthfully.

6.   Tell me about your extra-curricular activities.

Discuss briefly. If they reflect favorably on your current work, go into more detail (member of industry club, work-study program, honor societies).

7.   What have you done to stay current in your field?

Mention training courses, journals you read, etc.

8. What kind of on-the-job train-   Describe briefly.
ing have you experienced?

Dealing with the Salary Question

You don't want to get into the salary question early in the interview. You want an opportunity to show the interviewer your qualifications first. A good time to deal with the salary question is sometime toward the end of the first interview, although the question can be held until a second or third interview if the rest of the interview is going well. If the interviewer appears to be rushing into the salary discussion before you know enough about the position or have had an adequate opportunity to present your qualifications, you can stall the discussion for a while by saying something like:

> It would be easier for me to discuss my salary needs if I understood more about the job and how my qualifications might fit in. Could we discuss the job in more detail?

> I would expect a salary that's commensurate with my experience and is appropriate to the duties and responsibilities of the job.

> I imagine that the company has already established a salary range for that position. What did you have in mind?

You should have a figure in mind that's a minimum you'd accept. Generally, that would be somewhere between 10 and 20 percent more than you got in your previous position. Don't let the interviewer maneuver you into a box where you state a salary that's too low for the position or that's tied to what you made on your last job.

If, on the other hand, the interviewer appears to be stalling on the salary question, you may be spinning your wheels on the interview. Try a tactical question to try to find out where you stand.

Coping with Questions about Career Problems

How do you handle those really tough questions when you've had some problems during your career? The toughest areas to handle:

1. You had trouble on your last job(s) and know you'll have one or more poor references.

2. You've been unemployed for a long period of time.

3. You've had a number of jobs recently. You've either been job-hopping or you've had trouble handling the job and have been let go.

4. You are obviously overqualified for the position for which you are applying.

You can't minimize the problems. They're real and the interviewer's concerns have to be addressed. Essentially, you can handle these problems in three ways: 1) you can waste a lot of time trying to justify yourself (usually an unproductive approach); 2) you may refuse to discuss the problem in a vain hope that if you don't talk about it, the problem will "go away" (also unproductive—it isn't going away); or 3) you can try to get some kind of benefit from the situation that will be an advantage to an employer. In other words, try to turn a weakness into a strength.

A long period of unemployment might be turned to advantage by pointing out that you'd used that time period to learn new skills and update existing ones.

If you don't want to be questioned about a problem area or areas in an interview, you can be sure the interviewer will question you about it or them. Whatever the problem, try to meet it head on. Don't try to evade the question, remain silent, exhibit fear or become angry.

Those are the questions to practice answering with family members or friends until you come with responses that will put you in the most favorable light, without lying, yet will honestly answer the interviewer's question.

Handling Questions Related to Age

Another batch of really tough questions relate directly or indirectly to your age. They are tough to answer, and you have to prepare some kind of response in advance.

In the first, you are asked questions about your profession or career area to determine whether or not you've kept your skills up to date. (The prospective employer is afraid that your skills are obsolete.) The easiest answer to this kind of question is to be able to respond that you've kept current by taking seminars, by self-study, or by keeping your department at state-of-the-art level. If, however, you've been managing people and haven't stayed current, you'll use a different type of response. You say that on your most recent job assignments, you've been managing people (or worked in planning, or whatever). In essence, you made a career change and haven't been working at your original profession. You could expand by saying that you could certainly, however, manage professionals in that area.

As you already know, you can't be asked directly how old you are. But if the potential employer *thinks* you're too old or has a general prejudice against hiring older employees, you may be asked questions that skirt the topic. Many employers still work on the false assumption that older executives have reduced capabilities. Point out that some of the world's sharpest business people are old. Mention that as a mature person, you're more stable and would be less likely to job-hop than would a younger person. Older executives also have fewer distractions than younger executives; they have maturity and judgment; they've learned to focus on the job at hand and have positive experiences they can use as guidance.

But the best way to get around this whole area is to present an appearance and general demeanor that negates the stereotypes of age. Project vitality, energy and enthusiasm. Then, the interviewer is less likely to even consider age as a deselector.

Pension

Your potential employer may be worried about providing your pension. You won't have enough time to provide an adequate "cushion" of covered work. Currently, about a third of the workers in most companies stay long enough to be fully vested in the company's pension plan. Most pension plans also make payouts that are proportional to the number of years an individual has worked and been covered under the plan. You might ask the interviewer to calculate the cost of the pension to the company in comparison to someone making a comparable salary, but working there for more years.

Many companies are also turning to alternative methods of financing their pensions. They may have 401 K plans, where the employees save a portion of their salaries, which are then matched by the company after the employee has stayed a certain length of time. Some creative use has been made of IRAs, with the company contributing partially to IRAs specifically purchased on your behalf. Some companies have other types of deferred compensation or insurance plans for older executives, which have been developed to take care of some of the pension problems involved with hiring older workers. These plans are cost effective for the companies, for younger workers who have been job hunting, and they're also good for you. When you get down to the nitty gritty job negotiations, you can suggest something like this yourself. (See Chapter 13 for further discussion on negotiating salary and benefits.)

The Interview, Part III

Techniques to Keep the Interview under Control

An interview is a communication interaction between you and the interviewer. Both of you want to present yourselves in the best possible light and want the interview to be successful. Some of the communication skills that will help you bring your interviews to a successful and desired conclusion include answering questions to give information (as in the last chapter); asking questions while still presenting what's most beneficial to you (this chapter); being able to summarize the topics covered during the interview (this is a device that will also help you keep the interview on a track that's favorable to you); and listening carefully to the interviewer, to "read between the lines" and think along with the interviewer so that you don't miscommunicate.

One of the best techniques you can use to present yourself most favorably is the sales and marketing technique known as the "Needs/Benefits Link-Up." You use this technique by:

1. Determining what skills, background and experience are needed to fill the position (the "needs");

2. Showing how your skills, background and experience match or exceed those skills (the "benefits");

3. Demonstrating how hiring you can benefit the interviewer's company (the "link-up").

This technique is widely used by salespeople in selling products and services, and it's also used in advertising. And, of course, that's what you're doing during an interview —trying to present the benefits of your services to the company.

Needs/Benefits Link-Ups

As soon as you can during the interview, tie in your skills, background and experience to your potential employer's needs. In almost every situation, you should be able to link an employer's needs to the benefits your qualifications offer in a persuasive statement. For example: If the interviewer explained that the company is looking for someone with experience in planning and starting up an automated factory, you might say something like:

> Mrs. Baker, you need someone with experience setting up and operating an automated factory. In my last position, I evaluated the existing production system at the XYZ Company. On the basis of that evaluation, we completely revamped the production lines, reworking and automating what equipment could be salvaged, and installing the needed new equipment. We retrained existing personnel rather than hiring technicians from the outside. After the production lines were in full operation, we increased production 275 percent, improved quality and cut the reject and rework rate, while at the same time, we were able to substantially reduce unit production costs.

This statement illustrates the two steps you use in a good needs/benefits link-up statement. You begin with a brief statement of the employer's need. Then continue with the related benefits your qualifications can provide. (In the statement above, there were actually several related benefits.)

Another example:

> Mr. Forbes, Charles Peck from University Associates told me that you're looking for someone with a background in specialty chemical sales and sales management to head up your new telemarketing department. I sold specialty chemicals and then was a regional manager for 10 years with Reem and Speas. In addition, three years ago I started a telemarketing operation targeted specifically to our marginal customers who had been unprofitable to call on in person. The telemarketing operation increased our sales with these marginal customers by 78 percent, at a lower sales call cost per sales dollar.

Look for opportunities to use needs/benefits link-up statements. Use one during the interview as soon as you have a reasonable opportunity to do so. Do this as soon as the interviewer finishes a preliminary statement describing the position. Make your statement agree with the interviewer's definition of the job. Normally, you will find several opportunities to make needs/benefits link-up statements during the course of an interview. You will be able to show how several different aspects of your abilities could benefit an employer.

Summaries Keep Interviews on Track

One of the best ways to build empathy and understanding is to periodically summarize or paraphrase the meaning or main idea of different parts of the conversation. By doing this, you can: confirm that you understood what was said, define an attitude or restate a fact and/or place a statement of the interviewer on record. You use a *confirmatory paraphrase* for those purposes. Or, you can use a paraphrase to suggest disagreement without actually contradicting the interviewer or to force the interviewer to reexamine a previously stated position or premise. You use a *leading paraphrase* for this second purpose.

When you are making a confirmatory paraphrase, use some of the interviewer's same words, almost like an echo. Or you can rephrase completely, using your own words to summarize the gist or main thought. When you're receiving an intuitive message from the interviewer that is not stated in words but implied, trying a confirmatory paraphrase can let you off the hook. It allows you to ask for verification of what you are feeling, but which wasn't said.

Examples of confirmatory paraphrases:

> What you're looking for, then, is someone to revamp the department, cutting down on expenses while continuing to maintain high standards.
> In this position, then, I would be expected to introduce new products into existing markets, increase the sales on your current products as well as help open new markets.

A leading paraphrase, on the other hand, summarizes something which has been said, but does it in such a way that it brings the interviewer's position into question. Imagine, for instance, that you've applied for a position in the business school of your state university. The school is looking for someone with business experience, at least a master's degree and ability to make presentations to local businesses. You have all of the stated requirements in addition to years of business training experience. In your conversation with the interviewer, it suddenly dawns on you that they're interested only in a local person with an MBA (preferably from their institution) and aren't really interested in considering anyone with an MS or MA degree regardless of background and experience. A leading paraphrase in this instance might be:

> If I understand you correctly, it's more important to you that the person filling this position be a local resident and have an MBA, preferably from this school, than that they have a proven business record as well as experience making presentations before large groups.

A leading paraphrase is a good way to counter the age question. For instance, if an interviewer comments, "Your background is certainly impressive and you have the breadth of experience we need for the position. But, to be honest, we were looking for someone younger to fill the position."

A leading paraphrase directed toward countering this bias might be, "Oh, you feel that my background and experience are less important to your company than my age?"

You'll use other kinds of summaries during the interview. A summary is useful, for instance, to get an interview back on track after it has been interrupted for some reason. You can summarize briefly the topic of conversation that was interrupted, then continue in the line you'd like conversation to continue. You can: 1) Reemphasize and expand upon the remark you made just prior to interruption; 2) redirect the conversation into other channels; or 3) ask the interviewer a question to obtain information you'd like to have.

> Just before your secretary interrupted us, you'd asked me what experience I'd had in managing a clerical staff. In my last position, I managed a professional staff of 15 accountants and two lawyers as well as three secretaries, a file clerk, a word processor and a receptionist.

> Before the telephone rang, we were talking about the lack of up-to-date written corporate policies and procedures. Is one of your goals to have these revised or developed for this division?

When the interview ends, you want to have a reasonably firm understanding of what the next step will be. Frequently, interviewers clearly state what they have in mind and make some kind of commitment. But if they don't—they've made no offer or suggested a second meeting—or they've stated a conclusion that is unacceptable to you, you'll want to try an *interview conclusion statement.*

You begin an interview conclusion statement with an assumptive summary of at least two important benefits which the company would get if they hired you. You *assume* that the interviewer recognizes the value of those benefits. Then you continue by requesting some kind of commitment, even if it's just another meeting with a different interviewer—perhaps another manager mentioned by the interviewer. The request for commitment should be appropriate to the situation, but is not a push to try to get the interviewer to commit to hiring you.

> Mr. Adams, we've agreed that my recent hands-on experience in computer auditing is the kind of experience that your company is looking for. Also, my experience in working with outside audit firms would be useful to you in cutting down on the time and expense of your annual auditing procedures. When might it be convenient for me to speak with your chief financial officer?

Note that in the example, there's no element of pleading. There's a definite request for further action. Notice the difference in wording and in effect between the example above and the poor interview conclusion statement below:

> Mr. Adams, if you feel my qualifications in auditing are adequate, perhaps I could call you next Tuesday to see whether or not I could meet with your chief financial officer.

The latter statement is tentative, almost whining and obsequious in tone. The person making that statement comes across as a real wimp— and probably just blew the opportunity to interview further.

Questions You Should Ask

In Chapter 10, we discussed answering questions the interviewer asked. But during the interview, you also need to be a questioner. You will use your questions to gather enough information to allow yourself to make a considered judgment first about whether you are even interested in the job at all; and second, whether or not to accept the position if it is offered to you. Some of the information you receive may have no particular relevance for you—and some you may already have gathered from other information sources. You do need to spend time before the interview thinking about the things you want to find out about the organization with whom you are interviewing. Prepare a list of questions, then take it along with you to use as a prompt- sheet or notes.

The questions listed below are some that you might want to consider asking. Many of the questions are job specific (such as those included for someone seeking a human resources position), but others apply to jobs in general.

Questions Related to Performance on the Job

❒ Would you describe the duties of the job for me, please?
❒ Where and how does this job fit into the organization?
❒ What are the most important characteristics you are looking for in the person who holds this job?
❒ What are the most important skills for success on this job?
❒ What would be the ideal experience for this job?
❒ Was the person holding this position promoted? To what?
❒ Is this a new position? If not, why are you looking for someone? How many people have been in this position in the last three (or more) years? If several, why so many?
❒ Are you satisfied with the performance of the department staff?
❒ What is the size of the personnel (engineering, accounting, planning, etc.) department?
❒ Will I have a staff? How large is this staff? Will I be allowed to hire and fire, or otherwise make changes in this staff?
❒ How much autonomy would I have to make decisions?
❒ What is your single greatest expectation of me in this job?
❒ Would you like to see this position expanded? Improved? How?
❒ What might a typical day be for me in this position?
❒ How do you think a person in this position should function?
❒ Where would you like to see the person in this position five or ten years from now?
❒ What is the company's philosophy about how a human resources (engineering, accounting, planning, purchasing, etc.) department should function?
❒ What is the biggest problem facing the department staff now?
❒ What unusual demands does the job have that I should know about?
❒ Have there been outstanding results produced by people in this position? This department? This staff?
❒ What are my opportunities for growth from this position?

General Questions Related to the Company

❒ May I have a copy of the company's annual report? May I see a copy of the company's policy manual?

❐ Are the company's personnel records on computer?

❐ What is the company's philosophy on training? Do you encourage and pay for learning within the company and within the personnel (engineering, accounting, etc.) department?

❐ What in-house training programs do you have?

❐ What is your policy on funding outside training and learning programs?

❐ Do you find membership in local or national organizations pertinent to this position?

❐ Does the company have written guidelines for expense reimbursement?

❐ Because this is a private company, I was unable to find any published financial information. Is the company profitable? Are the sales and earnings trends upward, level or down? What is your relationship with your suppliers and vendors? Are you paying your sales commissions on time?

❐ What are your stated long-term and short-term goals? Do you have a written mission statement?

❐ Do you have a written business plan? Do you operate from a budget? Do your managers have an opportunity to contribute to the development of the budget, and do they know what budgetary amounts they control?

Questions about Interpersonal Relationships

❐ Who will I report to?

❐ What kind of manager is the person I would report to?

❐ Would I be expected to consult with my manager every step of the way?

❐ Would my manager prefer to be kept informed as I go along?

❐ Would my manager expect me to make decisions and act upon them independently of him (or her)?

❐ Would my manager prefer to make the decisions himself (herself)?

❐ To whom in the company does the job relate most importantly? Any unusual problems in these relationships?

❐ May I talk with the person who held this job? Other members of the staff?

❐ What is your concept of teamwork? Do you practice participatory management? If yes, discuss how you practice it.

Subjects Open to Negotiation

❐ What salary range are you considering for this position?

❐ Would I have a secretary or administrative assistant?

❐ What financial assistance do you provide for relocation?

❐ What productivity aids will I have available to me? Does that include a personal computer? Where is it located?

❐ What type of financial incentives would I have in this position for top performance?

❐ (You are not in agreement with the dollar amount of the salary offered, but you like the position, and are definitely interested.) Could you provide a company car? A performance bonus? Membership in a local club? Extra life insurance? Stock options? Profit participation? Extra vacation time?

❐ (You would have to relocate.) Would the company provide assistance in selling my current home and buying a new one? Would you provide (or make arrangements for) a low-interest-rate loan to purchase this new home?

Questions about the Future of the Company

❐ Are you facing challenges in the area of waste/quality/scheduling/market share/motivation/public relations/customer service/maintenance, etc.?

❐ Have you thought about...(some strategy to solve the problem)? Are there substantial factors preventing this course of action?

❐ Are you considering the new...(machine/process/system/approach)?

❐ How is the current_____program going?

❐ Would this approach produce good results?

Employee and Labor Relations (Job-Related questions you develop)

❐ What kind of employee relations program does the company have?

❐ What would be my role in employee relations?

❐ What is the biggest employee relations problem you are having right now?

❐ What are some of the typical ongoing employee relations problems you have?

❐ What kind of formal employee recognition policy do you have?

❐ What process does management have to meet with employees and exchange ideas on an informal basis?

❐ Does the company have a high turnover rate?

❐ What is the greatest reason for employee turnover?

❐ What are you doing to reduce turnover?

❐ Are you a union shop? In what classifications? Nationally? Which unions?

❒ What is the state of the relationship of the company with its unions?

❒ What is the process for dismissing a staffer?

❒ What resources are available for a staffer to respond to a reprimand or warning? A dismissal?

❒ What resources are available for a manager with the same problems as a staffer?

❒ What kind of psychological tests does the company give to job applicants and/or employees?

❒ Does the company give tests at all? Are they standard in all of the company offices?

❒ Does the company give polygraph tests? (These are illegal in many states.)

Recruiting, EEO and Affirmative Action Questions (For people applying for a human resources position)

❒ Does the company hire management personnel from outside?

❒ How does the company recruit now?

❒ Are all positions recruited through the personnel department?

❒ Does the company recruit through free agencies, such as the YWCA displaced homemaker program or 40 Plus?

❒ Is the company required to recruit certain protected group members due to a suit, charge or settlement of a charge from that group?

❒ Does the company have a recruitment program for protected group candidates?

❒ Is the company active in affirmative action?

❒ What are the provisions of the company's current affirmative action plan?

❒ Has the company ever been reviewed for compliance?

❒ Does the company currently have an EEO or other personnel-related suit or charge pending? In what area(s)?

❒ Does the company directly contract with governments (federal, state and/or local)? Indirectly through subcontractors or clients?

Benefits Questions (Only if it looks as though you might be hired)

❒ What kinds of insurance benefits do you have?

❒ Medical?

❒ Major medical?

❒ Dental?

❒ Eye care?

❒ Short-term disability?

❐ Long-term disability?
❐ Sick leave policy?
❐ Pregnancy sick leave policy?
❐ Paternity leave policy?
❐ What are your vacation policies?
   1. Based on length of service?
   2. How many days after how much service?
   3. Which holidays?
❐ What are your policies on "personal days"?
❐ What are the normal working hours? Lunch break?
❐ What type of pension plan do you have? Vested after how long? Do you offer a 401K option?
❐ Is there a stock option plan? To whom available? At reduced rates?
❐ Do you offer a profit-sharing plan?
❐ Do you have a credit union? Is there a payroll deduction plan?

Illegal Topics

Recent employment laws have made certain topics illegal for discussion. The Equal Employment Opportunities Act restricted topics that could be asked of minority groups and women. Later, laws restricted questions about age, health and physical disabilities. Briefly stated, the restrictions on questions that can be asked, either on application forms or in personal interviews prior to employment are as follows:

Topics that can't be asked about or discussed in any form

1. Race or color
2. Religion or creed
3. National origin
4. Sex (male, female)
5. Marital status
6. Birth Control
7. Age (other than to ask if the applicant is between 18 and 70).
8. Birthplace
9. Birthdate (This and the question on marital status can be asked after you're employed.)
10. Photograph
11. Who to notify in case of an emergency. (This question can be asked after you've been employed.)
12. Sexual orientation

Topics with restrictions

Topic	Can ask	Can't ask
1. Name	Have you ever worked for this company under	What is your maiden name? Have you ever

	another name? Will we need any other information such as a change of name or use of a nickname to check on your work record?	worked under another name?
2. Criminal or arrest	Have you ever been convicted of a crime? If so, give details.	Have you ever been arrested?
3. Physical, mental or medical disability	Do you have any impairment that might interfere with your ability to perform the job? Is there any type of position you can't hold or job duties you can't perform because of a physical, mental or medical disability? If so, describe.	What diseases have you had? What disabilities do you have?
4. Citizenship	Are you a citizen or do you intend to become one?	When were you naturalized? Are your parents or is your spouse naturalized or native born?
5. Languages	What languages can you speak?	What is your native language? Where did you learn to read and speak the languages you know?
6. Relatives	What relatives other than your spouse are presently employed by our company?	What are the names, addresses or other information about spouse, children, parents or other relatives not employed by this company. Any question about a spouse.
7. Military	In what branch of the U.S. Armed Forces of (state) militia have you served?	Any question about general military experience.

| 8. Member-ships | To what professional or-ganizations related to this kind of work do you be-long? | To what clubs, societies or lodges do you belong? |

Topics that can be discussed in detail:

| 1. Education | What schools, colleges and so on did you attend? What are their names and locations? When did you attend? When did you graduate? What other special-ized training or courses related to work have you taken? |

| 2. Work ex-perience | Where have you worked? When did you work there? What was your position and what work did you do? |

Responding to Illegal Questions

Most companies are aware of what they can and can't ask on applications. However, if the organization does not have a human resources depart-ment or legal department that sees that the organization doesn't open itself to possible litigation, you may find an application containing illegal questions. And you'll almost certainly come up against illegal questions in interviews. How do you handle these?

1. If you come up against an illegal question on an application, ignore the question and don't answer it, or put an "NA" (not applicable) in the blank. Be aware, however, that after the company has made you a job offer, you are required to answer many of those same questions for insurance purposes and to show that the company is in compliance with state and federal regulations.

2. When you are asked an illegal question in an interview, you can try any of these strategies:

❑ Counter the question with a question: "Do you believe that my ability to do this job is contingent on that factor?"
❑ Go ahead and answer the question as though it is no big deal. Get off it as fast as you can.
❑ Don't pontificate, or call the interviewer's attention to the fact that the question is illegal, unless you have definitely decided

you don't want the job, and don't want anything more to do with that organization.

❐ A suggestion: Do write down the interviewer's name and the exact question you were asked, with the date, location and the job you applied for, just for your own possible protection.

Post Mortem

Regardless of what kind of interview(s) you have undergone, consider the activity a learning experience. When you leave the site of the interview, take time to make notes on how you did. Before you forget, note the areas you thought you handled well, the areas where your answers were not what you would have liked. Also make notes of anything else that you think you should work on.

Debriefing. Convene your support group. If you are a member of a job search group, that support group would be the strategy group to which you belong. Discuss your feelings about the interview, and try to reconstruct the interview for the others. Describe the interviewer. What communications style did you observe? Were your responses appropriate for that style? Talk about the chemistry of the interaction. How did the two of you get along?

Describe the organization and the work climate that you could observe. What did the organization do? If the interview was not good, tell the group why, and try to look on it as a practice session.

Develop Strategies for Improvement. Discuss whatever negatives there were. Get feedback from the group on possible ways to turn those negatives into positives. Work out better responses together on the tough questions you may have fluffed.

Follow-up. Then, honestly, answer for yourself, "Do I really want to work there?" If you do, and you feel you have an honest chance at the job, ask the strategy group to suggest ways you can further your "suit" for the job. Write your follow-up letter(s) and ask them to evaluate the letter(s) before you send them. What other suggestions do they have for you? If they seem reasonable, do them.

Evaluating the Job Offer, Making the Decision and Beginning Work

Almost the worst part of being unemployed is being on tenterhooks after you've had one or several interviews that seemed favorable. You want to get back to work. Remaining unemployed is too emotionally draining. But until the job offer is in hand, you can't let down. You must continue to look and not put all your eggs in one basket. How will you deal with the disappointment if the offer you're depending on doesn't materialize? The situation is a little like the favorite vaudeville saying: "It isn't over until the fat lady sings." In this instance, the "fat lady" is the job offer and your acceptance.

You can you get the "fat lady" to sing earlier? Let's say you just completed one or several interviews with a company. You haven't received a job offer yet, but you know the interviewer was interested. Can you do anything to push for the offer without seeming pushy. Yes. You have several options, all of which fall in the area of "asking for the job."

Write an enthusiastic letter. Tell the interviewer how impressed you were with the company. Tell him/her that you're "raring to go." You really are interested in the job.

Telephone the interviewer every five to 10 working days. (If you can't reach them, leave a message with the secretary.) Explain who you are. Tell who you are and that after the interview, you really think you are the right person for the job. You're calling to see if a decision has been made. If not, when will it be made? If you have had to leave a message, you may not get an immediate return call. If your call isn't returned, at least you've left the message that you are interested.

According to Marilyn Moats Kennedy[1], managing partner of Career Strategies in Wilmette, Illinois:

> When you're told that someone will be in touch, don't wait for them to call. Call every five to 10 working days...Don't apologize for calling or suggest that you're being a nuisance. You are a serious job hunter and seriously interested in the job...Write a letter. Restate your interest in the job, desire to work for the company and belief you can make a contribution. Give some examples based on your observations during on-site interviews. Don't assume that unless you're invited back, you're out. Consider how tedious and time-consuming interviews are from the other side of the desk. Persistent, low-pressure wooing works best...Recontact the company by telephone or letter every 10 days, probably every other Friday...The longer the delay, the more likely some of your competition will evaporate. Six weeks from now, you may be the only remaining candidate—if you have the patience to wait that long...But while you're looking, following up isn't wasted time.

If your interview was arranged by an agency, follow-up with the counselor. Ask to talk with the counselor, either in person or on the telephone as a debriefing. Tell him or her the full results of the interview. Then, follow up with the employer yourself.

You'll know a company is serious when it asks for your references and begins to check them.

Evaluating the Job Offer

An employer (or two or three) makes you a job offer. Before you say, "Fine, I accept and will start immediately," seriously evaluate the firm, the offer and the match between you and them. Is this job really what you want? Or are you accepting it because you're desperate? Invariably, if you accept a job for the latter reason, you'll be back on the street again within a year because you don't fit them or they don't fit you.

How well do you fit the job characteristics? If you can get a job description or a copy of the job requisition from the person who offered you the job, go back to Chapter 6, "What Kind of Job Should You Search For?" and make an estimate of the various job characteristics using the

---

[1] Marilyn Moats Kennedy, "When the offer doesn't come," *National Business Employment Weekly*, Spring, 1987, pp. 31-33.

Position Concept Form, Figure 6.2. Score the form and compare the profile of the offered job with the profile of the one you said you wanted, Figure 5.2. Also, check the position profile of the job with your own communications style (the Public Concept profile you completed in Figure 5.6). What problems might you have?

Find out everything you can about the job. Do some additional research on the company, using the resources mentioned in Chapter 4, "Finding Out Where the Jobs Are." What would your duties be, who would you report to, what is the work climate? If you know someone who works there, ask some discreet questions about general conditions at the firm. Ask knowledgeable people in the community—bankers, lawyers, stockbrokers—about the company's general reputation. Try to do as much cross-checking as you can. If the answers vary widely, be careful.

Check out what you've learned about the job with what you learned about yourself. Would it require some skills you don't have or require that you upgrade existing skills? Would it play to your weaknesses instead of your strengths? Is it a detail job or a broad-picture job? (Which are you—a detail person or a broad-picture person?) Would you be working with things or with people? Which do you do best? Do you have the necessary background and experience to do the job well without a long learning period?

Will the job give you the satisfactions you require? How does each offer you've received stack up against the criteria you developed earlier in your job search? Up to the time of the offer, you were selling yourself. Now, you're being sold to. Don't buy a lemon. Take the time to really think about the job. Photocopy the checklist in Figure 13.1. Cross out any items that don't pertain to the job and add any other criteria that are important to the job.

Then evaluate the job in relation to the criteria. Look at each criterion and make a judgment about its importance to the job. In column 1, rate it a 5 if that characteristic of the job is extremely high, a 4 if it's high, 3 if it's average, 2 or 1 if it is low. After you have rated the job, go back over the list. Decide which of these factors is especially important to you—would, in fact, be a critical factor. In the second column, rate the importance of that factor to you on the same 1 to 5 scale. Then compare your responses about yourself with your responses about the job in column 1. If any of the scores in this column were low—say 1 or 2, and you have rated this factor a 5, it is a deselector. That part of the job doesn't meet your criteria. Have you rated each critical item a 4 or 5? If you have more than one critical factor that's rated 3 or less, don't accept the position.

Should you have more than one offer, you do the same kind of scoring on each position. If you don't have any serious deselectors, then you complete your rating of the other characteristics, and do a weighted score for that job. Multiply the job rating in column 1 times the importance rating in column 2. Place the answer in column 3. After you have scored all the factors for the position, sum the responses in column 3. Repeat the scoring with the second position (and the third, if you're so lucky.) Then compare the scores for each offer. You'll have a combination quantitative/qualitative measure that will be of more value than just your intuition. The job with the highest score should be the one you accept.

Keep in mind that the most significant factor of your performance on the job is apt to be your boss. If you have any reservations about this person—does he or she play by the rules, will your personalities clash, do your work styles mesh - -think long and hard about accepting the position. You may have been made an offer you can't refuse. But if the chemistry just isn't there, you may not last on the job—or worse yet, you'll stay and be miserable.

Negotiating Compensation

The decline in inflation, increased worldwide competition, and the need to keep fixed costs as low as possible has had a dramatic effect on executive compensation, according to a recent survey by the Arthur Young organization.[2] U.S. companies have adopted a compensation strategy designed to stabilize fixed compensation costs and place greater emphasis on variable pay-for-performance compensation programs. Salary administration programs are being restructured to de-emphasize base salary as a component of executive pay by giving increases less frequently, perhaps only when the market changes significantly. Still, base salary ranges will continue to be determined by what it takes to attract and retain the kind of executives a company needs to implement its long-term strategic plan.

It is now unusual for an executive, especially at the top management level, not to participate in a short-term incentive program. Bonus payments play a key role in the total compensation package, and will represent an increasingly significant portion of an executive's total cash compensation. In many industries, CEO bonus payments now exceed 50 percent of base pay for achieving corporate targets, but average between

---

[2]*The 1988 National Survey of Executive Compensation*, 2nd Edition, Arthur Young, pp. 13-28. The information in this section is based on the massive survey on compensation trends conducted by the Arthur Young organization. The previous survey was conducted 20 years earlier.

Figure 13.1. Checklist to Evaluate Job Offers

Checklist Items	Position 1			Position 2			Position 3		
	Score (1 to 5)	Critical factor or weight	Total Score	Score (1 to 5)	Critical factor or weight	Total Score	Score (1 to 5)	Critical factor or weight	Total Score
The company:									
Stability									
Reputation									
Quality of products or services									
Competitive position									
Fiscal condition									
Corporate climate									
Quality of management									
The position:									
Relationship to career goals									
Compensation (salary)									
Bonus arrangements									
Benefits									
Perquisites									
Status									
Creativity									
Flexibility									

Autonomy
Variety
Growth potential
Opportunity for advancement
Intellectual challenge
Quality of staff
Quality of co-workers
Social contacts
Meets personal values
Life style
Relocation
Family disruption
Commuting distance
Travel
Time requirements
Community
Other: list

30 percent to 40 percent of base salary. At the middle management level, bonuses average 20 percent to 30 percent of base pay. However, the bonus payments are income at risk. You must meet or exceed the specific goals established in the strategic plan before the bonus plan kicks in.

While short-term pay-for-performance bonuses play a key role in today's executive strategy, U.S. companies recognize the need for a balance between short- and long-term capital performance awards. These long-term incentives in the past generally took the form of stock options. However, the collapse of the bull market combined with the changes in the federal tax treatment of capital accumulation plans caused by the 1986 Tax Reform Act has changed the kinds of plans that companies use to reward executives. Companies are trying a variety of approaches, some of which are performance-based programs (such as performance shares) that do not have some of the disadvantages to the company and to the executive of the stock options plans. The long- term compensation plans will continue to change, especially with the changes in accounting procedures being initiated by the Financial Accounting Standards Board (FASB). Companies seeking to implement entrepreneurial spirit inside the corporation (i.e., to create entrepreneurs) will continue to structure their compensation packages so that they provide significant long-term rewards to those producing significant results for the company.

In the area of benefits, the 1986 and 1987 Tax Acts have had some impact on perquisites. However, companies continue to provide basic medical, death and retirement benefits for employees and executives, but shift some costs back to the employee through flexible or cafeteria programs. And, executives still have a number of options (cars, extra life insurance, participation in 401K, Matched Savings Plans, Supplementary Retirement Plans, etc.) which can be negotiated as perquisites.

The average executive compensation package in 1988 consisted of 40 percent base salary, 20 percent short-term incentives, 20 percent long-term incentives, 15 percent benefits, and 5 percent perquisites. Within those averages is a large area for negotiation. What you can't get in base salary, you may be able to negotiate in one of the other areas—and ultimately end up with more growth opportunities than if the base salary were larger.

Employment Contracts

With the increase in competition, few top executives or professionals will be offered jobs without an employment contract. Many organizations have begun to insist on contracts for their protection since recent court cases have said that offering employment is an implied contract. Even at middle management levels, and certainly at the top levels, the employ-ment contract is almost de rigueur. But this is an area where your negotiating skills must come to the fore. You want to negotiate a contract that is equally advantageous to you. You want to begin by assessing if the job calls for a contract.

According to Catherine H. Rubenstone, head of CR Associates, a management consultancy firm in Malvern, Pennsylvania,[3] you need to look at five key questions:

1. Is the industry particularly volatile?

2. Does the organization have a history of picking employees' brains, then getting rid of them?

3. Is the company ripe for merger or acquisition?

4. Will a non-compete clause severely restrict you as a job candidate in the future?

5. Are contracts the norm in the industry or firm?

You may request the contract yourself, after you have negotiated your compensation package and other perks. You may ask simply to have your verbal agreement placed on paper. Or the company may request the contract. Three- to five-year contracts are typical, although companies generally prefer the shorter term. The basic elements of the contract are:

1. The employment offered—the position/title and duties of the position, (these duties can be more generalized than a job description, or may be the actual job description) and reporting relationships.

2. The term or length of the contract, including termination date, renewal provisions, and any special provisions for early termination.

3. Compensation. This section generally includes a general state-ment about the company's right to deduct or withhold all taxes, specifics about the salary (for a specific time period, how payable—weekly,

[3] Catherine H. Rubenstone, "The Employment Contract: When and How to Negotiate It," *Management Solutions*, March 1988, pp. 17-21.

monthly, annually, if any adjustments are applicable—who determines and how often); bonus determination and when payable; stock options or other opportunities for capital accumulation; benefits offered; car or car allowance; expense reimbursement; vacations; and any other negotiated perquisites.

4. Restrictive Covenants

❏ Covenants not to compete with specific time frames and the specifics of what is covered. You may want to check with a lawyer on this part, since some non-compete clauses have been held to be in restraint of your legitimate right to earn a living.
❏ Trade secrets. A commonly accepted definition of a trade secret: A trade secret may consist of any formula, pattern, device or compilation of information which is used in one's business, and which gives an opportunity to obtain an advantage over competitors who do not know or use it. It may be a formula or a chemical compound, a process of manufacturing, treating or preserving materials, a pattern for a machine or other device, or a list of customers.

5. Termination (when, how and why)

❏ By mutual consent of the parties
❏ Upon the death of the employee (you)
❏ At the company's option (with or without cause). This clause now appears because the company wants to retain employment-at-will rights.
❏ Upon the dissolution, merger, termination of existence, insolvency or other reason for failure of the business
❏ Other miscellaneous reasons (relocation, change in scope of the employee's duties, etc.)
❏ If the contract is for a short-term project, this will be included in this section.
❏ Severance pay.

6. Miscellaneous General Contract Provisions

❏ The contract supersedes any and all prior agreements
❏ The contract can be modified only in writing

❑ If any portion of the agreement is void, illegal or unenforceable, that portion may be excluded and the balance of the contract will be enforceable

❑ A notice clause—where, when and how any notice required by the contract will be given

❑ A government law clause which states what jurisdiction's laws will govern the contract (i.e., the laws of Texas, California, Illinois, etc.)

For additional information on job contracts and job offers, check *The Employee Rights Handbook* by Steven Mitchell Sack (Facts On File).

The contract is brought just as you would negotiate any element of the package. Realize that you won't get everything you want, so be prepared for trade-offs. What are the key elements of successfully negotiating your contract? According to Rubenstone, they are the same ones that work in any negotiation:

1. Be confident—you're selling yourself. Rehearse your phrasing with a friend who can play devil's advocate.

2. Be patient—time for consideration on both sides can be worthwhile.

3. Ask questions—they keep the process moving.

4. Make your opponent (in this instance the person with whom you're negotiating) look good—give in on minor issues.

But even if you've done a good job on assessment and negotiation, the company may still refuse what you consider your main demands. You have three choices: Accept the job and forego the contract; refuse the job; or accept the job and in a few years renegotiate from an established position of power.

Making the Decision

You have to fish or cut bait. Do you take the job or don't you? If the offer is mediocre and you have other activity going on, you can probably take the risk and turn the offer down.

But if you've been out of work a long time, you'll be tempted to accept. Hold off a few days if you can before you give your final acceptance. You want to be as sure as you can. Don't let your panic about the need to work push you into a rash decision. You can end up in a trap, and in a job no better than what you left.

Involving your family in the decision. When the job offer requires relocation or a change in life style, working hours or anything which will impact upon your family life, involve your family in the decisions. This is an absolute essential if your spouse works. The decision must be a joint one. If you must move to accept the job, has provision been made for relocating your spouse and helping him or her find adequate employment? Discuss the pros and cons of the offer with every member of the family, and consider how each might be affected. Consider carefully the personal ramifications of the change. Are the advantages of the offer worth the upheaval? Or are the opportunities and changes so attractive that everyone looks forward to the move?

Family members can also help when the decision is difficult even when no move is contemplated. Should you hold out longer? Are they willing to continue making the sacrifices they've been making? Having an opportunity to be in on the decision is important to family members.

Notifying the interviewing company of the decision. After you've made your decision, notify each company you were considering and tell them what you've decided to do. If you're turning down their offer, do it tactfully. Tell them that you were impressed with their company and with their offer. You're sorry, but another company's offer was more attractive (or offered you more opportunity for growth, or didn't require that you relocate).

Finally, notify your friends that you're starting work. Thank again the people who helped you with your campaign.

Was There Any Age Discrimination?

What do you do if you didn't get a job that you were fully qualified for and wanted, and you think that age discrimination is the reason why? It's difficult to decide whether or not you were the victim of age discrimination. Fortunately, the climate on age is changing as employers discover that older employees have some advantages over young employees. Older employees are more reliable, are absent less, have fewer drug- and alcohol-related problems, work steadier with fewer emotional problems and are less likely to quit.

However, that said, age and other types of discrimination still occur. You can suspect it if any of the following occurs:

❒ You pass all of the required qualifying tests and are still refused (or not offered) a job.

❏ You don't get an opportunity to take the tests.

❏ You take the tests and are sure you did well. You're told that you didn't pass, but are denied proof.

❏ Your credentials are more than adequate, but you're told your education is inadequate, or you lack the necessary formal education.

❏ You noted during the interview that everyone in the company is under 40. You check around and discover that the firm never hires anyone over 40.

❏ You're asked to take a physical exam before a job is offered, or some other test that has no relationship to the demands of the job.

❏ During the interview, and before you've been made an offer, you're asked how old you are.

❏ You unfortunately reveal during the interview that you have a minor handicap, but that it doesn't interfere with your ability to do the job.

❏ You mention in passing during the interview that you're a member of the American Association of Retired Persons, a political action group, or some other political or religious group.

❏ To discourage you from accepting the job, the employer falsely tells you that you won't be covered by their benefit programs because your spouse is covered on his or her job.

Older women executives and professionals run into both age and sex discrimination, although it is much better and certainly less obvious than it was even five or ten years ago. Women and minorities are protected against discrimination by the Age Discrimination in Employment Act, Title VII of the Civil Rights Act of 1964, Title VII of the Civil Rights Act of 1967, and the Equal Pay Act. If older women and minority members feel they've been discriminated against, they have advocacy groups that are willing to take up the cudgel on their behalf.

Where to go for help if you think you've been discriminated against. Discuss your situation first with an advocacy group. Don't go to a lawyer and spend your own hard-earned cash. Many counties have a Family Service League which will help. The U.S. Equal Employment Opportunity Commission is willing to give you advice and help, either at their local office in your area, or you can write to the Commission's main office at 2401 E. St., NW, Washington, DC 20506.

The American Civil Liberties Union has offices all over and can give you help if they think you have a worthy suit. The National Legal Aid and Defender Association can refer you to attorneys who specialize in age and other discrimination suits. The National Employment Law

Project also provides attorney referral, as will a local law school and your local county bar association. And the AARP can give you help if you happen to be over 55.

All that said, the record on suits for age discrimination is abysmal. The agencies that are supposed to pursue discrimination suits are under-staffed, and the suits languish in the courts. If the suit does finally get to trial, the full proof that age discrimination has occurred appears to rest with you, the plaintiff. The legal process may drag on for months and years. In the meantime, you need to have an income from a job. So—continue your search.

Getting Off on the Right Foot

Good. You accepted a job (let's hope it was the one you wanted) and the starting day has arrived. Regardless of how long you've worked and how many jobs you've held, beginning a new one is stressful. You're going into a new environment and will be working with new people. They don't do things the way you're used to doing them, and vice versa. You're bound to have mixed emotions. You're excited because you have a new job, but also anxious because you want to do your best—and you want to keep the job.

When you accept a job, you go into partnership with your new employer. You agree to do a job for them, and they agree to pay you for your services. It's to both of your advantages to work out the job details as quickly as possible so that you can "get on with it."

Focus on asking and learning. Your first few days on the job, focus on asking questions of your boss, your coworkers and subordinates. In most instances, even if you're the new boss of the whole department, you aren't expected, and frankly shouldn't, begin to completely revamp operations on the first day. There's too much danger that you'll end up throwing out the baby with the bath water. Regardless of what you were told when you were hired, most of the employees are probably competent and trying to do their jobs. During the first few weeks, find out what they are doing and observe who's doing it well. Find out as much as you can. Assume the learner's role, and let department employees know that you appreciate their help. Do a lot of managing by "wandering around."

Investigate and ask about duties and responsibilities. If your new employer doesn't make arrangements for your training, you'll have to take the bull by the horns yourself. Introduce yourself around. Ask if anyone else has essentially the same kind of job. If so, ask them to describe their job and how they approach their work. Ask them to show you how they do some of the specifics.

Look for written job descriptions, training manuals or handbooks, catalogs of the company's products or services. Read everything you can find about the company and the department. Find out what the department's existing goals and objectives are and its purpose for the company. If you're at a higher level, find out what goals and objectives were for the preceding years, and what has been already set for this year. Find out if the company has any purpose statements. Investigate the various budgets for which you're responsible. In short, find out as much as you can as fast as you can.

Determine formal and informal power structures. A first order of business is to find out about the reporting relationships in your department, division or company. Who reports to whom and how is the company structured? What do the organizational charts look like? Get a copy of the company policies and procedures, if one is available. If these are not written down, find out what policies and procedures are understood.

In major companies, you'll likely be given an orientation session and a booklet or employee handbook describing the company, the benefits programs and the basic corporate personnel policies. If the company doesn't have these policies and procedures in writing, ask to discuss them with your immediate superior so that you won't make mistakes. Then take complete notes to use for reference purposes.

In addition to the formal power structure, every organization has an informal social structure that wields a good amount of power. What are the social norms for the organization? Who's friends with whom? What about coffee breaks, lunches, general socializing? Make an effort to be friendly, to become acquainted. It's tough to ease into a group. You don't want to be considered standoffish, but neither do you want to blunder. The best way to begin is to observe carefully. With whom do you seem to have rapport? Which people seem to be the key players, regardless of their job descriptions and formal titles?

Notice who talks with whom, who appear to be the advice givers and the advice takers. Meetings are an excellent opportunity to get a feel for these arrangements. Who sits with whom, who speaks up and commands attention, who speaks up and gets groans (or inattention). Unless you're in charge of the meeting, you're better off observing the first few times before you begin to speak out.

Managing Your New Employees
It's a truism that you've been aware of for a long time. Managers don't *motivate* employees; they simply create a good working climate where

employees can motivate themselves. As the new executive, you've got to get out of the blocks fast and create that kind of environment.

The same techniques you used earlier to identify and match the communication style of an interviewer will also work in managing employees and in interacting with your superiors and peers. Read over what you've read about the various communication styles—High D, High I, High S and High C—and begin applying this on the job. You don't just manage and encourage people *down*. You can manage and encourage *up*, and laterally as well.

Remember that most people have two main communications styles: the one they use in a favorable environment, and one they use in an unfavorable environment. As you get to know the other executives/professionals and your subordinates better, and have an opportunity to see them in both favorable and unfavorable environments, you will begin to see them as whole people. You'll have a better picture of their total communications style, the highs and lows as well as their strengths and weaknesses. By remaining alert and adjusting only those aspects of your personal and managerial style that will impact most on a particular individual, you'll be able to communicate better and more productively, develop your subordinates better and get the work done. You may find it helpful to keep notes about each individual's probable style, to "red flag" potential conflict areas and to plan ways to modify the way you work or manage each.

What Have You Accomplished?

If you got this far in the book, you should be employed in a position that will give you satisfaction, while at the same time provide financial rewards—or you are at least well on your way with your search. Let's hope that you haven't just given in and "settled" for work that will merely keep you busy.

You should also have learned a new set of coping and management skills. And you should have learned a lot more about yourself through your job search process. Your depression (if you were depressed) should be gone. It usually disappears just about the time you begin working, although you may still experience anxiety from time to time.

Much about your life should be in better shape than it was before you became unemployed. Above all, you should feel better about your age. Being an older *employed* executive feels a whole lot better than being an older *unemployed* executive!

Appendix

The Forty Plus Clubs

In 1989, the Forty Plus Club of New York celebrated its 50th birthday. It is the oldest executive self-help, job-seeking organization in the United States. Currently, sixteen Forty Plus Clubs are in existence around the country, and more have been chartered.

The Forty Plus Clubs are nonprofit, member-operated cooperatives, dedicated to helping unemployed managers, executives and professionals, forty years of age or older, to conduct an effective job search campaign and locate jobs commensurate with, if not better than, the ones they left. Forty Plus has strict entrance requirements since it also functions as a quasi-executive recruitment organization, and wants to assure potential "clients" that the members it recommends for positions exemplify a high standard of excellence. Six references from former employers are required—and they are checked. Members agree to attend weekly membership meetings and to spend two days a week helping the club operate—and helping themselves and other members find jobs quickly.

Forty Plus has no paid employees. Its staff is made up of members who have a 150 percent turnover each year. Unlike other organizations, this rapid turnover shows that the club has been successful. Its membership has returned to work.

During the first four weeks of membership, new members are put through an in-depth personal examination of their career skills, record and achievements. They are asked to define their career goals and objectives, and to write an Achievement Resume, putting their chief career achievements into a concrete form. During this phase, they will be coached by members of one of the club committees. After they develop what they believe to be an effective resume, they present it for review and suggestions for improvement before a Job Jury composed of members with similar backgrounds. The Job Jury goes over the resume with a fine-tooth comb, locating and beefing up the weak spots and suggesting ways to make the strong points stronger. During this early period, members also receive help in setting up their job campaign and participate in optional classes such as interviewing skills or communication skills. A bank of personal computers is a fairly recent addition to each club. Members with computer skills teach other executives and professionals how to use this essential business tool. They give classes, at very nominal fees, on Lotus 1-2-3, on databases, on various word processing packages, and on basic computer skills in general. People who came in not knowing anything about computer use leave fully computer-literate.

After members complete their resumes, they're assigned to a committee or given a special assignment to operate the club and help each other. One of the committees is responsible for contacting potential employers to locate jobs that club members might fill. The club does not charge placement fees, though, either to club members or employers. However, it does contact companies where downsizing is occurring, and will make financial arrangements for the company to pay for and sponsor membership for qualified departing employees.

But these activities are not the main advantages of this kind of club. For most members, the real advantage is in their contacts with other unemployed executives and professionals like themselves—and in the benefits they get from helping each other. The club also forces people to look at their real accomplishments—what they did for their company, and to see that they have real value. It helps members in four ways: 1) in writing resumes, cover letters, and other types of communications; 2) through access to the club's job bank, and sometimes, to temporary jobs which come in to the club; 3) through the relationships established with other club members, from which they get moral support—help with interviews, with job strategies through membership in Strategy Groups, self-evaluation and financial problems, and practical support—which is one more aspect of networking activities (club members often forward leads to each other); and 4) because they're expected to work at the club two days a week, they have some place to go, something to do, and can keep their minds active.

The surroundings at the clubs are not fancy—they are obviously places where work occurs. Membership dues plus donations from former members are the clubs' primary sources of financial support. Still, the clubs have the necessary physical equipment for conducting the job search, including access to the word processing mentioned so frequently in this book. And as the most important aspect to club membership is that of support, members don't seem to mind the lack of luxurious surroundings.

The addresses and telephone numbers of the active Forty Plus Clubs follow.

CALIFORNIA

Forty Plus of North America
7440 Lockheed Street
Oakland, CA 94603
(415) 430-2400

Forty Plus of Southern California
3450 Wilshire Boulevard
Los Angeles, CA 90010
(213) 388-2301

Orange County Division
23151 Verduga Drive, #114
Laguna Hills, CA 92653
(714) 581-7990

COLORADO

Forty Plus of Colorado
639 East 18th Avenue
Denver, CO 80203
(303) 830-3040

Northern Division
3840 South Mason Street
Fort Collins, CO 80525
(303) 223-2470, Ext. 261

Southern Division
2555 Airport Road
Colorado Springs, CO 80910
(303) 473-6220, Ext. 271

HAWAII

Forty Plus of Hawaii
126 Queen Street, #227
Honolulu, HI 96813
(808) 531-0896

ILLINOIS

Forty Plus of Chicago
53 West Jackson Boulevard
Chicago, IL 60604
(312) 922-0285

NEW YORK

Forty Plus of Buffalo
701 Seneca Street
Buffalo, NY 14210
(716) 856-0491

Forty Plus of New York
15 Park Row
New York, NY 10038
(212) 233-6086

OHIO

Forty Plus of Central Ohio
1700 Arlingate Drive
Columbus, OH 43328
(614) 275-0040

PENNSYLVANIA

Forty Plus of Philadelphia
1218 Chestnut Street
Philadelphia, PA 19107
(215) 923-2074

TEXAS

Forty Plus of Dallas
13601 Preston Road, #402
Dallas, TX 75240
(214) 991-9917

Forty Plus of Houston
3935 Westheimer, #205
Houston, TX 77027
(713) 850-7830

UTAH

Forty Plus of Utah
1234 Main Street
Salt Lake City, UT 84117
(801) 533-2191

WASHINGTON, DC

Forty Plus of Greater Washington
1718 P Street, NW
Washington, DC 20036
(202) 387-1562

Forty Plus of Puget Sound in Seattle, Washington, has been chartered, and expects to be in operation soon. Check the local phone book in the Seattle area for the telephone number and address.

INDEX